While America Sleeps

... The Coming Judgment

While America Sleeps

... The Coming Judgment

Helaine Mercer

Scripture quotations in this book are taken from the King James Version (KJV) of The Holy Bible.

Copyright © 2011 by Helaine Mercer
ALL RIGHTS RESERVED

Published by:

Joy of Jerusalem Ministries
P.O. Box 197
Salem, OH 44460
www.JoyofJerusalemMinistries.com

ISBN 978-0-578-09259-1

Printed in the United States of America
For Worldwide Distribution

Dedication

This book is dedicated to the Living God of Israel, in memory of my mother, Lorna Hamilton. Her faith in our Lord, and the extraordinary examples of answered prayers in her life, made the difference in my life. I am honored to be able to use her hand-drawn illustrations in this book.

To my children and my family for all the love we share one with the other. Special thanks to my nephew, James Barnes, for his editing skills and able assistance. His guidance in the spirit of love and encouragement helped me greatly in the completion of this work.

Table of Contents

Chapter 1:	Midnight in America	1
Chapter 2:	A Living Christ for a Dying World	21
Chapter 3:	Ezekiel's Wheel in the Middle of a Wheel	39
Chapter 4:	Grace versus the Law	45
Chapter 5:	Separation unto Sanctification	55
Chapter 6:	Pulpit Poison	71
Chapter 7:	A New Name for an Old Game	89
Chapter 8:	The Enemy Within	97
Chapter 9:	Sound the Alarm	101
Chapter 10:	Fishers of Men	109
Chapter 11:	The Proficiency of Prophecy	117
Chapter 12:	Mount of Slaughter	129
Chapter 13:	The Daniel Determinant	135
Chapter 14:	The Sting	147
Chapter 15:	The Black Horse and Rider	163
Chapter 16:	Day of Preparation	173
Chapter 17:	The Defeat of Satan	185
Chapter 18:	Fear Not Little Flock	195

Chapter One

Midnight in America

"And take heed to yourselves, lest at any time your hearts be overcharged with surfeiting, and drunkenness, and cares of this life, and so that day (Day of the Lord) come upon you unawares. For as a snare shall it come on all them that dwell on the face of the whole earth. Watch ye therefore, and pray always, that ye may be accounted worthy to escape all these things that shall come to pass, and to stand before the Son of man."

(Luke 21:34-36)

The changes taking place in today's world are fast and fascinating. The first decade of the twenty-first century brought significant changes to the world scene. There are no words of warning adequate to prepare the world for the fulfillment of Bible prophecy concerning these last days of this age, and the catastrophic events that must shortly come to pass. Christ gives warning to the slumbering masses in Ephesians 5:14-16, "Wherefore he saith, Awake thou that sleepest, and arise from the dead (spiritually dead), and Christ shall give thee light. See that ye walk circumspectly (utmost diligence), not as fools, but as wise, Redeeming the time, because the days are evil."

Has there ever been a time in American history when evil has been so unrestrained? Wickedness abounds everywhere. We must ask ourselves, what is wrong with a nation founded on Godly principles, yet has turned her back on morality? Many Christians have adopted a user-friendly gospel and live lukewarm, insipid lives where sin is overlooked and worse yet, excused. Sadly, righteousness has bowed her knee to political correctness. A term the far left has coined as not to offend anyone. What God condemns, no mere man can condone! Secular humanism and political correctness has brought forth moral decay. Evident in all aspects of life are crimes of self-indulgence and sexual deviances. America has become a product of all uncleanness. The culture we are living in today promotes sin. Sins of fornication, adultery, pornography, homosexuality and sexual deviances, murders, occult practices, greed, and cyber-crimes have all infiltrated and have saturated our society. According to recent statistics, America imprisons 756 inmates per one hundred thousand residents. That is an alarming number. Drugs, street gangs, sexual assaults, and the influx of illegal immigrants, many having criminal records, are largely responsible. United States abortion laws have made murder on demand legal. Over three thousand unborn babies are aborted daily. The latest unemployment statistics show approximately thirteen million Americans have lost their jobs and are unemployed. America is not only morally bankrupt, but our country is also financially bankrupt. Judgment has come to America!

The horror of September 11, 2001 is forever etched in our memories and indelibly stamped on our hearts. Al-Qaeda terrorists commandeered four United States commercial airplanes, all carrying civilian passengers. These Islamic extremists carried out barbaric crimes against the innocent people aboard these planes and their intended targets. The terrorists flew two of the hijacked planes into the Twin Towers of The World Trade Center in New York City. These terrorists, violently mass murdered over 3,000 innocent people as two of the planes crashed into the Twin Towers. Hijacked plane number three was flown into the Pentagon that caused a massive explosion on impact and there were many casualties. The fourth planes' intended target was the White House in Washington D.C. It crashed into a field in Pennsylvania and burnt on impact. The selfless and heroic passengers on board prevented the terrorists' plans from succeeding.

Radical Islamic extremists hate our beloved country because it was founded on Judeo-Christian beliefs and Godly principles. They refer to the United States as "Big Satan," and Israel as "Little Satan." They have vowed to annihilate us, calling us infidels and dogs. Arrogantly proclaiming that our blood will run in the streets of our cities and they will drive Israel into the sea! There are thirty-five known terrorist training camps on United States soil. Many terrorists have infiltrated the U.S. reportedly entering in through the unsecured Mexican-American border. Over the last thirty years many Muslim

Extremists have been born in the U.S. creating the problem of homegrown terrorists! In November 2009 Islamic terrorist, Nidal Malik Hasan was serving as a Major in the U.S. Army. Born in the U.S., of Palestinian decent and of the Muslim faith, Hasan went on a shooting spree at Fort Hood in Texas. He mass murdered 13 people and injured 31.

We are vulnerable to other terrorist attacks. May 2, 2010 a Muslim Pakistani-American, Faisal Shahzad, attempted to use a car as a weapon of mass destruction. He parked a car loaded with explosives at Times Square in New York City. Shahzad age 30, is described as a naturalized American citizen, born in Pakistan and appeared to be living a typical American lifestyle in Connecticut.

The Homeland Security's recent threat assessment 2008-2013: "Chemical, biological, radiological and nuclear attacks are considered the most dangerous that could be carried out against the U.S. The Al-Qaeda terrorist network continues to focus on United States targets. We are vulnerable to massive economic losses, casualties, and political turmoil."

Cyber-warfare is raging. Important government information was breached when China hacked into our National Defense Department. This infringement seriously compromised our nation's security. Communist China and Russia are believed responsible for also embedding a devious code into our nations' electrical grid. Utilities engineers were warned that a cyber-attack against the United States could turn off our electrical systems and has the potential to prevent us from retaliation during a nuclear strike.

In December 2010, an encrypted code was successful in the disruption of Iran's nuclear uranium enrichment program. This cyber-attack was described as effective as a digital warhead and is being credited for creating a possible two year delay in Iran's nuclear program which presented a viable threat to Israel and The United States. This malicious code has been dubbed the Stuxnet Worm, and reportedly has shown up not only in Iran, but also in Indonesia, India, and the U.S.

A call for repentance of sin and turning back to a loving and merciful God is our only assurance in these troublesome and dangerous times. God has warned us through many irrefutable proofs that the end of the Gentile World Dominion and the end of the Church Age is at hand.

Americans are reaping the consequences of practicing commerce without conscious. Politicians and corporate heads have become mercenaries of greed! This is a major factor in our ever-worsening economy. The collapse of government mega-lenders, Fannie Mae and Freddy Mac are prime examples. Their unconscionable lending practices have paved the way for the mortgage crisis. Millions have lost their homes due to foreclosure. Owning one's home has always been the "The American Dream." In light of these shoddy and questionable lending practices, for millions, this American Dream has become a nightmare! There were not adequate checks and balances in place to prevent corporate greed and corruption. Corporate leaders have accepted billions in bailout monies from the government. To prevent bankruptcy and cover reported losses, Troubled Asset Relief Program (TARP) has to-date paid out seven hundred billion to some of the largest corporations in the U.S. These federal bailouts have been at the taxpayer's expense. Insurance giant, AIG, paid out $165 million dollars in bonuses to its corporate executives with procured TARP bailout money. These bailouts under any name remain "redistribution of wealth." It appears many politicians and corporate leaders are in a moral free-fall. Political corruption in America has become epidemic.

The current chairman of The United States Federal Reserve, Ben Bernanke recently stated that the U.S. is close to a second depression. Bernanke is brilliant and capable, but cannot change governmental malaise alone. Some companies are being propped up by the government and this creates reluctance in prospective investors, not knowing which companies are solvent and which are not. Chairman Bernanke conveyed a need for tougher regulations of larger firms perhaps even a systemic regulator. Bernanke warns: "the biggest risk is that the U.S. does not have the political will and we do not have the commitment to solve this problem and we just let the problem continue and consequently we cannot count on financial recovery."

The imbalance of trade has been blatantly disregarded since the early 1980s. Enticing tax-credits and incentives for businesses were offered to companies to move overseas. This was once again lucrative for large corporations, but diminished U.S. jobs. Former President, Bill Clinton (1993-2001) signed into effect the North America Free Trade Agreement, known as NAFTA. This imbalance of foreign trade has created irreparable ruin to our nation's prosperity. We have become a nation of consumers, no longer leaders in the world of manufacturers. America has descended from her high position of world's largest creditor to one of the world's largest debtors! The Congressional Budget Office estimates our government will have to borrow 40 cents for every dollar it spends this fiscal year which ends in September of 2011. It is also reported that tax revenues are expected to drop to the lowest level since 1950. Unemployment, the shaky stock market, the mortgage crisis, the failing auto industries, the soaring cost of healthcare and the energy crisis, are all ingredients for a toxic stew. We are striving for economic survival. However, in all probability we are slated for total economic collapse.

Our present-day economy appears to have set a clandestine course with disaster. Economists are now concerned we may be headed into a "double-dip" recession with the potential to surpass the severity of the great depression of the 1930s. The ensuing circumstances will have a global effect. It is said, "If America sneezes the world catches a cold." Out of this global economic chaos, the one world leader, Antichrist, will rise to power, fulfilling Bible prophecy!

America's financial foundation was built on free enterprise. We were a prosperous industrious nation. America was a cornucopia for small business owners and entrepreneurship. There has been a recent shift in government. The current president of the United States, Barack Hussein Obama's administration has used deceptive tactics while in effect working to dismantle capitalism in America. A reported spending bill that triples the budget deficit is dangerous. It created a $1.8 trillion dollar deficit for 2009 alone. This deficit is now greater than ever before in American history, it is reported to be close to the $14.3 trillion cap set by law. This reckless spending bill allocates monies for studies such as why do pigs stink, the Salt-Marsh mouse, and other national absurdities! Big government is destroying the sovereignty of America and drawing us into a global government. Unprecedented in American history, the government has taken over Wall Street and Main Street.

The passing of Obama's healthcare reform bill signified a government takeover of our healthcare system and was accompanied by a mandatory medical insurance program that was to be publicly funded. The process used by Congress to force this bill onto the American people, was rammed through on a Christmas Eve, and incited civil unrest. This healthcare reform bill by any other name was also a redistribution of wealth! As of this writing the constitutionality of the healthcare bill is still being challenged in our court system. Obama's campaign proposal of a "Civilian Para-Military" warns of a future government with the capability to exercise forced control over the general public. America is rapidly being propelled into Socialism.

The New World Order, first called for by Former President George Herbert Bush (1989-1993), once seemed impossible. Now, this once extreme statement is becoming reality. We are witnesses to ancient Biblical prophecies being fulfilled before our eyes. We are going to see new boundaries being formed throughout Europe, Asia and North America. The fall of the Berlin Wall took the world by surprise, its rise happened as suddenly as did its fall. With almost unbelievable swiftness, the domino effect swept through the communist countries. New borders were formed throughout Europe and Asia. There is once again a United Germany. Man cannot take credit for the dissolution of the Berlin Wall. What would have taken mortal man many bloody wars, and lengthy negotiations, was accomplished by the will of God. When the Soviet Union collapsed, the Ukraine gained its independence from Russia. At present, the Ukrainian President is proposing to join NATO. Giant steps are now being taken for a united Europe. Remembering the former Soviet Union, the former Yugoslavia, the former Czechoslovakia are all predictors of what is to come. Proverbs 8:15, "By me (God) kings reign, and princes decree justice."

A new world currency made its debut onto the world scene in 2002. When the Euro became the centralized currency for most of Europe, the American dollar began to decline in value. The U.S. trade and budget deficits continue to increase, further inflating the value of the euro. The demise of the dollar is evident as it declines in value against all major world currencies. In September 2007, former Federal Reserve Chairman, Alan Greenspan stated that the euro could replace the U.S. dollar as the world's primary reserve currency. Further stating, "It is absolutely conceivable that the euro will replace the dollar as reserve currency, or will be traded as an equally important reserve currency." This is a precursor to the one-world (or centralized) currency which will help set the stage for "the beast" to rise to power. He is the evil one described in the Book of Revelation, as having all power and persuasion to control our money system at the end of Gentile world domination! Revelation 13:16-17, "And he (the beast) causeth all, both small and great, rich and poor, free and bond (prisoners), to receive a mark in their right hand, or in their foreheads: And that no man might buy or sell, save (except) he that had the mark, or the name of the beast, or the number of his name."

Former Prime Minister of England, Margaret Thatcher, resigned her post because she would not concede to a United Europe. Another of England's former Prime Ministers, Gordon Brown, spoke of a "New Deal." President Obama and the former Prime Minister Brown were featured on television, sitting together, and in agreement concerning A New World Order. New boundaries will be forthcoming as the amalgamation of North America is instituted. During the administration of former President George Walker Bush (2000-2008) son of George Herbert Bush, American government officials had secret meetings with government leaders of Canada, England, and Mexico. In that time period, U.S. Secretary of State, Condoleezza Rice and President G.W. Bush had many covert meetings. Their common goal was to unite America with Canada and Mexico, literally laying the groundwork for the New Global Community. There will be new boundaries, new money, a new one-world government, and a call for a one-world religion. The Prophets of old foretold many of these things would happen before the return of Jesus Christ.

Recent events in the Middle East have given us a commanding view of Bible prophecy being fulfilled before our eyes. Perhaps, Desert Storm, Shock and Awe, the Wars in Iraq and Afghanistan are a prelude to the final and fateful "Battle of Armageddon" foretold by the Bible prophets. These wars have been successful in gaining the world's attention, by gathering a great army of men and munitions to the area where all Bible prophecy will culminate, true to God's Word. His word tells us in Luke 21:20-22, "And when ye shall see Jerusalem compassed with armies, then know that the desolation thereof is nigh. Then let them which are in Judaea flee to the mountains; and let them which are in the midst of it depart out; and let not them that are in the countries enter thereinto. For these be the days of vengeance, that all things which are written may be fulfilled."

The Arab Nations are calling for Israel to give up God's Holy City Jerusalem and for Israel to submit to a Palestinian State. The call for the New World Order will result in a seven-year peace treaty; possibly demanding Israel to give up the West Bank or be forced to participate in a bi-national state.

In 2005, under the presidency of George Walker Bush, Israel was pressured by the United States Government to give up the Gaza Strip. This resulted in 8,100 Israelis being forced to leave their homes in Gaza through the dismantling of twenty-one Israeli settlements. This exacerbated the ancient conflict between the Arabs and the Jews. The Israeli withdraw strengthened radical jihadist Islam. The terrorist organization Hamas was emboldened and gained a vantage point from which to launch rockets from Gaza itself into Israeli blocs. The Arabs currently occupying that region are not the rightful owners of that land. God gave that land to Abraham and his seed, and it is to be Israel's everlasting Covenant possession! Careful study of scripture proves Jesus will rule and reign from the throne of David in Jerusalem during Jesus' Second Advent. It will be a time of peace foretold by both Old and New Testament prophets.

Mahmoud Abbas, current President of the Palestinian National Authority, recently demanded that Israel stop building their settlements. Yet, the Palestinians continue to build unabated and are not held accountable to the same mandate. President Barack Obama's administration is pressuring Israel to stop building settlements on their own God-given historic land. The White House press secretary released a statement in September 2009: "As the President has said before, the United States does not accept the legitimacy of continued settlement expansion and we urge that it stop. We are working to create a climate in which negotiations can take place, and such actions make it harder to create such a climate." President Obama's hard stance against Israel is cause for unease. In March of 2010, while visiting the White House, Israeli Prime Minister Benjamin Netanyahu endured an abrupt, and unprecedented, political snub by President Obama. Reportedly, Mr. Obama was trying to obtain a written promise from Netanyahu of concessions on the settlements in Israel. Prayerfully, Prime Minister Netanyahu will stand resolute against the enemies of Israel. It is evident Israel's enemies are many, and to be an enemy of Israel is to be an enemy of God! The Bible proclaims 930 times that Israel belongs to the Jews, yet, Mr. Obama has promised East Jerusalem to the Palestinians.

In June 2010, The United Nations Security Council passed a resolution to impose sanctions that would restrict arms being imported to the Islamic nation of Iran. Iran not only poses a threat to Israel, but to The United States as well. The meeting at the UN headquarters in New York City resulted in an international standoff over Iran's refusal to stop their nuclear program. Iran's current President Ahmadinejad arrogantly stated, "The proposed denuclearization process is worth nothing and the sanctions are laughable." Russia, Turkey, and China support Iran's right for peaceful use of nuclear energy.

The recent revolution in Egypt is alarmingly significant. Longtime Egyptian President, Mubarak was forced to resign. In the 1980s Anwar Sadat of Egypt, signed a peace treaty with the U.S. and Israel. Sadat, Mubarak's predecessor, was shortly thereafter assassinated. Mubarak honored the peace agreement and has been our ally for 30 years. The day before Mubarak stepped down, it was reported on television that U.S. President Barack Obama advised Egyptian leader Mubarak to "step down" citing "it is time for change." The country is now in transition and reportedly seeking a democratic Egypt. The presence of deep-seated radical Islamic fundamentalists, "The Muslim Brotherhood" poses a serious threat to a future democratic Egypt and would most assuredly promote hostility and present a viable threat against Israel and the U.S.

In 1948 Israel once again became a Nation. God re-gathered the Hebrew people back to Israel from every corner of the world. Prophecy is always threefold: Primary, secondary, and has an ultimate fulfillment. God's chosen children have experienced three expulsions from Israel. First, they went into Egyptian bondage because of disobedience. Secondly, they were carried away captives into Babylon, because of national sins. Lastly, the city of Jerusalem fell in A.D. 70 because of their rejection of Jesus Christ as Messiah.

The rightful heirs of that land were once again dispersed throughout the world. God promised the Jews would be restored back to Jerusalem and ultimately back to right standing with Him. Scripture proves scripture. In Exodus 19:4 "Ye have seen what I did unto the Egyptians, and how I bare you on eagles' wings, and brought you unto myself." Clearly, in this passage of scripture, we have an example of the power and accuracy of Bible prophecy. These words first spoken by God were for that time period. Moses, as deliverer, was bringing God's children out of Egyptian bondage.

God was also speaking prophetically to the Jews of this age. Airplanes were yet far into the future. Many were witnesses via television, seeing the Jews being re-gathered from every corner of the world. The return of hundreds of thousands of Soviet and Ethiopian Jews proved to be a successful airlift campaign (on eagle's wings) back to Jerusalem. This ancient Bible prophecy recorded in Exodus was ultimately fulfilled!

The land was also made desolate after A.D. 70. It became rocks and barren stubble, where almost nothing would grow. Prophecy also told us the land of Israel would once again be restored. Ezekiel 36:34-36, "And the desolate land shall be tilled, whereas it lay desolate in the sight of all that passed by. And they shall say, This land that was desolate is become like the garden of Eden; and the waste and desolate and ruined cities are become fenced, and inhabited. Then the heathen that are left round about you shall know that I the LORD build the ruined places, and plant that that was desolate: I the LORD have spoken it, and I will do it." Since the return of the Jewish people to their homeland, the once barren desert land has become lush and fruitful.

After centuries of dissension and bitter enmity between the Arabs and the Jews, the prophesied seven year peace treaty will have the appearance of being the sought-after political solution. Three major components of this evil amalgamation will make up a united world system, being economic, political, and religious. The religious faction will be the confederation of all apostate religions of the world. All aspects of this treaty will come together through the alliance and under the control of the unholy-trinity. There will be three distinct aspects: the beast (the economic world system), the false prophet (the one world religion) and the Antichrist (the one world leader). This world stronghold will be the unparalleled manifestation of the evils of the ages. This evil alliance will continue in force until Antichrist breaks the seven year peace treaty, after three and one-half years. All God's fury, at that time, will be unleashed upon the inhabitants of the earth. It is then that pandemonium will reign upon the earth. God is going to allow mankind to do his worst to mankind. There will also be wickedness, plagues, diseases, and catastrophic upheavals in nature. It is then that Jesus, The Messiah, will return to earth with a Heavenly Host, as The King of Kings and Lord of Lords. At the end of the appointed seven years, Jesus will put an end to Antichrists' evil dictatorial reign and finish the Battle of Armageddon, raging in the Valley of Megiddo in Israel.

Zechariah 12:1-3, "The burden of the word of the LORD for Israel, saith the LORD, which stretcheth forth the heavens, and layeth the foundation of the earth, and formeth the spirit of man within him. Behold, I will make Jerusalem a cup of trembling unto all the people round about, when they shall be in the siege both against Judah and against Jerusalem. And in that day will I make Jerusalem a burdensome stone for all people: all that burden themselves with it shall be cut in pieces, though all the people of the earth be gathered together against it."

America should learn an invaluable lesson from history. In 1918 during World War One, Palestine came under the control of Great Britain. In the late 1930s Great Britain tried to neutralize the strength of the Jews by restricting their emigration to Israel. This resolution was racist and an attempt to appease the oil rich Arab nations. As a result millions of Jews and many Christians died in concentration camps in Germany under the evil Hitler regime!

Genesis 12:1-3, "Now the LORD had said unto Abram (Abraham), Get thee out of thy country, and from thy kindred, and from thy father's house, unto a land that I will shew thee (land of Canaan, later Palestine, now Israel): And I will make of thee a great nation, and I will bless thee, and make thy name great; and shalt be a blessing: And I will bless them that bless thee, and curse him that curseth thee: and in thee shall all families of the earth be blessed."

We, as a people or a nation, cannot compromise, hinder, or harm Israel. We must not, through ignorance, coercion or intentionally, prostitute ourselves to any situation or condition that would threaten or weaken the welfare of the Nation of Israel. We cannot even afford neutrality. It would be an affront to God to come against God's city of Jerusalem or oppose God's people the Jews!

The Old Testament prophet Ezekiel in chapter 38 forewarns that God himself is going to fight against the enemies of Israel. Bible scholars believe these referenced in the following scriptures is to be a confederated northern (to Israel) European army. Ezekiel 38:1-6, "And the word of the LORD came unto me, saying, Son of man, set thy face against Gog (yet future, but probably Russian, leader), the land of Magog (perhaps Russia), the chief prince of Meshech (Perhaps Moscow), and Tubal (perhaps Tobolsk), and prophesy against him, And say, Thus saith the Lord GOD; Behold I am against thee, O Gog, the chief prince of Meshech and Tubal: And I (God) will turn thee back, and put hooks into thy jaws, and I will bring thee forth, and all thine army, horses and horsemen, all of them clothed with all sorts of armour, even a great company with bucklers and shields, all of them handling swords: Persia (now Iran), Ethiopia, and Libya with them; all of them with shield and helmet: Gomer (perhaps Germany), and all his bands; the house of Togarmah (Heb. root word–son of Gomer) of the north quarters, and all his bands: and many people with thee." The terminology horse and horsemen could be symbolic of warriors, but there is always a literal fulfillment of scripture. These scriptures indicate there will be a shortage of oil for fuels. A shortage of oil, or greed for oil, may hasten this end-time army of horsemen.

During Desert Storm, Iraq's Saddam Hussein, set Kuwait's oil fields on fire. This was a deliberate assault on the earth and its natural resources, and demonstrated a contemptible disregard for the earth and its inhabitants. Hussein was executed December 30, 2006 for crimes against humanity. Ezekiel 38:11-13, "And thou shalt say, I (enemies of Israel) will go up to the land of unwalled villages; I will go to them that are at rest, that dwell safely, all of them dwelling without walls, and having neither bars nor gates, To take a spoil, and to take a prey; and to turn thine hand upon the desolate places that are now inhabited, and upon the people that are gathered out of the nations (re-gathered Israel), which have gotten cattle and goods, that dwell in the midst of the land. Sheba, and Dedan, and the merchants of Tarshish, with all the young lions (sadly, perhaps England and America) thereof, shall say unto thee, Art thou come to take a spoil? hast thou gathered thy company to take a prey? to carry away silver and gold, to take away cattle and goods, to take away a great spoil?" Perhaps this great spoil is the costly and precious oil necessary for energy, machinery, transportation, and multiple military conveyances. August 17, 2010 it was reported that Israel discovered over 1.5 billion barrels of oil called the Rosh HaAyin Discovery. The find is located on the edge of Samaria in Central Israel and could be the costly and precious spoil that draws the enemies of Israel to her very door.

On April 20, 2010, one of the worst environmental disasters in American history occurred as a fire caused an explosion on a BP (British Petroleum) offshore drilling rig located off our Gulf Coast region, and tragically killed 11 workers. As the damaged rig sunk, the oil started gushing from the damaged well 5,000 feet below the surface and 13,000 feet back under the seabed. Scientists estimate the well spewed between 94 million and 184 million gallons of crude oil into our beautiful Gulf waters for 3 months before BP successfully placed a 75-ton cap onto the mile-deep, blown out well. This estimate translates to nearly $4 billion dollars of damage to the once beautiful waters of the Gulf of Mexico. Heavy oil polluted the waters, marshlands, and destroyed fish, shrimp, oysters, crabs, sea turtles, and pelicans. We are all saddened by the loss of lives and disheartened by the detrimental effect on the region and the economy. Approximately one-third of our fish and seafood supply comes from our once beautiful Gulf region. The catastrophe in the Gulf started April 20th just 3 weeks after the March 26th diplomatic snub to Israel's Prime Minister Netanyahu, by President Obama. This is a significant timeframe because Israel celebrates their Nation's Independence Day on May 16. In Hebrew it is called Yom Ha'Atzmaut. During the crisis in the Gulf, the Governor of Mississippi, Haley Barbour, and several other gulf coast governors proclaimed June 27th a day of prayer, asking for prayer for the Gulf Coast states affected by the oil gushing from the blown-out undersea well. 2 Chronicles 7:14, "If my people, which are called by my name, shall humble themselves, and pray, and seek my face, and turn from their wicked ways; then will I hear from heaven, and will forgive their sin, and will heal their land." If this was a chastisement of America from God, it is not because the people of the Gulf Coast are more iniquitous than any other people or region in our country.

In 2005 Hurricane Katrina, and the subsequent flooding that left 3,000 people dead and tens of thousands Americans homeless in the New Orleans area, came on the heels of President G.W. Bush's pressuring Israel to give up the Gaza Strip. This mandate called for the evacuation of the Jews from the Gaza Strip and resulted in over 8,000 Israeli people being displaced and homeless. Could these remedial judgments being visited on us as a nation be the result of America's insensitivity to Israel and their needs? Sadly, if America continues her arrogance and hard stance against the nation Israel and God's people the Jews, it most assuredly will result in <u>catastrophic judgments</u> of apocalyptic proportions coming to America.

Remember, America was established as a Democratic Republic. The three branches of government are Executive, Legislative and Judicial. These three are to represent "We The People." America votes in the men and women who write our laws and appoint our judges, but the righteous Godly principles on which this nation was founded have been usurped. The present condition of our nation is indicative of our departure from God. We, as a nation and a people, must turn back to God, and turn away from wickedness. Luke 10:12, "But I say unto you, that it shall be more tolerable in that day (Day of the Lord's return) for Sodom, than for that city." God is a loving and merciful Father, but there is coming a time when continued willful rebellion against God and God's ways will be final. God's Word (The Holy Bible) is not like Burger King, you can't have it <u>your</u> way! Rejection of God and perversion of His Truths cannot continue without consequences.

Ezekiel 38:16-18, "And thou shalt come up against my people of Israel, as a cloud to cover the land; it shall be in the latter days (the end of the Gentile world rule), and I will bring thee against my land (Israel is God's land), that the heathen may know me, when I shall be sanctified in thee, O Gog, before their eyes. Thus saith the Lord GOD; Art thou he of whom I have spoken in old time by my servants the prophets of Israel, which prophesied in those days many years that I would bring thee against them? And it shall come to pass at the same time when Gog (powers headed by Russia) shall come against the land of Israel, saith the Lord GOD, that my fury shall come up in my face." All advanced modern technology and our space-age weaponry is going to wane in comparison to the wrath Almighty God will pour out upon the enemies of Israel. We as a people must guard Israel with gusto!

Traditionally, a Hebrew father pronounced blessings upon his sons while placing his right hand on the head of the first born who by birthright, was to receive the greatest blessing and inheritance. In Genesis chapter 48, there is an account of Jacob (God later changed his name to Israel) blessing his two grandsons, Ephraim and Manasseh, sons of Joseph and his <u>Gentile wife</u>, Asenath.

Genesis 48:13-14, "And Joseph took them both, Ephraim in his right hand toward Israel's (Jacob's) left hand, and Manasseh in his left hand toward Israel's right hand, and brought them near unto him. And Israel stretched out his right hand, and laid it upon Ephraim's head, who was the younger, and his left hand upon Manasseh's head, guiding his hands wittingly (by the crossing over of his hands); for Manasseh was the firstborn."

It appeared to Joseph that his father was, unwittingly, about to give the greater blessing to the younger son. Joseph, thinking to correct his father's error, asked Jacob (Israel) to place his right hand on Manasseh, the elder. Continuing in verse 19, "And his father refused, and said, I know it, my son, I know it: he also shall become a people, and he also shall be great: but truly his younger brother shall be greater (in number) than he, and his seed shall become a multitude of nations."

Some mistakenly believe that the Gentiles have replaced the Jews as God's chosen people. This replacement theory is wrong. Former President James Carter (1977-1981) has for this reason, or perhaps some other misguided belief system, positioned himself against the Nation Israel. He has proven himself to be a Palestinian sympathizer. He is a professing Christian, but his position against Israel indicates a lack of understanding of God's purpose and God's harmony with Israel. God's plan miraculously included the Gentiles, never to the exclusion of the Jews. Jesus died to make Jew and Gentile one people. The crossing of Israel's (Jacob's) hands has a great and significant meaning. It was a symbolic foreshadow of the Cross. God reversed the greater blessing from his Jewish children to His Gentile children. In a spiritual sense God crossed hands and, through the Blood that Jesus shed while on the cross of Calvary, blessed <u>also</u> the Gentile Nations. <u>Greater in number only!</u>

Ephesians 3:2-6, "If ye have heard of the dispensation of the grace of God which is given me to you-ward: How that by revelation he made known unto me the mystery; (as I wrote afore in few words, Whereby, when ye read, ye may understand my knowledge in the mystery of Christ) Which in other ages was not made known unto the sons of men, as it is now revealed unto his holy apostles and prophets by the Spirit; That the Gentiles should be fellowheirs, and of the same body, and partakers of his promise in Christ by the gospel."

Never in eternity past has there ever been, nor in eternity future shall there ever be, an act of such inordinately supreme importance as that which Emmanuel (God with us) accomplished while on the cross. This merciful plan of salvation for both the Jew and the Gentile surpasses finite understanding or logic. By His supreme and willing Blood Sacrifice, Jesus changed man's destiny from inevitable destruction to everlasting life. God redeemed man while bringing unity to Jew and Gentile.

Romans 11:11, "I say then, Have they (Jewish children) stumbled that they should fall? God forbid: but rather through their fall salvation has come unto the Gentiles, for to provoke them (the Hebrews) to jealousy."

The Gentiles could then also receive, through adoption, the blessings of Abraham. This redemption plan was first to the Jew, and then to the Gentile, and to whosoever will. Romans 9:30-33, "What shall we say then? That the Gentiles, which followed not after righteousness, have attained to righteousness, even the righteousness which is of faith. But Israel, which followed after the law of righteousness, hath not attained to the law of righteousness Wherefore (why)? Because they sought it not by faith, but as it were by the works of the law. For they stumbled at the stumblingstone (Jesus Christ); As it is written, Behold, I lay in Sion a stumblingstone and rock of offence: and whosoever believeth on him (Jesus Christ) shall not be ashamed."

The birthright and greatest blessings belong to God's Hebrew children, but by His mercy and grace, Gentiles were afforded the blessings of Abraham and through adoption were brought into the family of God. Continuing the analogy concerning the reversed-hand blessing of Jacob (who God later changed his name to Israel) upon his grandsons, we see the blessing return to the Jews as recorded in Genesis 48:21, "And Israel (Jacob) said unto Joseph, Behold I die: but God shall be with you, and bring you again unto the land of your fathers (the re-gathering of the Jews to their homeland)."

We've seen the world-wide re-gathering of Jews to Israel, the land of their fathers, thus fulfilling in part this obscure prophecy which will culminate with the fullness of the blessing reverting to the Jews. God's divine judgment has started on the Gentile World powers. We are witnessing the conclusion of this dispensation of God's grace to the Gentile nations.

Romans 11:25, "For I would not, brethren, that ye should be ignorant of this mystery, lest ye should be wise in your own conceits; that blindness in part is happened to Israel, until the fullness of the Gentiles be come in."

While in prayer, God revealed to me, that we, as the Gentile nations, have woefully failed God. Tragically, the Judeo-Christian Church that began on the Day of Pentecost has fallen asleep! As a watchman cries out a warning of impending doom to a slumbering city, the angel of the church of Laodicea is crying out a warning today, admonishing those who are spiritually asleep, careless, lukewarm, and indifferent to the Gospel of Jesus Christ. This present day, apostate church is unacceptable to a holy and righteous God.

In Revelation 3:15-16, Jesus said to the church of Laodicea, "I know thy works, that thou art neither cold nor hot: I would that thou wert (were) cold or hot. So then because thou art lukewarm (spiritually), and neither cold nor hot, I (God) will spue thee out of my mouth."

In April of 2009, President Obama delivered a speech at Georgetown University in Washington D.C. Georgetown is a Christian college. The Obama administration requested that Christian emblems be covered or draped. The emblem representing Jesus' name in Greek "I H S" was inscribed high on a wall in the lecture hall. A piece of plywood, painted black and triangular in shape was boarded over the inscription and blotted out the name of Jesus! Those who are responsible for allowing this irreverence at Georgetown University have compromised their Christian stance!

Titus 1:16, "They profess that they know God; but in works they deny him, being abominable, and disobedient, and unto every good work reprobate."

Sadly, America promotes the ideologies of the false gods of mammon (material wealth) and diversion. In our quest for material possessions, and an insatiable need for mindless entertainment, America has departed from the God of our fathers; Jehovah God. We are prostituting ourselves and substituting our God-directed mission of furthering the Gospel of Jesus Christ for immediate gratification of our fleshly appetites. America must have revival! We have neglected our call to righteousness. The need in this midnight hour calls for repentance of sin and Godly sorrow.

We are on the threshold of a mighty awakening, and by many signs all around us, we know a powerful shaking has already started. Christians must arise from spiritual apathy to truth and shake off the heavy bands of sin and slothfulness!

Jesus Christ is coming soon to rapture (catch away) the waiting church of the redeemed. Those found worthy to be translated alive into heaven, will be the ones who have repented of their sins and donned the righteousness of Jesus Christ. Keep looking up! He is coming soon!

1 Thessalonians 4:15-18, "For this we say unto you by the word of the Lord, that we which are alive and remain unto the coming of the Lord shall not prevent (preclude) them which are asleep. For the

Lord himself shall descend from heaven with a shout, with the voice of the archangel, and with the trump of God: and the dead in Christ (the righteous ones who have already died) shall rise first: Then we which are alive and remain shall be caught up (translated) together with them in the clouds, to meet the Lord in the air: and so shall we ever be with the Lord. Wherefore comfort one another with these words." The Church is Jesus' bride, living a life of purity through the indwelling of the Holy Ghost. The Church is comprised of both Jew and Gentile, all who have accepted Jesus Christ as Messiah and have made Him Lord of their lives.

The disappearance of multitudes of people, caught up alive into heaven with Jesus, may be masked by a worldwide earthquake. It is interesting that at the completion of the Old Testament there was a great earthquake. Perhaps at the completion of the New Testament there will also be a great earthquake.

Matthew 27:50-52, "Jesus, when he had cried with a loud voice, yielded up the ghost. And, behold the veil of the temple was rent in twain (torn in half) from the top to the bottom; and the earth did quake, and the rocks rent; And the graves were opened; and many bodies of the saints which slept (in death) arose."

When Jesus fulfilled The Old Testament (Covenant) the curtain where God's presence dwelt was split in half. He dwelt in The Holy of Holies in The Temple, but as The New Testament (Covenant) came into existence, God departed there and now dwells within man! The New Covenant made with God's own Blood (body of Jesus) will perhaps also end with an earthquake.

Revelation 6:12, "And I (John) beheld when he had opened the sixth seal, and, lo, there was <u>a great earthquake;</u> and the sun became black as sackcloth of hair, and the moon became as blood."

The Book of Revelation is a prophetic book and this great earthquake is yet in the future. We don't know when these events will take place. We do know they will happen, because God is forewarning us and is preparing us through His word. This earthquake, yet future, will leave in its wake missing multitudes, injury, diseases, and death! It could contaminate water and food sources. It could leave the world with little or no communication! These horrendous happenings may present an apparent need for the man of sin, the Antichrist, causing him to seize the advantage and further his dictatorial reign. Through tyranny, and much deception, he will eventually falsely proclaim himself to be the Messiah!

Jesus himself warned us of this coming deception. John 5:43, "I am come in my Father's name, and ye received me not: if another shall come in his own name, him ye will receive." This international personality, will first present himself as a man of peace. He will act expeditiously, capably, and perform miracles by his deceptions, with lying signs and wonders. In reality he will be the son of perdition, a counterfeit Christ, and all who follow him will be destroyed!

It will be the time of the seven years of the Great Tribulation. This prophesied seven year time period, will bring unsurpassed suffering and horrors as the world has never experienced before, or ever shall again. One must not be lulled into a false sense of security and be deceived by the pseudo-peace system brought into existence by the man of sin.

The Bible forewarns in 1 Thessalonians 5:3-4, "For when they shall say, Peace and safety; then sudden destruction cometh upon them, as travail upon a woman with child; and they shall not escape. But ye, brethren, are not in darkness, that that day should overtake you as a thief." Indeed it is true the events taking place in today's world are fast and fascinating!

This world is being readied for the culmination of this dispensation of God's Grace known also as the Church Age and the culmination of this Gentile world rule. The inhabitants of the world will be propelled into seven years of tribulation. Everyone must look to Jesus who has provided the way of escape. One must stand fast when the entire world is in great disorder.

Luke 21:25-28, "And there shall be signs in the sun, and in the moon, and in the stars; and upon the earth distress of nations, with perplexity; the sea and the waves roaring; Men's hearts failing them for fear, and for looking after those things which are coming on the earth: for the powers of heaven shall be shaken. And then shall they see the Son of man coming in a cloud with power and great glory. And when these things <u>begin</u> to come to pass, then look up, and lift up your heads; for your redemption draweth nigh."

We are living in a world that is poised on the brink of destruction. Sadly, man faces man as opponents. Good versus evil, and we are suspended over a moral abyss. Countries all over the world are procuring and putting into place weapons of mass destruction, with lethal intent! Christians must stand strong in knowing that righteousness through Jesus will ultimately prevail. God's Word has declared it!

Chapter Two

A Living Christ for a Dying World

"For as by one man's (Adam's) disobedience many were made sinners, so by the obedience of one (Jesus) shall many be made righteous."

(Romans 5:19)

How can we survive and spiritually prosper in a world where everything seems to be raging out of control? The morals and high ideals we, as people, once held are apparently forgotten. Situational ethics have, for so many, become a mode of life.

The breakup of the traditional family has left many people unanchored, and adrift in a harsh environment. One out of every three marriages ends in divorce. Today, many couples choose not to marry. They live together without the sanctity of the marriage ceremony and the blessing of God. The absence and apathy of parents has produced a dangerous culture. Drug and alcohol abuse have become epidemic in America. Televisions, movie theaters, home videos, and the home computer have created a medium for one to view violence, murder, sexual perversions and all manner of depravity. Music often contains demoralizing and uncensored language. Many of the youth in our culture are disobedient and disrespectful to those in authority.

In the United States, murder is the number one cause of death for pregnant women. These crimes are, almost without exception, committed by their husbands or a boyfriend. In Tracy, California, an eight-year-old girl was abducted, raped, and murdered. A 28-year-old female was charged with these heinous crimes against nature. Initial investigation of the child's disappearance revealed that in a five-mile radius of her home there were eighty known sexual offenders. We have become an odious, violent, and sexually oriented society.

Sin seems to reign supreme. Can we agree that these are sufficient reasons to bring us back to the basics our country was wonderfully founded upon? Originally, America abided by precepts that harmonized with the commandments of God. The disastrous circumstances around us should not have dominion over us. God did not create us to be mastered by the diverse and perplexing problems of life. God is the answer to obtaining deliverance from the curse of sin, and its end result, that was visited upon man.

Mankind is sinful and responsible for the calamitous condition of the world, not God! God created man for His pleasure, and life in the Garden was to be pleasant and peaceful. Adam and Eve were created to enjoy the beauty and serenity of life complete with God's fellowship. God walked and talked with them, and there was never to be any separation between the Creator God and His creation, man. Man was never to have known any woes, sickness, sorrows, pain, nor experience death. God had commanded Adam and Eve, as recorded in Genesis 2:16-17, "And the LORD God commanded the man, saying, Of every tree of the Garden thou mayest freely eat: But of the tree of the knowledge of good and evil, thou shalt not eat of it: for in the day that thou eatest thereof thou shalt surely die." This was the first law, or commandment, that was given to mankind. The definition of sin is very simple. Sin is disobedience to God's word.

Reading further in Genesis, we see the temptation that caused the fall of man. Genesis 3:4-5, "And the serpent said unto the woman, Ye shall not surely die: For God doth know that in the day ye eat thereof, then your eyes shall be opened, and ye shall be as gods, knowing good and evil." Then Eve, seeing the tree was good for food, ate of the forbidden fruit, and gave some to her husband and he ate the fruit as well. The commandment given by God to Adam and Eve was a type of providential care, as are all God's commandments that are given to man. God's instruction not to eat of the tree was for their benefit. God created Adam and Eve innocent as little children, having no carnal knowledge. After eating of the forbidden fruit, their eyes were opened to discern the difference between good and evil and thus became accountable for sin. In the temptation to which Eve, and then Adam yielded, Satan won a temporary victory. Man had obeyed the enemy instead of his Creator. The folly of listening, and yielding, to Satan's temptations always has, and always will, result in disaster. For man's disobedience to God's commandment, he not only received the forewarned death sentence, but also a fallen sin nature.

A very sad scene shortly followed. As God came down to fellowship with Adam and Eve, we see the beginning of sorrows to be visited upon mankind. Genesis 3:8-10, "And they heard the voice of the LORD God walking in the Garden in the cool of the day: and Adam and his wife hid themselves from the presence of the LORD God amongst the trees of the garden. And the LORD God called unto Adam, and said unto him, Where art thou? And he (Adam) said, I heard thy voice in the garden, and I was afraid, because I was naked; and I hid myself."

Sin always has consequences. Here we see the first three consequences garnered by man. First, was guilt, second was fear, and third was separation from God! Until this time, the emotions and the effects of sin were totally alien to man. We were not created to bear guilt, shame, fear, reproach, death, or separation from God. In Genesis 3:14-19, God cursed Adam, Eve, and the serpent, "And the LORD God said unto the serpent, Because thou hast done this, thou art cursed above all cattle, and above every beast of the field, upon thy belly shalt thou go, and dust shalt thou eat all the days of thy life: And I will put enmity between thee and the woman, and between thy seed and her seed; it shall bruise thy head, and thou shalt bruise his heel." God told Eve, "… in sorrow thou shalt bring forth children …" and He told Adam, "… Because thou hast hearkened unto the voice of thy wife, and hast eaten of the tree, of which I commanded thee, saying, Thou shalt not eat of it: cursed is the ground for thy sake; in sorrow shalt thou eat of it all the days of thy life; Thorns also and thistles shall it bring forth to thee … In the sweat of thy face shalt thou eat bread, till thou return to the ground; for out of it wast thou taken: for dust thou art, and unto dust shalt thou return." Despite inflation, the wages of sin remain the same-death. Romans 6:23. "For the wages of sin is death; but the gift of God is eternal life through Jesus Christ our Lord."

All of these dire pronouncements were a direct result of man's original sin. Genesis 3:22-23, "And the LORD God said, Behold, the man is become as one of us, to know good and evil: and now, lest he put forth his hand, and take also of the tree of life, and eat, and live forever: Therefore the LORD God sent him (man) forth from the garden of Eden, to till the ground from whence he was taken." We see God's mercy laced with His judgment. In this instance "judgment" means punishment. God sent them out of the garden, in part, for their own good. Had they stayed in the garden and eaten of the "Tree of Life," their immortal souls would have strayed beyond salvation, reprobate! The souls of mankind would have gone into the realm of eternal life, in an unredeemable state, trapped in eternal damnation in hell. There were more consequences of sin yet to come. The anguish and heartbreak Adam and Eve suffered as their firstborn son, Cain, rose up and killed his brother Abel. In all probability, they knew this murder was a direct result of the sin-nature that had taken over all mankind. All these sorrows were a result of Adam and Eve's direct disobedience to the Living God.

Satan, in the guise or embodiment of the serpent, beguiled Eve to obey him instead of God. In a shrouded mystery God declared a grand plan to redeem His beloved creation man, back from Satan. Genesis 3:15, "And I will put enmity between thee and the woman, and between thy seed and her seed; it (seed of the woman–Jesus) shall bruise thy head (Jesus destroyed the headship of Satan) and thou shall bruise his heel." God in a prophetic decree, shrouded in profound mystery, declared the seed of the woman would win back the souls of men, in victory over Satan. God being omniscient (having all knowledge) knew He would send Jesus to the earth as the Redeemer. Jesus would buy back the souls of men from the wicked deceiver, at the cost of Jesus Christ's own blood. This atoning sacrifice would contain all the necessary properties to restore fallen man back to full fellowship to God.

The prophet Isaiah foretold of this coming savior in Isaiah 9:6-7, "For unto us a child is born, unto us a son is given: and the government shall be upon his shoulder: and his name shall be called Wonderful, Counsellor, The mighty God, The everlasting Father, and the Prince of Peace. Of the increase of his government and peace there shall be no end, upon the throne of David, and upon his kingdom, to order it, and to establish it with judgment and with justice from henceforth even for ever. The zeal of the LORD of hosts will perform this." Glory to God for the salvation plan that destroyed Satan's temporary victory over mankind! At the appointed time, God put into action His grand plan to save us from our sins. Jesus Christ who was God's sacrificial Lamb, died on the cross of Calvary and spanned the gulf of separation created by man's sin. This sacrifice reconciled the fallen creation back to the Creator. Man could not attain to the heights of God, so God-Himself put on the garment of flesh and came down to man. The love and sacrifice of our gracious Savior is awesome. The miraculous plan was hidden so deep in mystery, that Satan missed it. Satan thought he was stopping God's plan when Jesus was crucified on the cross. In actuality, it is and always will be the resounding victory over sin and Satan.

In the New Testament (Covenant) we see the Righteous God, who pronounced the death sentence on mankind, now putting in motion His veiled plan of salvation. Matthew 1:18-25, "Now the birth of Jesus Christ was on this wise: When as his mother Mary was espoused to Joseph, before they came together (in a marital union of the flesh), she was found with child of the Holy Ghost. Then Joseph her husband, being a just man, and not willing to make her a public example, was minded (decided) to put her away privily (privately). But while he thought on these things, behold, the angel of the LORD appeared unto him in a dream, saying, Joseph, thou son of David, fear not to take unto thee Mary thy wife: for that which is conceived in her is of the Holy Ghost. And she shall bring forth a son, and thou shalt call his name JESUS (Greek form of Hebrew Jehoshua, meaning Jehovah is salvation): for he shall save his people from their sins. Now all this was done, that it might be fulfilled which was spoken of the Lord by the prophet, saying, Behold, a virgin shall be with child, and shall bring forth a son, and they shall call his name Emmanuel, which being interpreted is, God with us. Then Joseph being raised from sleep did as the angel of the Lord had bidden him, and took unto him his wife: And knew her not (in the marital union of the flesh) till she had brought forth her firstborn son: and he called his name JESUS."

Scripture proves scripture! Isaiah was the Old Testament prophet referenced in Matthew 1:22–23. He prophesied the birth of Jesus in the eighth century before Jesus' birth. Isaiah 7:14, "Therefore the Lord himself shall give you a sign; Behold, a virgin shall conceive, and bear a son, and shall call his name Immanuel." Could the sign Isaiah prophesied be that Jesus was to be born in a stable? The sign of Jesus' birth was shrouded in mystery for He was born God's Sacrificial Lamb! The mystery was that Jesus' sacrificial blood would be shed on the cross to take away the sins of the world. A stable is the appropriate place for a baby lamb to be born. Jesus' birth was first announced to local shepherds; they being the first and appropriate persons to know when baby lambs were born. He was born in a stable and laid in a manger. A manger is a feeding trough and was the appropriate placement for Jesus who is the Bread of Life and it was there that He was "symbolically," first presented to the world. John 6:35, "And Jesus said unto them, I am the bread of life: he that cometh to me shall never hunger; and he that believeth on me shall never thirst." His birth had been announced to the shepherds by the angel of the Lord. Joining the angel of the Lord was a heavenly host and the glory of the Lord shown all about, for Jesus was the Son of God. Luke 2:4-14, "And Joseph also went up from Galilee, out of the city of Nazareth, into Judaea, unto the city of David, which is called Bethlehem (because he was of the house and lineage of David); To be taxed (everyone according to a decree by Caesar Augustus) with Mary his espoused wife, being great with child. And so it was, that, while they were there, the days were accomplished that she should be delivered. And she brought forth her firstborn son, and wrapped him in swaddling clothes, and laid him in a manger; because there was no room for them in the inn. And there were in the same country shepherds abiding in the field, keeping watch over their flock by night. And, lo, the angel of the Lord came upon them, and the glory of the Lord shone round about them: and they were sore afraid. And the angel said unto them, Fear not: for, behold, I bring you good tidings of great joy, which shall be to all people. For unto you is born this day in the city of David a Saviour, which is Christ the Lord. And this shall be a sign unto you; Ye shall find the babe wrapped in swaddling clothes, lying in a manger. And suddenly there was with the angel a multitude of the heavenly host praising God, and saying, Glory to God in the highest, and on earth peace, good will toward men." God's salvation plan had literally been born!

Prophet Isaiah prophesied that Jesus would be born as a baby to a virgin. The prophecy continued that as an adult, Jesus would be revealed as the suffering Messiah. Isaiah 53:6-11, "All we like sheep have gone astray; we have turned every one to his own way; and the LORD hath laid on him the iniquity of us all. He was oppressed, and he was afflicted, yet he opened not his mouth: he is brought as a lamb to the slaughter, and as a sheep before her shearers is dumb (silent), so he openeth not his mouth. He was taken from prison and from judgment: and who shall declare his generation? For he was cut off out of the land of the living (died on the cross): for the transgression (sins) of my people was he stricken. And he made his grave with the wicked, (the two thieves on the other two crosses) and with the rich in his death (Jesus' tomb was donated by a rich man of

Arimathaea); because he had done no violence, neither was any deceit in his mouth (Jesus was sinless). Yet it pleased the LORD to bruise him (God foretold that Satan would bruise the heel of the seed of the woman); he hath put him to grief (Jesus was acquainted with grief): when thou shalt make his soul an offering for sin (on the cross), he shall see his seed, he shall prolong his days (Jesus arose from the dead), and the pleasure (Jesus' sinless blood sacrifice was pleasing to God) of the LORD shall prosper in his hand. He shall see of the travail of his soul (Jesus agonized in death for us sinners), and shall be satisfied: by his knowledge shall my righteous servant (Jesus) justify many; for he shall bear their iniquities."

By His own miraculous plan, the great and loving Jehovah God put on the garment of flesh, and through Jesus became the son of man that the sons of men might become the sons of God. Romans 5:18-19 "Therefore as by the offence of one (Adam), judgment (punishment) came upon all men to condemnation; even so by the righteousness of one (Jesus) the free gift (salvation) came upon all men unto justification of life. For as by one man's disobedience (Adam's) many were made sinners, so by the obedience of one (Jesus) shall many be made righteous." Jesus was obedient unto the course of salvation, even unto his death.

Leviticus 17:11, "For the life of the flesh is in the blood: and I have given it to you upon the altar to make an atonement for your souls ..." The Edenic covenant was broken. Mankind had tragically fallen prey to Satan by rebelling against God's commands. Obeying Satan instead of God caused man's souls to become a pawn of the enemy. At that time our merciful God provided a temporary sacrifice for a covering for Adam and Eve. Genesis 3:21, "Unto Adam also and to his wife did the LORD God make coats of skins, and clothed them." This blood sacrifice was a fore type of Christ, and proved our need of atonement from sin. Recorded in the Old Testament, Isaiah realized man's need of redemption, and prophesied God's plan for the coming Savior. Isaiah 59:16-17, "And he (God) saw that there was no man, and wondered that there was no intercessor: therefore his arm brought salvation unto him; and his righteousness, it sustained him. For he put on righteousness as a breastplate, and an helmet of salvation upon his head; and he put on the garments of vengeance for clothing, and was clad with zeal as a cloak." The blood sacrifice of animals was to be a temporary covenant. At that time, God provided temporary security for mankind, utilizing both the blood to cover sins and the skins as garments for a physical covering for Adam and Eve. God knew, and ordained, that He would send Jesus "The Sacrificial Lamb" whose sinless blood would take away the sins of the world. Jesus' righteousness would then be the necessary covering garment for mankind. God's Deity was manifested in the flesh and blood of Jesus Christ.

Man's mortal enemy, Satan, has always warred against God and His righteous love and perfect plan for mankind! At the time of Jesus' birth, Satan devised a plan to destroy the newly born baby and, if successful, would have destroyed the only chance of man's redemption. The fall of mankind came through man, so man was the only avenue of redemption! Matthew 2:1-6, "Now when Jesus was born in Bethlehem of Judaea in the days of Herod the king, behold, there came wise men from the east to Jerusalem, Saying, Where is he that is born King of the Jews? for we have seen his star in the east, and we are come to worship him. When Herod the king had heard these things, he was troubled, and all Jerusalem with him. And when he had gathered all the chief priests and scribes of the people together, he demanded of them where Christ should be born. And they said unto him, In Bethlehem of Judaea: for thus it is written by the prophet, And thou Bethlehem, in the land of Juda, art not the least among the princes of Juda: for out of thee shall come a Governor, that shall rule my people Israel." Herod was fearful for his position as ruler, prompting inquiries concerning the birth of Jesus, and used a deceitful pretense of desired worship. After finding the baby Jesus, and bestowing him with gifts, the wise men received a warning concerning Herod. Matthew 2:12-15, "And being warned of God in a dream that they should not return to Herod, they departed into their own country another way. And when they were departed, behold, the angel of the Lord appeareth to Joseph in a dream, saying, Arise and take the young child and his mother, and flee into Egypt, and be thou there until I bring thee word: for Herod will seek the young child to destroy him. When he arose, he took the young child and his mother by night, and departed into Egypt: And was there until the death of Herod: that it might be fulfilled which was spoken of the Lord by the prophet, saying, Out of Egypt have I called my son."

Prophecy proves prophecy. Matthew chapter 2, verses 5 and 15 reference Old Testament prophet Hosea. Recorded in Hosea 11:1, "When Israel was a child, then I loved him, and called my son out of

Egypt." Old Testament prophecy concerning the birthplace of Messiah is also recorded in the Book of Micah 5:2, "But thou, Bethlehem Ephratah, though thou be little among the thousands of Judah, yet out of thee shall he (Jesus) come forth unto me that is to be ruler in Israel; whose goings forth have been from of old, from everlasting." Glory to God who causes his prophets to speak, and has all power to cause every word to be fulfilled! Matthew 2:16-23, "Then Herod, when he saw that he was mocked of the wise men, was exceeding wroth, and sent forth, and slew, all the children that were in Bethlehem, and in all the coasts thereof, from two years old and under, according to the time which he had diligently enquired of the wise men. Then was fulfilled that which was spoken by Jeremy (Old Testament prophet Jeremiah) the prophet, saying, In Rama was there a voice heard, lamentation, and weeping, and great mourning, Rachel weeping for her children, and would not be comforted, because they are not. But when Herod was dead, behold an angel of the Lord appeareth in a dream to Joseph in Egypt, Saying, Arise, and take the young child and his mother, and go into the land of Israel: for they are dead which sought the young child's life. And he arose, and took the young child and his mother, and came into the land of Israel. But when he heard that Archelaus did reign in Judaea in the room of his father Herod, he was afraid to go thither: notwithstanding, being warned of God in a dream, he turned aside into the parts of Galilee: And he came and dwelt in a city called Nazareth: that it might be fulfilled which was spoken by the prophets, he shall be called a Nazarene."

Firsthand testimony and eyewitness testimony is the only acceptable testimony in a courtroom. An attorney once told me that he had only read the New Testament once and that he had only read the words printed in red ink. He knew the words printed in red ink indicate the words spoken by Jesus only. Obviously, he was interested in firsthand testimony. I realized John the Baptist, gave eyewitness testimony of the deity and office of Jesus. He recognized Jesus as the prophesied Messiah. An account of John baptizing Jesus is recorded in Matthew 3:13-17, "Then cometh Jesus from Galilee to Jordan unto John, to be baptized of him. But John forbad him, saying, I have need to be baptized of thee, and comest thou to me? And Jesus answering said unto him, Suffer it to be so now: for thus it becometh us to fulfil all righteousness. Then he suffered him. And Jesus, when he was baptized, went straightway out of the water: and, lo, the heavens were opened unto him, and he (John) saw the Spirit of God descending like a dove, and lighting upon him: And lo a voice from heaven, saying, This is my beloved Son, in whom I am well pleased." God was pleased with Jesus and endued Him with power as The Holy Ghost descended on Him. This equipped Jesus with all power to withstand the assaults of the enemy. Matthew 4:1-4, "Then was Jesus led up of the Spirit into the wilderness to be tempted of the devil. And when he had fasted forty days and forty nights, he was afterward an hungred. And when the tempter (Satan, the one who had tempted Eve in the garden) came to him, he said, If thou be the Son of God, command that these stones be made bread. But he answered and said, it is written, Man shall not live by bread alone, but by every word that proceedeth out of the mouth of God." It is worth noting that Jesus conveyed obedience to the commandments of God, obedience is more important to the body than food. It is also spiritually significant that Jesus is the "Bread of Life" for the "Word" is sustenance for our very souls!

The temptation continues. Matthew 4:5-11, "Then the devil taketh him up into the holy city, and setteth him on a pinnacle of the temple, And saith unto him, If thou be the Son of God, cast thyself down: for it is written, He shall give his angels charge concerning thee: and in their hands they shall bear thee up, lest at any time thou dash thy foot against a stone. Jesus said unto him, It is written again, Thou shalt not tempt the Lord thy God. Again, the devil taketh him up into an exceeding high mountain, and sheweth him all the kingdoms of the world, and the glory of them; And saith unto him, All these things will I give thee, if thou wilt fall down and worship me. Then saith Jesus unto him, Get thee hence, Satan: for it is written, Thou shalt worship the Lord God, and him only shalt thou serve. Then the devil leaveth him, and behold, angels came and ministered unto him." Jesus' victory over Satan and his temptations secured His right to buy back the souls of mankind. Satan had procured ownership of man through man's own disobedience to God. Jesus' obedience to God, and God's word, qualified Him as the only proper candidate. Because of God's unfathomable love for mankind, the price of redeeming fallen man back from the devil was paid by Christ's own holy blood. If Jesus had yielded to the Devil's temptations, the souls of mankind would have been unredeemable. Satan set a snare showing the allures of this world. Jesus knew the things of this world are temporary and subject to the order of this world and will pass away. Matthew 6:19-20, "Lay not up for yourselves treasures upon earth, where moth and rust doth corrupt, and where thieves break through and steal: But lay up for yourselves treasures in heaven, where neither moth nor rust doth corrupt, and where thieves do not break through nor steal."

Jesus has a Kingdom that is eternal, unequaled in beauty and splendor. The word tells us "Eye hath not seen, nor ear heard, neither have entered into the heart of man, the things which God hath prepared for them that love him." We also can resist the devils snares. It is written in James 4:7, "Submit yourselves therefore to God. Resist the devil, and he will flee from you." Scriptures prove we are overcomers, and equipped with power to resist our enemy. Satan is the enemy of God and the enemy of our mortal souls. 1 Corinthians 10:13-14, "There hath no temptation taken you but such as is common to man: but God is faithful, who will not suffer you to be tempted above that ye are able; but will with the temptation also make a way to escape, that ye may be able to bear it. Wherefore, my dearly beloved, flee from idolatry." Anything that we put before God and His word is idolatry; it could be a loved one, our home, a job, worldly success, money, sports, television, or possibly another pastime. For many Americans, entertainment and obtaining worldly possessions are given first place, and have taken precedence over God. We must not be subject to the allures and idols of this world, for they are soon to pass away. God demands, and deserves, first place in our lives and is necessary for us to live a victorious Christian life.

John 1:29-34, "The next day John seeth (eyewitness) Jesus coming unto him, and saith, Behold the Lamb of God, which taketh away the sin of the world. This is he of whom I said, After me cometh a man which is preferred before me: for he was before me (Jesus is eternal and was in eternity past). And I knew him not: but that he should be made manifest to Israel, therefore am I come baptizing with water. And John bare record, saying (firsthand eyewitness testimony), I saw the Spirit descending from heaven like a dove, and it abode upon him. And I knew him not: but he that sent me to baptize with water, the same said unto me, Upon whom thou shalt see the Spirit descending, and remaining on him, the same is he which baptizeth with the Holy Ghost. And I saw, and bare record that this is the Son of God." John's eyewitness testimony is of great worth and most valuable. John testifies that Jesus is the Lamb of God that takes away the sins of the world. He baptized Jesus with water and was privileged to witness Jesus' baptism with God's Holy Spirit. This is of paramount importance for us today. The infilling of the Holy Spirit is the avenue and order God set up for man to receive this power also. The salvation plan is accepting Jesus as God's Sacrificial Lamb, repentance and remission of our sins in Jesus' name, water baptism, and the complete infilling of the Holy Ghost.

1 Corinthians 6:19-20, "What? know ye not that your body is the temple of the Holy Ghost which is in you, which ye have of God, and ye are not your own? For ye have been bought with a price: therefore glorify God in your body, and in your spirit, which are God's." He made available that overcoming power to the "Blood-Bought Church." Satan has waged an effective campaign to discredit, mock, and malign the true and complete redemption plan. For centuries, the Devil has waged war against this order and provision God miraculously instituted for His believers. Through ignorance or unbelief, people often shun or malign the Spirit-filled believers. The wicked one does not want believers to know about, accept, or to be filled with the Holy Ghost, for He (the Holy Ghost) provides us overcoming power within! The Christian believer is incomplete without the baptism of the Holy Ghost. It is comparable to one building a home, but leaving it incomplete, without the roof! The indwelling Holy Ghost is our Comforter, Counselor, Guide, and God-given Wisdom. The baptism of the Holy Spirit is the avenue from which the gifts of the Spirit are demonstrated here on earth. He made available this power to the Blood-Bought Church.

We Gentile believers have sorely failed God in His perfect plan for our sanctification and service to a Holy God! God's unfathomable love and mercy toward mankind transcends human comprehension. His love is limitless and without boundaries. Jesus demonstrated God's love by personally dying for each and every one of us. He took our sin-debt onto himself and died in our place. He was judged and suffered the penalty of sin, yet He was sinless. He loves and pardons mankind regardless of the depths of sin one has yielded to. His nail-scarred hand extends down to lift out that one from the depths and dregs of depravity; that one who society shuns and describes as the worst of the worst. God's love saves us, baptism seals us, the reading of The Word reproves, corrects, and cleanses us, and The Holy Spirit empowers us to change from a sinner to a saint.

Recorded in the Gospel of John we have an account of a ruler of the Jews searching for answers pertaining to life's most serious questions. John 3:2-7, "The same came to Jesus by night, and said unto him, Rabbi, we know that thou art a teacher come from God: for no man can do these miracles that thou doest, except God be with him. Jesus answered and said unto him, Verily, verily, I say unto thee, Except a man be born again, he cannot see the kingdom of God. Nicodemus saith unto him, How can a man be born when he is old? can he enter the second time into his mother's womb, and be born? Jesus answered, Verily, verily, I say unto thee, Except a man be born of water and of the Spirit, he cannot enter into the kingdom of God. That which is born of the flesh is flesh; and that which is born of the Spirit (Holy Ghost) is spirit. Marvel not that I said unto thee, Ye must be born again." The Jewish ruler asked Jesus questions concerning eternal life. Continuing with verses 14-20, "And as Moses lifted up the serpent in the wilderness, even so must the Son of man be lifted up (on the cross): That whosoever believeth in him should not perish, but have eternal life. For God so loved the world, that he gave his only begotten Son, that whosoever believeth in him should not perish, but have everlasting life. For God sent not his Son into the world to condemn the world; but that the world through him might be saved. He that believeth on him is not condemned: but he that believeth not is condemned already, because he hath not believed in the name of the only begotten Son of God. And this is the condemnation, that light is come into the world, and men loved darkness rather than light, because their deeds were evil. For every one who doeth evil hateth the light, neither cometh to the light, lest his deeds should be reproved."

Understand (without exception) all men are sinners and all need salvation. We must repent of our sins and true repentance means developing a Godly sorrow and Godly hatred of sin. God's nature and realm is holiness. He has a righteous holy-hatred of sin. Amazingly, God loves the sinner, but abhors the sins men commit. After salvation one must not misuse the cleansing blood of Jesus. God accepts the sinner, but never the sin.

Grace means unmerited, undeserved favor with God! There is not one of us who deserves salvation and we cannot earn it. It is a free gift from God accepted and instituted through faith. Faith that Jesus Christ is the Son of God, and that Jesus overcame Satan and destroyed that headship Satan procured through man's disobedience.

Jesus, who knew no sin, took on Himself the sin-debt of the world. As we remit our sins to Jesus, we have assurance in the efficacy of the blood. Jesus' last words to the church are relevant for the church today. Acts 1:8-9, "But ye shall receive power, after that the Holy Ghost is come upon you: and ye shall be witnesses unto me both in Jerusalem, and in all Judaea and in Samaria, and unto the uttermost part of the earth. And when he had spoken these things, while they beheld, he was taken up (into heaven); and a cloud received him out of their sight."

We must all be very diligent concerning the word of God. We must all read and study the Bible and search out these immutable truths for ones' self! Knowledge of Jesus as the Messiah produces repentance of sins, and true repentance produces obedience to God's word. We follow Jesus' example of water baptism and His example of being filled with the Holy Ghost. John 14:15-21, "If you love me, keep my commandments. And I will pray the Father, and he shall give you another Comforter (this is capitalized because it references the Holy Spirit as the Comforter, and the part of God's deity that God ordained to dwell within man), that he may abide with you for ever; Even the Spirit of truth; whom the world cannot receive, because it seeth him (Holy Spirit/Ghost) not, neither knoweth him: but ye know him; for he dwelleth with you, and shall be in you. I will not leave you comfortless: I will come to you (through the indwelling of His Holy Spirit). Yet a little while, and the world seeth me no more; but ye see me: because I live, ye shall live also. At that day ye shall know that I am in my Father, and ye in me, and I in you. He that hath my commandments, and keepeth them, he it is that loveth me: and he that loveth me shall be loved of my Father, and I will love him, and will manifest (make known) myself to him."

It requires faith to be saved and proper faith produces obedience. Remember to be pleasing to the Father, we follow Jesus' example of obedience, refusing to bow down to the weak and beggarly elements of this earth that are passing away. Jesus was filled with the indwelling power of the Holy Ghost, and this mandate provides us with that same overcoming power because it is the same Spirit that dwells within us. He understands that we are weak and lack strength in our own selves. This plan ensures that we can overcome temptations and withstand the attacks sent by the enemy.

The Roman government, the Pharisees, and the Sadducees resented Jesus. As Herod before them, they too feared for their positions. The Pharisees were expecting a majestic type of Messiah. They looked for one who would present himself as a king, regal in manner, for they measured worthiness by outward appearances. They also resented Jesus because He did not commend them. Jesus recognized the Pharisees as hypocrites. He proclaimed them to be a "generation of vipers." He denounced their wicked ways saying that on the outside they were scrupulously clean, but inside their hearts they were corrupt. They were spiritually unclean and an abomination to God.

It was politics at its worst: corrupt spiritual leaders and an incited crowd that brought the arrest of Jesus. He was not guilty of any crime, nor had He ever sinned. Jesus willingly laid down His life, as atonement for our sins. He, being sinless, would have lived forever because the consequence of sin is death. Jesus was sinless and therefore would never have died; it is written when sin is through it brings forth death. Jesus willingly laid down His life to redeem fallen man. Matthew 21:1-9, "And when they drew nigh unto Jerusalem, and were come to Bethphage, unto the mount of Olives, then sent Jesus two disciples, Saying unto them, Go into the village over against you, and straightway ye shall find an ass (donkey) tied, and a colt with her: loose them, and bring them unto me. And if any man say ought unto you, ye shall say, The Lord hath need of them; and straightway he will send them. All this was done, that it might be fulfilled which was spoken by the prophet (Zechariah), saying, Tell ye the daughter of Sion, Behold, thy King cometh unto thee, meek, and sitting upon an ass, and a colt the foal of an ass. And the disciples went, and did as Jesus commanded them, And brought the ass, and the colt, and put on them their clothes, and they set him thereon. And a very great multitude spread their garments in the way; others cut down branches (palm) from the trees, and strawed them in the way. And the multitudes that went before, and that followed, cried, saying, Hosanna to the son of David: Blessed is he that cometh in the name of the Lord; Hosanna in the highest."

Nothing in the Bible is insignificant. Scriptures that sound odd or superfluous often have deep and significant meaning. Jesus instructed that He should be brought the ass and the foal of the ass, and where they were to be found. All scripture is the inspired word of God and this is an example of Jesus' authority and His omniscience. This scripture, as does all scripture, contains deep and profound mysteries. Prophesied by Zechariah in the Old Testament, Zechariah 9:9,

"Rejoice greatly, O daughter of Zion; shout, O daughter of Jerusalem: behold, thy King cometh unto thee: he is just, and having salvation; lowly, and riding upon an ass, and upon a colt the foal of an ass." As Jesus made His triumphal entry into Jerusalem, He was riding on a lowly donkey and following was her offspring. A donkey is a beast of burden and Jesus was carrying the burden of fulfilling the Old Testament, for He came not to destroy the law, but to fulfill it. He was bringing to completion the Old Testament, and was ushering in the New Testament, ordained of God that it would be signed in Jesus' sinless Holy Blood. Jesus, the Sacrificial Lamb of God, was taking upon Himself the sin-debt of the entire world. The mother, or mature donkey, was representative of the Old Testament giving birth to the New Testament, and her young foal was representative of the birth of the New Testament (Blood Covenant) being ushered in by Jesus. As Jesus entered into Jerusalem the crowds cried "Hosanna," meaning save us! Many people in the crowd had been healed and many had witnessed the miracles Jesus performed in the few short years of His ministry. It is recorded in John 21:24-25, "This is the disciple which testifieth of these things, and wrote these things: and we know that his testimony is true. And there are also many other things which Jesus did, the which, if they should be written every one, I suppose that even the world itself could not contain the books that should be written. Amen."

Jesus foretold His disciples often and recorded in many scriptures that He was to be crucified, and He would be raised from the dead. They heard, but did not understand these mysteries that He spoke to them. Jesus instituted the Lord's Supper (Communion) In Jerusalem at the last Passover. He again forewarned them that He would be betrayed by one of them and would be crucified. Matthew 26:26-29, "And as they were eating, Jesus took bread, and blessed it, and brake it, and gave it to the disciples, and said, Take, eat; this is my body (symbolic of). And he took the cup, and gave thanks, and gave it to them, saying, Drink ye all of it; For this is my blood (symbolic) of the new testament, which is shed for many for the remission of sins. But I say unto you, I will not drink henceforth of this fruit of the vine, until that day when I drink it new with you in my Father's kingdom." The bread was unleavened, for leaven is symbolic of sin. The cup that they drank was unfermented red wine and is symbolic of His blood. It is significant that His first miracle was turning water into wine for a wedding. He will not drink of the new wine until we are with Him as His bride in heaven. It will be at the great marriage feast, prepared by the Father. Jesus was obedient to the Father, resisted the devil, turned the water into wine, opened blind eyes, unstopped deaf ears, made the lame to walk, cast out devils and demons, fed a multitude with five loaves and a few fishes, walked on water, forgave sins, healed the sick, cleansed the leper, and raised the dead to life again! Many in the crowd, as Jesus made His triumphal entry into Jerusalem, were eyewitnesses to these miracles. The crowd crying Hosanna would soon turn riotous and scream: "crucify him." Judas Iscariot, one of His twelve disciples, betrayed Him. Peter denied Him and Pilot washed his hands of Him. The chief priests and elders sought to put Him to death and He endured being beaten with thirty-nine lashes of a vicious cruel whip. Jesus' death on the cross was preceded by a sham trial. It was the greatest mockery of justice in Biblical or secular history. Crucifixion was a common type of capital punishment in those days. The fact that Jesus was innocent of any crime and never committed sin, qualified Him as God's Perfect Sacrificial Lamb. We, you and I, owed a debt we could not pay and Jesus paid a debt He did not owe.

Every year at the feast it was customary that the governor would release one prisoner. One prisoner, whomever the people chose, would be released unpunished. When Jesus was brought bound before Pontius Pilate, there was also in custody an infamous criminal named Barabbas. It is very significant the crowd would ask that Barabbas be set free and Jesus would take his place. Barabbas, perhaps guilty of breaking every commandment and God's laws, represents all sinners and man's proclivity to sin. Pilate asked the crowd who should be freed. Matthew 27:17, "...Whom will ye that I release unto you? Barabbas, or Jesus which is called Christ?" The frenzied crowd shouted Barabbas! Pilate called for a basin of water to be brought and washed his hands in the presence of those gathered, saying "I am innocent of the blood of this just person, see ye to it."

Old Testament prophet Isaiah prophesied every aspect of Jesus as Messiah. Isaiah 50:6, "I (Jesus) gave my back to the smiters (he was lashed with a whip), and my cheeks to them that plucked off the hair: I hid not my face from shame and spitting." He was scourged, bruised, mocked, and carried a heavy wooden cross to Calvary's hill. 1 Peter 2:24, "Who his own self bare our sins in his own body on the tree (cross), that we, being dead to sins, should live unto righteousness: by whose stripes (lash wounds) ye were healed." He was nailed to the cross between two thieves. One thief also mocked Him, but the other recognized His deity. Luke 23:42-43, "And he said unto Jesus, Lord, remember me when thou comest into thy kingdom. And Jesus said unto him, Verily I say unto thee, Today shalt thou be with me in paradise." What a merciful, magnificent Savior and what a merciful, magnificent salvation plan.

We know there is life after death and there are only two places where one spends eternity-Heaven or Hell. Just as Pilate and the two thieves made their decisions, we also must decide what we are going to do with this man called Jesus. Are we going to accept Him as savior of our souls, the Messiah, as did the one thief who entered Paradise with Him? Two choices remain, refuse Him, as did the other thief, or wash our hands of Him and do nothing as did Pilate. There is only one wise choice, and that is the one made by the first thief that leads to everlasting life. Any other decision, or non-decision, is rejection of the salvation plan and results in death and hell. God's plan to redeem fallen, disobedient, sinful man continues in force today. The holy Blood of Jesus covers all sins. Jesus' Blood covered the sins of Barabbas and the sins of all men even to this day.

Romans 3:23, "For all have sinned, and come short of the glory of God." Not one is, or can one ever be, righteous enough to obtain salvation without the Blood of Jesus to wash away every sin and its guilty stain. John 19:30, "When Jesus therefore had received the vinegar, he said, It is finished: and he bowed his head, and gave up the ghost." Jesus' last words had deep and significant meaning. He proclaimed that the Old Testament was finished and the New Testament, signed in His Blood, was dawning. It is recorded in Isaiah 25:8, "He will swallow up death in victory ..." This scripture was fulfilled by Jesus and was reiterated in 1 Corinthians 15:55, "O death, where is thy sting? O grave, where is thy victory?" Jesus The Christ was victorious over sin, death, hell, and the grave.

Jesus is the living Savior for this dying world and He is the only answer to all of life's problems. Acts 1:10-11, "And while they looked stedfastly toward heaven as he (Jesus) went up, behold, two men (angels) stood by them in white apparel; Which also said, Ye men of Galilee, why stand ye gazing up into heaven? this same Jesus, which is taken up from you into heaven, shall so come in like manner as ye have seen him go into heaven." This same Jesus will soon return in clouds of glory to rapture the Blood-Bought Church of the redeemed.

Chapter Three

Ezekiel's Wheel in the Middle of a Wheel

"The appearance of the wheels and their work was like unto the colour of a beryl: and they four had one likeness: and their appearance and their work was as it were a wheel in the middle of a wheel."

(Ezekiel 1:16)

God can step out of time and into eternity. He is not limited to the timeframes and constraints that limit mere man to his mortal boundaries.

Ezekiel was a priest and a prophet of the one true Jehovah-God. He was among those exiled from Israel and led captive into Babylon. His visions are ripe with symbolism, relevant and up to date for our space-age society in which we live today.

First, Ezekiel was shown the divine glory and majesty of God. God revealed His deity manifested in the flesh of Jesus, the Messiah! Ezekiel 1:5-12, "Also out of the midst thereof came the likeness of four living creatures. And this was their appearance; they had the likeness of a man. And every one had four faces, and every one had four wings. And their feet were straight feet; and the sole of their feet was like the sole of a calf's foot: and they sparkled like the colour of burnished brass. And they had the hands of a man under their wings on their four sides; and they four had their faces and their wings. Their wings were joined one to another; they turned not when they went; they went every one straight forward. As for the likeness of their faces, they four had the face of a man (symbolic of Jesus as the "Son of man" revealed in the N.T. Gospel of Luke), and the face of a lion (symbolic of Jesus as "King" revealed in the N.T. Gospel of

Matthew), on the right side: and they four had the face of an ox (symbolic of Jesus as "Servant" revealed in the N.T. Gospel of Mark) on the left side; they four also had the face of an eagle (symbolic of Jesus revealed as the "Son of God" in the N.T. Gospel of John). Thus were their faces: and their wings were stretched upward; two wings of every one were joined one to another, and two covered their bodies. And they went every one straight forward: whither the spirit was to go, they went; and they turned not when they went." Some believe these creatures to be the same as described in Revelation 4:8, but they are dissimilar in the number of wings. God's Word has the power and the ability to appear in different forms to prove the purpose of symbolic revelation. A few examples to aid in our understanding: God appeared to Moses in "the burning bush," the Holy Spirit descending as "a dove" onto the scene at Jesus' baptism and the Holy Ghost appearing in the form of "tongues of fire" on the heads of all assembled in the upper room on the Day of Pentecost. God's Word is Holy and stands guarded and forever correct by His own righteous power and infallibility!

Ezekiel's visions and prophecies were six centuries before the birth of Christ, but they are still relevant today. The continuity of God's word is infallible and causes the prophecies of the Bible to come to fruition. In the four gospels written six hundred years later, Jesus fulfilled these four distinct offices that were foretold by God to Ezekiel. Holy Jehovah God used the title "son of man" 91 times while addressing Ezekiel, indicating God's concern for mankind.

Jesus is presented as "King" in Matthew, "Servant" in Mark, "Son of Man" in Luke, and "Son of God" in John. Each gospel has certain similarities, but each is unique and reveals Jesus in different aspects of His being. The four narratives that record the life of Christ are written to the four classes of men who made up the world in Jesus' day and are still relevant today. Matthew, to the Jews, Mark, to the Romans, Luke to the Greeks, and John, was written to all men, whosoever will.

In Matthew we see Jesus is King, not by ballot, but by birth. Jesus was a Jew. His genealogy is traced back to King David, thus giving Jesus legal right to the throne by natural lineage. The mother of Jesus, Mary, was of the tribe of Judah. Jesus has often been referred to as the Lion of the tribe Of Judah!

In Mark, no genealogy is given because we see Jesus portrayed as a servant. The purpose of Mark was to depict a word picture of

Christ's servitude. In the Book of Mark, we find no introduction, as servants are not introduced. There is no mention of His virgin birth, or the visit of wise men, and there is no mention of His childhood. No titles are used except in Mark 2:28, which states: "Therefore the Son of man is Lord also of the sabbath." In Mark's Gospel, the word "forthwith" is used forty times. It is a word that means "immediately" and is authoritative and a directive.

In the writings of Luke, we see Christ's genealogy going back to the beginning, even to Adam, verifying Jesus was the Son of man.

John reveals Jesus as God. John 1:1, "In the beginning was the Word, and the Word was with God, and the Word was God." In the book of 1 John 5:5-6, "Who is he that overcometh the world, but he that believeth that Jesus is the Son (flesh and blood) of God? This is he that came by water and blood, even Jesus Christ; not by water only, but by water and blood. And it is the Spirit that beareth witness, because the Spirit is truth."

The prophet Ezekiel's vision has proven accurate. Evidentiary are the four aspects of Jesus, which were prophesied and fulfilled. God revealed Jesus as being all things to all men, yet in tandem as "The Word" and the Word was with God, and the Word is God. Ezekiel 1:13-16, "As for the likeness of the living creatures, their appearance was like burning coals of fire (fire denotes God's presence and power), and like the appearance of lamps (God's word is a lamp unto our path): it went up and down among the living creatures; and the fire was bright, and out of the fire went forth lightning (God's word is quick and powerful). And the living creatures (God's Word revealed in the four aspects of Jesus) ran and returned as the appearance of a flash of lightning. Now as I (Ezekiel) beheld the living creatures, behold one wheel upon the earth by the living creatures, with his (Jesus') four faces. The appearance of the wheels and their work (carrying the Gospel of Jesus Christ throughout the world) was like unto the colour of a beryl: and they four had one likeness (all four gospels reveal Jesus in different aspects of His being): and their appearance and their work was as it were a wheel in the middle of a wheel."

The "work" of the wheels proved a purpose. Isaiah 55:11, "So shall my word be that goeth forth out of my mouth: it shall not return unto me void (Hebrew meaning empty, ineffective, or without cause), but it shall accomplish that which I please, and it shall prosper in the thing whereto I send it." The gospel message will never be outdated or unnecessary. Matthew 24:35, "Heaven and earth shall pass away, but my words shall not pass away." The word of God will be preached throughout the entire world, before the end of this age and will endure for all eternity. The four creatures are Jesus Christ as the Word of God going forth throughout the world via satellite in these last days, and accomplishing God's divine will and purpose.

Continuing in Ezekiel 1:17-25, "When they went, they went upon their four sides: and they turned not when they went. As for their rings (rims), they were so high that they were dreadful; and their rings (rims or outer edges) were full of eyes round about them four. And when the living creatures (the four gospels) went, the wheels went by them: and when the living creatures were lifted up from the earth, the wheels were lifted up (from the earth). Whithersoever the spirit (Holy Spirit of God) was to go, they (the four gospels) went, thither was their spirit to go; and the wheels were lifted up over against them: for the spirit (Holy Spirit) of the living creature was in the wheels. When those went, these went; and when those stood, these stood; and when those were lifted up from the earth, the wheels were lifted up over against them: for the spirit of the living creature (Jesus) was in the wheels (God's Holy Spirit goes before, and with, His Word). And the likeness of the firmament (Hebrew meaning: expanse, or visible arch of the sky) upon the heads of the living creature was as the colour of the terrible crystal, stretched forth over their heads above (in the air of the heavens). And under the firmament (even under the air) were their wings straight, the one toward the other: every one had two, which covered on this side, and every one had two, which covered on that side, their bodies. And when they went, I (Ezekiel) heard the noise of their wings, like the noise of great waters, as the voice of the Almighty, the voice of speech, as a noise of an host: when they stood, they let down their wings. And there was a voice from the firmament (sky) that was over their heads, when they stood, and had let down their wings (the gospel having an ability to transpire into a different realm)." The vision God gave Ezekiel was the Gospel of Jesus Christ yet in a future dimension! Reiterating the gospel of John explains that Jesus IS the Word of God and Jesus IS God. Matthew 24:14, "And this gospel of the kingdom shall be preached in all the world for a witness unto all nations; and then shall the end come."

Satellite has a base transmission station on the ground and is circular in shape; it has a receiver high in the heavens, which is also round in shape and loops the information back to earth. It is programmed to a specific destination as the above scripture stated, "they turned not when they went." The Gospel of Christ is going throughout the world via satellite and is, in part, a fulfillment of Ezekiel's vision! The gospel is as a wheel in the middle of a wheel, via satellite, circling the earth day and night. The Trinity Broadcasting Network (TBN) broadcasts the gospel that proclaims Jesus as Lord and Savior, twenty-four hours a day. The TBN network has one satellite named Angel! God's word is multi-faceted and this satellite is a partial fulfillment, in a very literal sense, of this ancient prophecy. Revelation 14:6-7, "And I (John) saw another angel fly in the midst of heaven, having the everlasting gospel to preach unto them that dwell on the earth, and to every nation, and kindred, and tongue, and people, Saying with a loud voice, Fear God, and give glory to him; for the hour of his judgment is come: and worship him (Jesus-the Word) that made heaven, and earth, and the sea, and the fountains of waters." The word is eternal and eternally with God. John 1:2-3, "The same was in the beginning with God. All things were made by him; and without him was not any thing made that was made." God the creator foreordained this to be so. The Holy Spirit of God goes before and with the gospel, for it is the creative power and presence of Almighty God even now broadcasting the everlasting gospel around the world.

As a rainbow is seen above the earth, it is circular and serves as a reminder of God's edict to Noah. Genesis 9:13-14, "I do set my bow in the cloud, and it shall be for a token of a covenant between me and the earth. And it shall come to pass, when I bring a cloud over the earth, that the bow shall be seen in the cloud." The bow has no beginning and no end for it exists as a circle. God's word is from everlasting to everlasting as God Himself exists and has no beginning and has no ending! Revelation 4:1-3, "After this I (John) looked, and, behold, a door (Jesus is the open door) was opened in heaven: and the first voice which I heard was as it were of a trumpet talking with me; which said, Come up hither (God's voice at the future rapture of the church), and I will shew thee things which must be hereafter. And immediately I (John was translated into heaven and is a fore type of the rapture) was in the spirit: and, behold, a throne was set in heaven, and one (God's deity: Father, Son and

Holy Ghost as the Ancient of Days) sat on the throne. And he that sat was to look upon like a jasper and a sardine stone: and there was a rainbow round about the throne, in sight like unto an emerald." The bow is symbolic that God is eternal, His word is eternal and His gospel is eternal! Just as the bow is in heaven circling the throne, the gospel, as an unending bow, is circling the earth with the good news of Jesus the Christ in the realm and dimension of satellites.

Ezekiel was first shown God's glory and majesty and we can see a wondrous correlation between Ezekiel's vision in the Old Testament, and John's glorious vision in the New Testament. Revelation 4:7-8, "And the first beast was like a lion, and the second beast like a calf, and the third beast had a face as a man, and the fourth beast was like a flying eagle. And the four beasts had each of them six wings about him, and they were full of eyes within: and they rest not (the Gospel never rests, and it never returns void to God) day and night, saying, Holy, holy, holy, Lord God Almighty, which was, and is, and is to come."

Ezekiel was called to be a watchman; a watchman is to cry out a warning of impending doom. We are being warned today that the last seven years of Israel's punishment is at the door! Ezekiel's warning is twofold. The Great Tribulation period lasting seven years will affect both Jew and Gentile. His visions are pertinent warnings to the Gentile nations that the allotted time for Gentile world domination is coming to completion. Jesus Christ will set up His throne and rule and reign from Jerusalem as King of the Jews.

Revelation 14:6-7, "And I saw another angel fly in the midst of heaven, having the everlasting gospel to preach unto them that dwell on the earth, and to every nation, and kindred, and tongue, and people, Saying with a loud voice, Fear God, and give glory to him; for the hour of his judgment is come: and worship him that made heaven, and earth, and the sea, and the fountains of waters."

Chapter Four

Grace versus the Law

"Think not that I (Jesus) am come to destroy the law, or the prophets: I am not come to destroy, but to fulfil."

(Matthew 5:17)

In this present time of apostate Christendom, man's understanding has been darkened, hindering us from comprehending that God is pluperfect (complete perfection)! Our finite minds cannot understand that Jehovah's realm, and actual Being, exists in holiness. He is the God of all creation and in Him is the beauty of holiness found complete.

God's presence was shown as fearful at the time God called Moses and the Israeli people to Mount Sinai. At this historic time, Moses was leading the Israelites out of Egyptian bondage. Moses, the deliverer of that time period, and the Israelites were camped before the mount.

Exodus 19:3-6, "And Moses went up unto God, and the LORD called unto him out of the mountain, saying, Thus shalt thou say to the house of Jacob, and tell the children of Israel; Ye have seen what I did unto the Egyptians, and how I bare you on eagles' wings, and brought you unto myself. Now therefore, if ye will obey my voice indeed, and keep my covenant, then ye shall be a peculiar treasure unto me above all people: for all the earth is mine: And ye shall be unto me a kingdom of priests, and an holy nation. These are the words which thou shalt speak unto the children of Israel." After hearing all the words of the Lord, the Israelites agreed to obey the Lord.

The Jews were, and always have been, God's chosen people. They were the first people to comprehend Monotheism, and served and worshipped the one and only true Jehovah-God! One must be careful to understand the Trinity. There is, and always has been, only "one" God. Deuteronomy 6:4, "Hear, O Israel: The LORD our God is one LORD." The mystery of God in Christ is revealed. God the Father is the soul of His Being demonstrated in the actuality of His eternal magnificence and glory. God the Son is God's creative authority revealed as the Word, Who presented God's physical body transpicuous as Jesus the Christ. God the Holy Ghost is His splendid holiness, all-encompassing sanctity and purifying power of Almighty God. God has a triune nature. He is Soul, Body, and Spirit yet eternally exists as One, and evidenced in plurality. Our unchanging God is revealed in the New Testament in Colossians 2:9, "For in him (Jesus) dwelleth all the fullness of the Godhead bodily." We were created in God's image and we too have a triune nature consisting of body, soul, and spirit.

Exodus 19:9, "And the LORD said unto Moses, Lo, I come unto thee in a thick cloud, that the people may hear when I speak with thee, and believe thee for ever. And Moses told the words of the people unto the LORD." 12-13, "And thou shalt set bounds unto the people round about, saying, Take heed to yourselves, that ye go not up into the mount, or touch the border of it: whosoever toucheth the mount shall be surely put to death: There shalt not an hand touch it, but he shall surely be stoned, or shot through; whether it be beast or man, it shall not live: when the trumpet soundeth long, they shall come up to the mount." God is holiness personified, and at His presence upon the third day, the mountain was shrouded in a cloud, the lightning flashed, and the thunder came crashing all around Mount Sinai. Same chapter verse 16, "And it came to pass on the third day in the morning, that there were thunders and lightnings, and a thick cloud (as a barrier between God and man) upon the mount, and the voice of the trumpet exceeding loud; so that all the people that was in the camp trembled."

What an awesome sight they saw and what wondrous and fearful things they heard as the voice of God sounded as a trumpet. Exodus 19:18-21, "And mount Sinai was altogether on a smoke, because the LORD descended upon it in fire: and the smoke thereof ascended as the smoke of a furnace, and the whole mount quaked greatly. And when the voice of the trumpet sounded long, and waxed louder and louder, Moses spake, and God answered him by a voice. And the LORD came down upon mount Sinai, on the top of the mount: and the LORD called Moses up to the top of the mount; and Moses went up. And the LORD said unto Moses, Go down, charge the people, lest they break through unto the LORD to gaze, and many of them perish." Understanding that sinful man could not ascend to the heights of God, so our wondrous God came down to man! His ways are far above our ways, and His thoughts are far above our thoughts. Moses' reply to God is recorded in Exodus 19:23, "And Moses said unto the LORD, The people cannot come up to mount Sinai: for thou chargedst us, saying, Set bounds about the mount and sanctify it."

Moses was the mediator between a righteous God and errant mankind and he explained to the Israelites God's Ten Commandments as recorded in the Bible. Exodus 20:1-2, "And God spake all these words, saying, I am the LORD thy God, which have brought thee out of the land of Egypt, out of the house of bondage."

I. Thou shalt have no other gods before me.

II. Thou shalt not make unto thee any graven image.

III. Thou shalt not take the name of the LORD thy God in vain. (God's name is holy. One must never use it in a fit of anger or as a casual exclamation.)

IV. Remember the sabbath day, to keep it holy. (Six days God has given us. One must not misuse His day.)

V. Honour thy father and thy mother. (One must be respectful of parents.)

VI. Thou shalt not kill. (One must not commit murder.)

VII. Thou shalt not commit adultery.

VIII. Thou shalt not steal. (One must not take anything; no item, whether large or small, is without consequence, not one penny or one billion dollars.)

IX. Thou shalt not bear false witness against thy neighbor. (One must not tell a lie, or falsely accuse, or relay untruths against another.)

X. Thou shalt not covet. (One must not wish longingly for anything that belongs to someone else.)

Exodus 20:6, "And shewing mercy unto thousands of them that love me, and keep my commandments." Scripture proves scripture. The New Testament reveals God's unchanging ways as Jesus' words are recorded in John 14:15, "If you love me, keep my commandments." Same chapter verse 21, "He that hath my commandments, and keepeth them, he it is that loveth me: and he that loveth me shall be loved of my Father, and I will love him, and will manifest myself to him." The commandments were not given to be grievous, but beneficial and are advantageous for our welfare. God was instructing mankind from the abundance of His love. God's commandments are the essential mandate from a holy God to Adamic man. God instructed Adam and Eve in the garden not to eat of the tree of knowledge because He knew it would bring destruction on mankind. Just as God gave them instructions, we also have been given instructions. We must understand the importance of His mandates, and the importance of obedience.

Obedience to a holy and just God is essential for life, and ensures everlasting life in heaven. Just as a loving parent would instruct a child not to cross a busy highway, for the child's own safety, so it is with the commandments to us. We benefit if we keep His commandments. They are a joy and a blessing to keep! It would be most unsettling if God were moody, indecisive, or given to whims. If God were not constant and unchanging we would continually be questioning His expectations. Hebrews 13:8, "Jesus Christ the same yesterday, and to day, and for ever." Thank God for His love that instructs, and makes known His proclamations for mankind. By His word we understand His nature and expectations. Matthew 24:35, "Heaven and earth shall pass away, but my words shall not pass away." Next to the salvation plan, I thank God above all, that we serve a God whom we can know His nature and in whom we can trust.

The law, not to be confused with the Ten Commandments, was God's laws for mankind. God handed down the laws to mankind through Moses. The laws were connected with works. It demanded righteousness from man, and that blessing be earned. Man, under the law, was born into a type of bondage. The law was not God's original intention for man, but it became a necessity. Mankind had received a fallen sin-nature through disobedience to God. Therefore, the law was instituted as necessary and designed as a temporary mandate for man.

There were varied classes of the law affecting every aspect of life whether religious, civil, dietary, or sanitary. The religious laws were distinguished as moral, ceremonial, and ritualistic. The law was to be temporary until the redemptive, yet future, work of the coming Messiah could be instituted. Galatians 3:23-24, "But before faith came, we were kept under the law, shut up unto the faith which should afterwards be revealed (made known). Wherefore the law was our schoolmaster to bring us unto Christ, that we might be justified by faith (cleared of guilt)."

The foundation of our modern civil laws go back to the Mosaic code, for all matters of business, commercial enterprise, crimes and misdemeanors, and to the rights of persons, and of property. Penalties were imposed for the violators of these laws, such as fines, corporal punishment, confinement, and even death.

Under the old covenant law, there had to be a shedding of blood to cover sins. The animal had to be without blemish. Oftentimes, a baby lamb was used. The offering implies confession of sin and its penalty, which was death. Every sacrificial death was the execution of the sentence of the law. The offering of the innocent animal took the place of the offerer in death. According to the scriptures, once the legal sacrifice was made, the offerer's sins were covered by the blood, and he received forgiveness. The sinner established the law by acknowledging that, by it, he is justly condemned. In Genesis chapter 4, Abel was a keeper of sheep and his brother Cain was a tiller of the ground. In time, Cain brought an offering of fruit of the ground unto the Lord, and Abel brought forth a lamb of his flock as an offering to God. God was not pleased with Cain's offerings, for it implied he had no sin and hence no need of shedding blood to cover his sins.

The Jews, knowing the law, were condemned by the law. The final verdict was that the entire world was guilty before God. Romans 3:23, "For all have sinned, and come short of the glory of God." Scripture proves scripture. Romans 3:10, "As it is written, There is none righteous, no, not one." Continuing in verse 20, "Therefore by the deeds of the law there shall no flesh be justified in his sight: for by the law is the knowledge of sin." Under the new covenant of grace, or love, Jesus Christ bore the curse of the law for us. Christ fulfilled all the law and redeemed us from its curse. Roman 1:16, "For I am not ashamed of the Gospel of Christ: for it is the power of God unto salvation to every one that believeth; to the Jew first, and also to the Greek (Gentile)."

In Christ's death the law is not evaded, but honored. Jesus was sinless (unblemished). He was tempted, but never yielded to the temptation, so His Blood was innocent. Man was guilty of sin, but Jesus, in His mercy and grace, became the innocent sacrifice for man. Christ shed His innocent Blood on the cross of Calvary, as the atonement for sin. The atonement, when translated from the Hebrew word means, "covered." Jesus, through His grace, "covered our sins" by the shedding of His innocent, pure Blood. The Atonement of Christ, as interpreted by the Old Testament, has all the necessary elements. Christ, on behalf of the sinner, established the law by enduring its penalty, which was death. Jesus said in Matthew 5:17, "Think not that I am come to destroy the law, or the prophets: I am not come to destroy but to fulfil."

Justification originated in grace through Christ. By faith, we are guiltless of our sins through Jesus. Romans 3:24, "Being justified freely by his grace through the redemption that is in Christ Jesus." We are justified by faith in Christ's crucifixion, the only remedy for sins.

Law and grace cannot co-exist. Grace is the kindness and love of God, our savior, toward mankind. No one can be saved by works, or by his own righteousness, for we have none. Man cannot work his way to heaven, and man does not have any righteousness. Isaiah 64:6-7, "But we are all as an unclean thing, and all our righteousness are as filthy rags; and we all do fade as a leaf; and our iniquities, like the wind, have taken us away. And there is none that calleth upon thy name, that stirreth up himself to take hold of thee: for thou hast hid thy face from us, and hast consumed us, because of our iniquities." There can be no fellowship between errant sinful mankind and a Holy God. Old Testament prophet Isaiah lamented over the separation sin had brought between God and man.

Grace is therefore always set in contrast to the law, under which God demanded righteousness from man. The law was given by God to Moses, and was connected with works. Grace and truth came by Jesus Christ. The law blesses the good, but grace saves the bad. Salvation is free to all who accept Jesus as the Lamb of God and His atoning Blood. The law demands that blessings be earned; grace is a free gift. It was purchased at the cost of Jesus' own Blood and given freely to all who accept.

The Bible explains that Jesus broke the yoke of bondage we bore under the law. Galatians 5:1, "Stand fast therefore in the liberty wherewith Christ hath made us free, and be not entangled again with the yoke of bondage." Sin itself is a type of bondage. Sin hinders, controls, demands, dictates, and dominates its host until sin overpowers, leaving the sinner completely subjugated. The only remedy against sin is Jesus Christ.

If, once again, we put ourselves under the law then we become subject to the law and its penalties. If the Spirit leads us, we are not under the law, but are under the love of grace. Jesus made us free, and we are free indeed. Galatians 5:14, "For all the law is fulfilled in one word, even in this; Thou shalt love thy neighbor as thyself."

"Love and Grace" are the sum of the law. Liberty in Christ means freedom from the Mosaic laws. People often misconstrue scripture as "liberty in Christ" as a license to sin. Jesus Christ made us free from the law and the penalty of sin, but He did not give us freedom to continue in sin.

Romans 6:14, "For sin shall not have dominion over you: for ye are not under the law, but under grace." Take heed and be warned. One must not misuse the acceptable, holy Blood of the covenant of love. Everything we say, and do, should be done for His glory. Only unbroken fellowship through our glorious redeemer, the Lord Jesus, produces true peace and contentment from within.

Reason can only take us so far, and then faith has to come in. Logic and faith will always collide. Hebrews 11:6, "But without faith it is impossible to please him ..." We must be careful to obey the Ten Commandments for all the basis of civilization comes from the Ten Commandments. However, we could not keep all the laws, which we were given, because of transgression (sin), until the Messiah came. The Ten Commandments were given in addition to "the law." The Ten Commandments are not laborsome nor grievous as is the whole letter of the law. The laws were difficult and many. To keep part of the Jewish law, makes one liable to keep all the law.

Apostle Paul, a Jew, was once Saul of Tarsus, a Pharisee of Pharisees. His testimony and admonitions are found in the New Testament. Romans 10:1-5, "Brethren my heart's desire and prayer to God for Israel is, that they might be saved. For I bear them record that they have a zeal (devotion) of God, but not according to knowledge. For they being ignorant of God's righteousness, and going about to establish (secure) their own righteousness, have not submitted themselves unto the righteousness of God. For Christ is the end of the law for righteousness to everyone that believeth. For Moses describeth the righteousness which is of the law, That the man which doeth those things shall live by them." Continuing with verses 9-14, "That if thou shalt confess with thy mouth the Lord Jesus, and shalt believe in thine heart that God hath raised him from the dead, thou shalt be saved. For with the heart man believeth unto righteousness; and with the mouth confession is made unto salvation. For the scripture saith, Whosoever believeth on him shall not be ashamed. For there is no difference between the Jew and the Greek

(Gentile): for the same Lord over all is rich unto all that call upon him. For whosoever shall call upon the name of the Lord shall be saved. How then shall they call on him in whom they have not believed? and how shall they believe in him of whom they have not heard? and how shall they hear without a preacher?"

Mankind could not keep all the laws, so God came to us again. This time not shrouded in smoke and the presence of fire as He did at Mount Sinai. Rather, He donned the flesh and blood of a man-child named Jesus. The mighty Messiah, Jesus Christ, is the flesh and blood of God. God is not "three persons," but rather has a triune nature consisting of Body, Soul, and Spirit. Isaiah 59:16, "And he (God) saw that there was no man (deliverer), and wondered that there was no intercessor (to plead man's case): therefore his arm (God's) brought salvation unto him (mankind); and his righteousness (Jesus'), it sustained him."

Recognizing our needs, God in His infinite love and wondrous mercy, made a way of deliverance from the sin-nature that had overtaken mankind and held him captive. God's mercy always triumphs over judgment! The law could not make imperfect man obedient, but grace made man blameless through the covenant of His love. This became possible as Jesus did not destroy the law, but fulfilled every letter of the law for man.

Two examples show the profound contrast of the law in the Old Testament and the grace of the New Testament. In the Old Testament, we see the incompatibility of the Holy God and unholy mankind. This breach was evident at Mount Sinai. The mountain was shrouded in smoke and did quake at God Jehovah's holy presence. Sin had caused separation, and created a need for a barrier or boundary so no man could come near, or gaze upon God and die. The hem of the mountain was the protective zone or boundary.

Unlike the border or boundary at Mount Sinai, Jesus (God in flesh) became accessible, even touchable. An example of God's accessibility through Jesus is recorded in the New Testament. Matthew 9:20-21, "And, behold, a woman, which was diseased with an issue of blood twelve years, came behind him (looked upon Jesus), and touched the hem of his garment: For she said within herself, if I may but touch his garment, I shall be whole." This is a glorious contrast between the old law and the new covenant: Grace! Before the covenant of grace, this woman's disease caused her to be considered unclean, and therefore untouchable. Before grace, God's holiness caused Him to be untouchable and inaccessible, because God is the absolute perfection of Holiness.

Grace performed what the law could not. God's covenant of Grace is undeserved, unmerited favor with God. It is a covenant of His love and signed in His own blood. It united God and man. Same God-New Covenant! Jesus provides the perfect balance, proving God is a combination of holiness and love. These two attributes express the very character of God. The same righteous God who manifested Himself on Mount Sinai once again came into the presence of man, this time accessible.

In the New Testament we find two revelations: unity and continuity. Both culminate in Christ. Luke 24:44, "And he (Jesus) said unto them, These are the words which I spake unto you while I was yet with you, that all things must be fulfilled, which were written in the law of Moses, and in the prophets, and in the psalms, concerning me."

Psalm 103:8-18, "The LORD is merciful and gracious, slow to anger, and plenteous in mercy. He will not always chide: neither will he keep his anger forever. He hath not dealt with us after our sins; nor rewarded us according to our iniquities. For as the heaven is high above the earth, so great is his mercy toward them that fear him. As far as the east is from the west, so far hath he removed our transgressions from us. Like as a father pitieth his children, so the LORD pitieth them that fear him. For he knoweth our frame; he remembereth that we are dust. As for man, his days are as grass: as a flower of the field, so he flourisheth. For the wind passeth over it, and it is gone; and the place thereof shall know it no more. But the mercy of the LORD is from everlasting to everlasting upon them that fear him, and his righteousness unto children's children; To such as keep his covenant, and to those that remember his commandments to do them."

Paul explains, by example, the new covenant between a holy God and a needy and sinful people. Galatians 2:21, "I do not frustrate the grace of God: for if righteousness come by the law, then Christ is dead in vain."

As Grace versus the Law, the verdict proclaimed through the corridors of time is: Grace wins with a resounding victory through the love of Jesus Christ the Righteous!

Chapter Five

Separation unto Sanctification

"For if we sin willfully after that we have received the knowledge of the truth, there remaineth no more sacrifice for sins." And "Of how much sorer punishment, suppose ye, shall he be thought worthy, who hath trodden under foot the Son of God, and hath counted the blood of the covenant (Jesus' Blood), wherewith he was sanctified, an unholy thing, and hath done despite unto the Spirit of grace?"

(Hebrews 10:26, 29)

The indwelling of the Holy Ghost is the divine impartation of God's Holy Spirit into these tabernacles of mortal flesh! Jesus' last instruction to mankind, spoken as He was preparing to be received up into heaven was, "wait for this promise." Acts 1:4-5, "And, (Jesus) being assembled together with them, commanded them that they should not depart from Jerusalem, but wait for the promise of the Father, which, saith he (Jesus), ye have heard of me. For John truly baptized with water; but ye shall be baptized with the Holy Ghost not many days hence." Jesus indisputably commanded believers to wait and expect the baptism of The Holy Ghost.

The Father ordained believers to be infused and empowered with the Holy Ghost. This is the preamble God established and instituted to follow salvation. The Father God, having all knowledge, understands the depths of Satan's inconceivable hatred for mankind. Satan despises God and stands in opposition to all God's love and good plans for man. While in the Garden of Eden, Satan, understanding man's God-given ability of the freedom of choice, instituted an evil plan to tempt God's treasured creation (man) to obey him (Satan) and thereby man became self-willed and possesses a proclivity for sin. Jesus overcame Satan and did not yield to Satan's temptations, but through obedience to God became the only avenue of salvation and sanctification. The Holy Spirit is the part of God's Deity sent down to earth on the Day of Pentecost to dwell within man and provide man with the necessary abilities to be overcomers in this world filled with temptations.

There is a difference in having the Holy Ghost and receiving the baptism of the Holy Ghost. There are gifts of the Spirit, and they will be manifested when a life is completely yielded to our Holy God, and a believer has received this baptism! We will become sanctified holy and effective in our work here on earth for God's glory and our good! One must not confuse works with sanctification. Works are works and cannot, and will not, ever get anyone into heaven. One could be a preacher, a Sunday school teacher, a deacon, a missionary, an evangelist or a faithful church worker but not be saved. Judas Iscariot is a prime example. Judas was an integral part of Jesus' own ministry and worked in the capacity as "the church treasurer." John 12:4-6, "Then saith one of his disciples, Judas Iscariot, Simon's son, which should betray him, Why was not this ointment sold for three hundred pence, and given to the poor? This he (Judas) said, not that he cared for the poor; but because he was a thief, and had the bag (the money bag), and bare what was put therein." Most are aware that Judas betrayed Jesus for thirty pieces of silver, but this should not be a surprise for Judas was, as scripture explains a hypocrite and a thief and his heart was corrupt. Judas had works, but apparently not salvation!

Once saved, God did not intend for the Christian believer to be weak and remain "marginally," saved! Many professing Christians morph from Sunday-morning-saint into Saturday-night-sinner! Woe to those who are comfortable in transgressions and have become apostate! We are to live as victors over sin in this world, fitting of the Church triumphant. 1 Corinthians 12:6-11, "And there are diversities of operations, but it is the same God which worketh all in all. But the manifestation of the Spirit is given to every man to profit withal. For to one is given by the Spirit the word of wisdom; to another the word of knowledge by the same Spirit; To another faith by the same Spirit; to another the gifts of healing by the same Spirit; To another the working of miracles; to another prophecy; to another discerning of spirits; to another divers (different) kinds of tongues; to another the interpretation of tongues: But all these worketh that one and the selfsame Spirit (Holy Spirit), dividing to every man severally as he (Holy Spirit) will." God ordained and commissioned the church of today, to do the same works as those of the apostles.

These miraculous gifts are available through the operation of the Holy Ghost. God infuses His wisdom, knowledge, understanding, and these marvelous operational gifts into our mortal bodies. We then become a proper temple fit for His service. These gifts are necessary for the individual Christian walk, and necessary for the body of Christ that comprises the church. To be effective, the church must have these gifts being demonstrated, and in proper working order. The scripture clearly states that God gives several to everyone! The apostate church of these last days of Gentile world dominion is sin-friendly and laced with apathy. It has been weakened by sins of commission and omission. The church has omitted the integral operation and gifts of the Holy Spirit. Apostate Christendom is the consequence.

Upon receiving the infilling of the Holy Ghost, a process of sanctification begins! Jesus explained that we were to wait for, and expect, this divine impartation. Pray, expect, and wait for the infilling. Jesus instructed the newly forming church to wait for this power and they were all praying, for it was their chief desire to receive this divine impartation. One must be praying and expecting. We are creatures of free will and our God will not intrude. He wants and waits to be invited. The baptism of the Holy Ghost creates oneness between mortal man and a holy God, resulting in the recipient being pliable and humbly yielded to God.

Sanctification is a characteristic of salvation just as wet is a characteristic of water. They cannot be separated. Salvation cannot be earned, bought, or bargained for. We cannot do anything to make ourselves worthy to be saved. It is a free gift, complete, when we repent (forsake) of our sins, and accept Jesus as Lord. We must be washed in the Blood and not just the water. Accepting Jesus' Blood sacrifice is the only remission or cleansing of sins. After being born again, we must then start to live a new life, a Christ-centered life. Romans 6:1-10, "What shall we say then? Shall we continue in sin, that grace may abound? God forbid. How shall we, that are dead to sin, live any longer therein? Know ye not, that so many of us as were baptized into Jesus Christ were baptized into his death? Therefore we are buried with him by baptism into death: that like as Christ was raised up from the dead by the glory of the Father, even so we also should walk in newness of life. For if we have been planted together in the likeness of his death, we shall be also in the likeness of his resurrection: Knowing this, that our old man is crucified with him, that the body of sin might be destroyed, that henceforth (after baptism) we should not serve sin. For he that is dead is freed from sin. Now if we be dead with Christ, we believe that we shall also live with him: Knowing that Christ being raised from the dead dieth no more; death hath no more dominion over him. For in that he died, he died unto sin once: but in that he liveth, he liveth unto God."

Scripture states we should submit to water baptism, a complete submersion in water, symbolic of a burial. The old man, our former sin-state, is dead and we become a new creature in Christ. As the newly baptized believer comes up out of the water, it is symbolic of a new spiritual birth and of resurrection. We are born again into fellowship and right-standing with God. We must pray expectantly, wait for, and allow the baptism of the Holy Spirit. God's Holy Spirit imparts wisdom and fortifies us with overcoming power. Most importantly, we become readied to do the work God has ordained for the Church. It also affords mankind the joy and sweet fellowship with the Creator God who fashioned us for companionship.

Old Testament prophet Joel urges people to repent of sin and turn to the Lord. Joel 2:12-13, "Therefore also now, saith the LORD, turn ye even to me with all your heart, and with fasting, and with weeping, and with mourning: And rend your heart, and not your garments, and turn unto the LORD your God: for he is gracious and merciful, slow to anger, and of great kindness, and repenteth him of the evil." Through Joel, God is revealed as the Restorer of the breach between God and wayward mankind. God restores contrite sinners back to Himself. He restores broken lives and He is the mender of broken dreams. Joel is referred to as the prophet of Pentecost. Joel 2:28-29, "And it shall come to pass afterward, that I will pour out my spirit upon all flesh; and your sons and your daughters shall prophesy, your old men shall dream dreams, your young men shall see visions: And also upon the servants and upon the handmaids in those days will I (God) pour out my spirit."

Acts 2:1-4, "And when the day of Pentecost was fully come, they were all in one accord in one place. And suddenly there came a sound from heaven as of a rushing mighty wind, and it filled all the house where they were sitting. And there appeared unto them cloven tongues like as of fire, and it sat upon each of them. And they were all filled with the Holy Ghost, and began to speak with other tongues, as the Spirit gave them utterance (speech)." Continuing with verses 7-11, "And they were all amazed and marveled, saying one to another, Behold are not all these which speak Galilaeans? And how hear we every man in our own tongue, wherein we were born? Parthians, and Medes, and Elamites, and the dwellers in Mesopotamia, and in Judaea, and Cappadocia, in Pontus, and Asia, Phrygia, and Pamphylia, in Egypt, and in the parts of Libya about Cyrene, and strangers of Rome, Jews and proselytes, Cretes and Arabians, we do hear them speak in our tongues the wonderful works of God." These scriptures indicate that the indwelling of the Holy Ghost with evidence of speaking in other tongues (and unknown languages), and other gifts of the Spirit, were ordained for everyone. The scriptures reveal some who were present mocked. There has always been in our midst doubters, unbelievers, scoffers, and mockers; some even mocked Jesus as He hung on the cross. Some present doubted, but Peter explained this was a fulfillment of prophecy. Acts 2:16-18, "But this is that which was spoken by the prophet Joel; And it shall come to pass in the last days, saith God, I will pour out of my Spirit upon all flesh: and your sons and your daughters shall prophesy, and your young men shall see visions, and your old men shall dream dreams: And on my servants and on my handmaidens I will pour out in those days of my Spirit; and they shall prophesy." Peter and those assembled were eyewitnesses to Joel's prophecy, in part, being fulfilled. The terminology "all flesh" proves this is God's desire for all men to come to repentance of sin, and turn to God with all their hearts, and be filled with the Holy Spirit. These scriptures also indicate the timeframe: "in the last days." This is the order our Lord set up for us. Satan has been all too often successful in dissuading men from fulfilling God's desire to tabernacle within mankind.

    Perfection is not found in the earth, but we must endeavor to be pleasing to God. If we do sin, we do have an advocate with the Father, who is the Lord Jesus Christ. We are human, prone to sin and vices, but sanctification must be our chief desire. If someone commits a sin, transgression, or an offense, repent, ask God to forgive you, and then forgive yourself because God forgives and even forgets! With a renewed mind, and born-again Spirit, our desire to be God-pleasers is greater than fulfilling the desire of our own selfish wants and former habits. Ephesians 4:30-32, "And grieve not the holy Spirit of God, whereby ye are sealed unto the day of redemption. Let all bitterness, and wrath, and anger, and clamor, and evil speaking, be put away from you, with all malice: And be ye kind one to another, tenderhearted, forgiving one another, even as God for Christ's sake hath forgiven you."

Sanctification is a process, which must follow salvation. It requires giving of one's self wholly and denying fleshly lusts. The power of the indwelling Holy Ghost enables us to resist worldly snares, because continued sin would result in a worse state of separation from our Holy God. 2 Timothy 2:19-26, "Nevertheless the foundation of God standeth sure, having this seal, The Lord knoweth them that are his. And, let every one that nameth the name of Christ depart from iniquity. But in a great house there are not only vessels of gold and of silver, but also of wood and of earth; and some to honour, and some to dishonour. If a man therefore purge himself from these, he shall be a vessel unto honour, sanctified, and meet for the master's use, and prepared unto every good work. Flee also youthful lusts: but follow righteousness, faith, charity (love), peace, with them that call on the Lord out of a pure heart. But foolish and unlearned questions avoid, knowing that they do gender strifes. And the servant of the Lord must not strive; but be gentle unto all men, apt to teach, patient, In meekness instructing those that oppose themselves; if God peradventure (or perhaps) will give them repentance to the acknowledging of the truth; And that they may recover themselves out of the snare of the devil, who are taken captive at his will." After becoming a child of God, there is a righteous standard! If we are to become sanctified, a vessel of honor to God, "we must purge ourselves" of unrighteousness. 1 John 3:3, "And every man that hath this hope in him purifieth himself, even as he (Jesus) is pure." God ordained our salvation, Jesus provided the way of salvation, and the Holy Ghost has fulfilled the office of providing the avenue of holiness. We must not misuse the Blood Covenant and profanely remain the same old weak, excuse making, sin-laden person we were before accepting the Covenant of Salvation!

As we surrender to a new and better life in Jesus, the Holy Ghost changes our desires! Galatians 2:16-20, "Knowing that a man is not justified by the works of the law, but by the faith of Jesus Christ, even we have believed in Jesus Christ, that we might be justified by the faith of Christ, and not by the works of the law: for by the works of the law shall no flesh be justified. But if, while we seek to be justified by Christ, we ourselves also are found sinners, is therefore Christ the minister of sin? God forbid. For if I build again the things which I destroyed, I make myself a transgressor. For I through the law am dead to the law, that I might live unto God. I am crucified with Christ: nevertheless I live; yet not I, but Christ liveth in me: and the life which I now live in the flesh I live by the faith of the Son of God, who loved me, and gave himself for me."

Sanctification is a process, just as a baby grows in the natural; the newly born-again in Christ grows in the Spirit. One must daily war against the flesh and the temptations of the flesh. As we develop in Christ through the Holy Spirit, we become stronger and He even changes our very desires! One does not have to do an in-depth study of God's word to understand that God detests sin. 1 John 3:8, "He that committeth sin is of the devil; for the devil sinneth from the beginning. For this purpose the Son of God was manifested (made known), that he might destroy the works of the devil."

As I prayed concerning this chapter, God spoke to my heart and said, one of three things occur after salvation. The first, and only winning choice, is to become sanctified, holy and acceptable unto God, by separating ourselves from the world and the evils thereof. 2 Corinthians 6:17-18, "Wherefore come out from among them (from sinners), and be ye separate, saith the Lord, and touch not the unclean thing; and I will receive you. And will be a Father unto you, and ye shall be my sons and daughters, saith the Lord Almighty." 2 Corinthians 7:1, "Having therefore these promises, dearly beloved, let us cleanse ourselves from all filthiness of the flesh and spirit, perfecting holiness (which is sanctification) in the fear of God."

The second thing that may happen after salvation is we become a hypocrite. Remaining the same, yet pretending to be holy. Matthew 23:25-28, "Woe unto you, scribes and Pharisees, hypocrites! for ye make clean the outside of the cup and of the platter, but within they are full of extortion and excess. Thou blind Pharisee (hypocrite), cleanse first that which is within the cup and platter, that the outside of them may be clean also. Woe unto you, scribes and Pharisees, hypocrites! for ye are like unto whited sepulchres (tombs), which indeed appear beautiful outward, but are within full of dead men's bones, and of all uncleanness. Even so ye also outwardly appear righteous unto men, but within ye are full of hypocrisy and iniquity."

Or, third, we become a heretic, changing God's Word and misconstruing scriptures to suit our lifestyle, to make our religion more comfortable. 2 Peter 2:1-6, "But there were false prophets also among the people, even as there shall be false teachers among you, who privily shall bring in damnable heresies (doctrines of deception), even denying the Lord that bought them, and bring upon themselves swift destruction. And many shall follow their pernicious (deadly) ways; by reason of whom the way of truth shall be evil spoke of. And through covetousness shall they with feigned words make merchandise of you (sell you out): whose judgment now of a long time lingereth not, and their damnation slumbereth not. For if God spared not the angels that sinned, but cast them down to hell, and delivered them into chains of darkness, to be reserved unto judgment; And spared not the old world, but saved Noah the eighth person, a preacher of righteousness, bringing in the flood upon the world of the ungodly; And turning the cities of Sodom and Gomorrha into ashes condemned them with an overthrow, making them an ensample unto those that after should live ungodly."

In light of this we must then ask ourselves, "Which of these three are we?" Are we sanctified holy? A hypocrite? Or a heretic? The test of truth is declared in the Bible: 1 John 2:3-6, "And hereby we do know that we know him (Jesus), if we keep his commandments. He that saith, I know him, and keepeth not his commandments, is a liar, and the truth is not in him. But whoso keepeth his word, in him verily is the love of God perfected (sanctified): hereby know we that we are in him. He that saith he abideth in him ought himself also so to walk, even as he (Jesus) walked."

Many wrongfully proclaim the infilling of the Holy Ghost is not for today. This heresy has brought into existence the modern day Church of Laodicea (Revelation 3:14-19). This heresy has fostered a school of thought that cause's sin-prone man to accept mediocrity. This falsehood, propagated by Satan, is an attempt to eliminate God's holiness and overcoming power from the lives of Christians.

Sadly, in the world in which we live, Christians are often mocked, ridiculed, and persecuted for sharing Christian beliefs or holding Godly morals. We see wicked people taking ungodly stances against God's laws and God's people. It is an attempt by Satan to stamp out the Word of God, and to eliminate Godliness off the face of the earth. Satan has been effective in his campaign to malign the

Holy Ghost and those possessing the gifts of the Spirit. Speaking in tongues is a wonderful gift from God, and is designed to edify the individual and the church! These people are mocked and inferences are made that these gifts from God are of the devil. This is a blasphemous heresy against the Deity of God. Mark 3:28-30, "Verily I say unto you, All sins shall be forgiven unto the sons of men, and blasphemies wherewith soever they shall blaspheme: But he that shall blaspheme against the Holy Ghost hath never forgiveness, but is in danger of eternal damnation. Because they said, he hath an unclean spirit." It is also a ridiculous assumption that God's holy power be attributed to Satan. Scripture proves scripture. Luke 12:10, "And whosoever shall speak a word against the Son of man (Jesus), it shall be forgiven him: but unto him that blasphemeth against the Holy Ghost it shall not be forgiven." It is one of Satan's most effective campaigns to discredit the gifts of the Spirit. 1 Corinthians 14:39, "Wherefore, brethren (the church), covet to prophesy, and forbid not to speak with tongues." God clearly states that speaking in tongues is an evidence of the complete infilling of the Holy Ghost. As demonstrated on the day of Pentecost "all" were filled with the Holy Ghost and "all" spoke in other tongues and languages! Everyone gathered there in obedience to Jesus' command, everyone was expecting, and everyone received Jesus' promise. The apostle Paul taught often on the gifts of the Spirit. The gifts of The Spirit are necessary for the Church Triumphant just as fuel and oil are for an engine.

Our minds are like computers. What we put in comes out personified! It we put in filth, filth and corruption will come out. If we put in hate, hate and violence will come out. All evil tends to magnify itself and take over its host, until evil is master. 2 Timothy 3:1-5, "This know also, that in the last days perilous times shall come. For men shall be lovers of their own selves, covetous, boasters, proud, blasphemers, disobedient to parents, unthankful, unholy, Without natural affection, trucebreakers, false accusers, incontinent, fierce, despisers of those that are good, Traitors, heady, highminded, lovers of pleasures more than lovers of God; Having a form of godliness, but denying the power (Holy Ghost) thereof: from such turn away."

God's desire for the Church is that we should be filled with His power and separated through sanctification for His service. Acts 13:2, "As they ministered to the Lord, and fasted, the Holy Ghost said, Separate (unto) me Barnabas and Saul (Paul) for the work whereunto I have called them."

The mystery of Jesus' love for the Church is revealed as the "Bride of Christ." Jesus often taught in parables, and the parable of the marriage feast is most significant. Matthew 22:1-14, "And Jesus answered and spake unto them again by parables, and said, The kingdom of heaven is like unto a certain king, which made a marriage for his son, And sent forth his servants to call them that were bidden to the wedding: and they would not come. Again, he sent forth other servants, saying, Tell them which are bidden, Behold, I have prepared my dinner: my oxen and my fatlings are killed, and all things are now ready: come unto the marriage. But they made light of it, and went their ways, one to his farm, another to his merchandise: And the remnant took his servants, and entreated them spitefully, and slew them. But when the king heard thereof, he was wroth: and he sent forth his armies, and destroyed those murderers, and burned up their city. Then saith he to his servants, The wedding is ready, but they which were bidden were not worthy. Go ye therefore into the highways, and as many as ye find, bid to the marriage. So those servants went out into the highways, and gathered together all as many as they found, both bad and good: and the wedding was furnished with guests. And when the king came to see the guests, he saw there was a man which had not on the wedding garment: And he saith unto him, Friend, how camest thou in hither not having a wedding garment? And he was speechless. Then said the king to the servants, Bind him hand and foot, and take him away, and cast him into outer darkness, there shall be weeping and gnashing of teeth. For many are called, but few are chosen." The parable Jesus shared teaches us that God is the King, Jesus is the Son and Bridegroom, and the invitation includes all. The willing ones are the Church, comprised of believers, and the wedding garment is the righteousness of Jesus Christ. The one not accepted by the Father, and sent into everlasting punishment, was representative of one who has not accepted Jesus as. Lord and has not donned, or availed, oneself of the Saviors' righteousness, symbolic of the wedding garment. The Church is Jesus' bride and He is the groom because we are to be in a oneness with Him through the indwelling of the Holy Ghost.

Marriage was instituted by God and is to be a holy union. At the consummation of the wedding, the earthly bride and groom become one through the union of their flesh. This act was designed to be complete with a blood covenant. Our union with the Holy Ghost has absolutely nothing to do in the earthly fleshly realm, but is completely holy in the Spiritual realm. As the Holy Ghost overshadowed Mary she conceived Jesus and this was absolutely not physical, but was purely Spiritual. God's "Word" was imputed within Mary as the Holy Ghost overshadowed her, much like the example of the Holy Spirit descending on Jesus as a dove. We also become Spiritually One with Jesus when we receive the infilling of the Holy Ghost. This is a Spiritual example of our union with God, and it has absolutely nothing to do with the physical union between an earthly man and woman. 2 Corinthians 6:16-17, "And what agreement hath the temple (Greek: the sanctuary itself) of God with idols? for ye are the temple of the living God; as God hath said, I will dwell in them, and walk in them, and I will be their God, and they shall be my people. Wherefore come out from among them (from worldly sinners), and be ye separate, saith the Lord, and touch not the unclean thing; and I will receive you." Scripture proves scripture. 1 Corinthians 6:19-20, "What? know ye not that your body is the temple of the Holy Ghost which is in you, which ye have of God, and ye are not your own? For ye are bought with a price (Jesus' Blood): therefore glorify God in your body, and in your spirit which are God's." The living God is holy and just. He abhors sin. Amazingly, He is a God of love and He loved us when we were yet sinners. After receiving the saving knowledge of Jesus Christ, one must not remain in sin.

Sin will separate us from God, or we will be separated by sanctification through the Spirit unto God. One must not believe that the infilling of the Holy Ghost with manifestation of His gifts, are not for the Church today. That heresy is ridiculous. God's word and constant ways are recorded for man's benefit. Joel continued his account of the Holy Ghost and makes known the timeframe is for the last days of this age. Joel 2:30-32, "And I will shew wonders in the heavens and in the earth, blood, and fire, and pillars of smoke. The sun shall be turned into darkness, and the moon into blood, before the great and the terrible day of the LORD come. And it shall come to pass, that whosoever shall call on the name of the LORD shall be delivered: for in mount Zion and in Jerusalem shall be deliverance, as the LORD hath said, and in the remnant whom the LORD shall call." God would not give the early church power for a while then take it away, when the time of the end is near. When in all eternity past, or in all eternity future, will mankind need the power of the Holy Ghost dwelling within our mortal body as the perilous times in which we live today?

There is a spiritual battle still raging today for the souls of men. Ephesians 6:12-19, "For we wrestle not against flesh and blood, but against principalities, against powers, against the rulers of the darkness of this world, against spiritual wickedness in high places. Wherefore take unto you the whole armour of God, that ye may be able to withstand in the evil day, and having done all, to stand. Stand therefore, having your loins girt about with truth, and having on the breastplate of righteousness; And your feet shod with the preparation of the gospel of peace; Above all, taking the shield of faith, wherewith ye shall be able to quench all the fiery darts of the wicked. And take the helmet of salvation, and the sword of the Spirit, which is the word of God: Praying always with all prayer and supplication in the Spirit, and watching thereunto with all perseverance and supplication for all saints; And for me, that utterance may be given unto me, that I may open my mouth boldly, to make known the mystery of the gospel."

We, who are living in the last days of the gentile world domination, must grasp the weight of the seriousness of the hour. We are in spiritual warfare and our God has provided us with the necessary weapons for this war. These weapons are supernatural endowments of God's order, enabling mortal man to do mighty works because of the blood of Jesus and the indwelling power of the Holy Spirit.

Acts 2:38-39, "Then Peter said unto them, Repent, and be baptized every one of you in the name of Jesus Christ for the remission of sins, and ye shall receive the gift of the Holy Ghost. For the promise is unto you, and to your children, and to all that are afar off (the Church today), even as many as the Lord our God shall call." After accepting Jesus, we must repent of sins, and then remit them (our sins) to the Blood and receive forgiveness. We must then submit to water baptism, symbolic of a dying to oneself, and being resurrected into our born-again life in Christ. We must then pray for, and wait for, the divine impartation of the Holy Ghost. We then receive God's promise of power, and the process of sanctification begins through the baptism of the Holy Ghost. It is a wondrous, essential gift and you will KNOW when you receive the full indwelling. There will be verification and evidences through the Spirit. This gift is too marvelous for words.

The apostle Paul asked certain disciples in Ephesus a crucial question concerning the Holy Ghost Acts 19:1-6, "And it came to pass, that, while Apollos was at Corinth, Paul having passed through the upper coasts came to Ephesus: and finding certain disciples, He said unto them, Have ye received the Holy Ghost since ye believed? And they said unto him, We have not so much as heard whether there be any Holy Ghost. And he said unto them, Unto what then were ye baptized? And they said, unto John's baptism. Then said Paul, John verily baptized with the baptism of repentance, saying unto the people, that they should believe on him which should come after him, that is, on Christ Jesus. When they heard this, they were baptized in the name of the Lord Jesus (water baptism). And when Paul had laid his hands upon them, the Holy Ghost came on them; and they spake with tongues, and prophesied." These believers repented, submitted to water baptism, and then received the baptism of the Holy Ghost with signs following. This scripture illustrates our need to be baptized in the Holy Ghost and have signs following us. The infusion of God's power is the remedy for everyone who claims the title of Christian. We must become Christ-like, following His examples and being yielded to the Holy Spirit, and have power to be overcomers in this world of chaos and woe.

Satan has waged an effective campaign through the ages to discredit those filled with the Holy Ghost. The Holy Ghost is of such utmost importance, that Jesus warned every sin is pardonable except for blasphemy against the Holy Ghost. Matthew 12:31-32, "Wherefore I say unto you, All manner of sin and blasphemy shall be forgiven unto men: but the blasphemy against the Holy Ghost shall not be forgiven unto men. And whosoever speaketh a word against the Son of man, it shall be forgiven him: but whosoever speaketh against the Holy Ghost, it shall not be forgiven him, neither in this world, neither in the world to come." One must not fear that perhaps, in times past, that you may have committed the unpardonable sin. This, I believe, is a deliberate act and one could not, just through ignorance, blunder into such dangerous and deadly territory.

As it was then, so it is even now. Today, many have only obtained the baptism of repentance and have not pursued the overcoming power, which is given to us through the baptism of fire, which can only come through the infilling of the Holy Ghost. Tragically, just as in the Apostle Paul's day, his words still ring true: Believers "have not so much as heard whether there be any Holy Ghost."

We are a jaded society, desensitized by sin and seduced by the world. We, in America, mistakenly perceive sin as something pleasurable and acceptable. In reality, without a renewed mind and the Holy Spirit, continued sin will lead to our ultimate destruction. Sin always brings devastating results, as is illustrated by the true story recorded in Acts Chapter 5. A man named Ananias and his wife Sapphira conspired together to sin. Their sins of hypocrisy and greed, led them to lie, and resulted in their deaths. For the wrong they conceived in their hearts, and carried out, God struck them dead within three hours of one another.

This example serves warning that our God is unchanging and His instant, righteous judgment can be visited upon sinful man today, just as in the Old Testament times. It is needful for us to recognize sin as our enemy, and if held in its sway, man is most wretched. Satan is the author of sin and, left unrepented and nurtured, sin is the destroyer of men's souls. How can one believe that sin is unacceptable to God in an unsaved, unrepented person, but after receiving Christ as Savior, it is acceptable? Sin is never acceptable to God. It is more dangerous to continue in sin after having once known the saving grace of Jesus, The Christ. Hebrews 10:26-29, "For if we sin willfully after that we have received the knowledge of the truth, there remaineth no more sacrifice for sins, But a certain fearful looking for of judgment and fiery indignation, which shall devour the adversaries. He that despised Moses' law died without mercy under two or three witnesses: Of how much sorer punishment, suppose ye, shall he be thought worthy, who hath trodden underfoot the Son of God, and hath counted the blood of the Covenant (Jesus' Blood), wherewith he was sanctified, an unholy thing, and hath done despite unto the Spirit of grace?" After salvation, one must not remain in sin. True repentance brings forth salvation, and salvation must be followed by sanctification. We have no righteousness of our own; the only righteousness we have is in Jesus! We have no power of our own; the only power we have, to become sanctified, is that of the Holy Ghost. One may be a decent citizen and accomplish many good things in one's lifetime, but if that person is depending on his own goodness, that one's end will be most wretched! Since the fall of man, everyone is in need of God's redemption plan. We must develop a God-like holy hatred for Satan, sin, and the penalty of sin!

Once, being cleansed from sin, we must not continue in sin or fellowship with those who do. Paul writes in 1 Corinthians 5:9-13, "I wrote unto you in an epistle not to company with fornicators (all sex outside of the marriage covenant between a man and woman). Yet not altogether with fornicators of this world, or with the covetous, or extortioners, or with idolaters; for then must ye needs go out of the world. But now I have written unto you not to keep company, if any man that is called a brother be a fornicator (sexually immoral), or covetous, or an idolater, or a railer (one who rages and rants), or a drunkard, or an extortioner; with such an one no not to eat. For what have I to do to judge them also that are without (nonbelievers)? do not ye judge them that are within (Christians)? But them that are without God judgeth. Therefore put away from among yourselves that wicked person."

Paul did not make excuses for, or gloss over, these sins. Nor did he call sin "weaknesses" or "faults" or "mistakes." Rather, he made it clear that one who is called a "brother" and still continues in sin is "wicked."

Countless people professing to be Christians, make excuses for themselves while practicing sin, and thereby misuse the blood of Jesus. Luke 12:51, "Suppose ye that I am come to give peace on earth? I tell you Nay; but rather division." It is evident Jesus knew his gospel would not be accepted by all, as his apostles had assumed. Jesus knew that the gospel would not only be rejected by many, but worse yet, would be opposed by some. His intention for the Church did not, and does not, include sin and hypocrisy. Instead, it affords overcoming power through the baptism of fire, which denotes God's presence. God's indwelling presence fans the flames of Holiness that burns off the dross of sin and impurities in our lives. Moses found himself in the presence of God as God spoke out of the burning bush, instructing Moses to take off his shoes, for he was standing on holy ground! The tongues of fire on the day of Pentecost denoted God's holy presence. 2 Corinthians 4:7, "But we have this treasure (Holy Ghost) in earthen vessels (our bodies), that the excellency of the power may be of God, and not of us." Acceptance or rejection of these immutable truths does not change God. God's Word and Will are set upon an eternal unchanging foundation. Unbelief in God's existence, or disbelief in the authority of the Bible (the Word), does not alter God or annul these truths. All, believers and nonbelievers, will be judged by the standard of the Bible.

Following Christ's resurrection, the gospel, which Jesus preached, confirms God's desire for His Church, which is to fulfill "His Great Commission." Mark 16:14-20, "Afterward (after Jesus' resurrection) he (Jesus) appeared unto the eleven as they sat at meat, and upbraided (corrected) them with their unbelief and hardness of heart, because they believed not them which had seen him after he was risen. And he (Jesus) said unto them, Go ye into all the world, and preach the gospel to every creature. He that believeth and is baptized shall be saved; but he that believeth not shall be damned. And these signs shall follow them that believe; In my name (the mighty name of Jesus) shall they cast out devils; they shall speak with new tongues (as on the day of Pentecost); They shall take up serpents (oppose false teachers); and if they drink any deadly thing (hear false doctrine), it shall not hurt them; they shall lay hands on the sick, and they shall recover. So then after the Lord had spoken unto them, he was received up into heaven, and sat on the right hand (given all authority) of God. And they went forth, and preached every where, the Lord working with them, and confirming the word with signs following. Amen." These signs that follow are mighty to the pulling down the strongholds of evil. 1 Thessalonians 3:13, "To the end he (Holy Ghost) may stablish your hearts unblameable in holiness before God, even our Father, at the coming of our Lord Jesus Christ with all his saints."

Chapter Six

Pulpit Poison

"My people are destroyed for lack of knowledge."

(Hosea 4:6)

Poison destroys and kills. It can bring deadly harm if taken accidentally or even intentionally administered by another. The results are the same-death.

There is a multitude of false doctrines being preached from behind the pulpits, which would send souls into eternal damnation. The most important task a man has in his lifetime is to prepare his soul for his death. We must be very careful of the spiritual food our souls are being fed. 2 Peter 2:1, "But there were false prophets also among the people, even as there shall be false teachers among you, who privily shall bring in damnable heresies, even denying the Lord that bought them, and bring upon themselves swift destruction."

It's imperative to study The Holy Bible for oneself. If you have difficulty understanding the Bible, stop reading, and pray. Ask God to give you understanding through the indwelling Holy Spirit. Read again and pray again. If you can't understand the Bible, perhaps you are not walking in the light, or the knowledge you have already obtained. If one hasn't applied the knowledge he or she has already been given, most likely God will not afford that one additional insights, understandings, or revelations. The Lord is faithful if we ask and He rewards those who diligently seek Him. Don't trust just anyone or just any religion. With so many churches, beliefs, and diverse doctrines flourishing today how do we know which is correct? We can know by the Word of God, recorded in The Holy Bible. The Bible is the only directive book that is prophetic. God instructs, warns, and foretells future events before they happen. Proving God IS God. He causes these prophecies, which are foretold often thousands of years in advance, to come to fulfillment, even down to minute details. God proves Himself and His Word trustworthy and infallible.

The Bible explains God's love, plan, and purpose for mankind, but forewarns there are false shepherds and deceivers out to seduce the souls of mankind. 2 Corinthians 11:13-15, "For such are false apostles, deceitful workers, transforming themselves into the apostles of Christ. And no marvel; for Satan himself is transformed into an angel of light. Therefore it is no great thing if his ministers also be transformed as the ministers of righteousness; whose end shall be according to their works." Mankind possesses an inner knowledge of the existence of a higher power. Nature itself dictates the existence of God, the Creator. It is He who set the boundaries of the vast seas and He who sculpted the imposing beauty in the solid lofty heights of the mountain ranges. There is a serene splendor in a sunset overlooking the snowy and desolate regions of the beautiful Alaskan coastline. God's mastery of creativity is seen in the Tropical Rainforest with its lush green foliage and the brilliant color of its exotic birds. There is a Creator, and man was created in His image, and deep within the heart of man is a God-given desire to search out and worship our Creator. There is a void and a longing instilled deep within man that only God can satisfy. Men have sought God and often settled for fabricated untruths and empty ideologies.

There are 22 major religions in the world today. Christianity ranks first in size with 2.1 billion, Islam ranks second with 1.5 billion, Secular and non-religious ranks third with 1.1 billion, Hinduism ranks fourth with 900 million, Chinese Traditional ranks fifth with 394 million, Buddhism ranks sixth with 376 million. There are so many diverse religions and recognized belief systems, or sects, abounding in the world today they are too numerous to list. But a few are: Humanists, Shinto, Unitarian Universalism, Baha'i, Neo-Paganism, Spiritualism, Satanism, Wiccan, New Age, and one of the newest being Scientology.

America allows and welcomes freedom of religion. Once again, America was founded on Judeo-Christian principles taught in The Holy Bible. Judaism ranks twelfth in the world with only 14 million Jews whose foundation, and Old Covenant with Jehovah God, is recorded in the Old Testament of The Holy Bible. The Hebrew people were the first Monotheists, meaning they were the first to recognize Jehovah God as the only ONE TRUE GOD. Jehovah's existence is eternal. He is in eternity past and exists in eternity future. His love for His creation, mankind is unfathomable. This one and only true God is the Creator of all things, but God created us to be free-will beings. It is a God given right to believe, or even not to believe. Diverse beliefs, or even unbelief itself, does not alter nor does it annul these foundational truths. Jehovah's desire is that all men everywhere repent of their sins and accept the salvation plan through the Blood Covenant of Jesus Christ (God's own blood and body) as presented in The New Testament, but was also prophesied throughout the Old Testament. 1 Timothy 3:16, "And without controversy great is the mystery of godliness: God was manifest (revealed) in the flesh, justified in the Spirit, seen of angels, preached unto the Gentiles, believed on in the world, received up into glory." The majority of the Jewish population has not, as yet, accepted Jesus' new covenant, but will because God's word declares "all Israel shall be saved." Zechariah 12:10 "And I will pour upon the house of David, and upon the inhabitants of Jerusalem, the spirit of grace and of supplications: and they shall look upon me (Jesus) whom they have pierced, and they shall mourn for him (Jesus), as one mourneth for his only son, and shall be in bitterness for him, as one that is in bitterness for his firstborn." Though many Jews have accepted Jesus as Messiah and are called Messianic Jews, or Completed Jews, many have not, as yet, understood this great salvation plan. All Hebrew people will come to full revelation knowledge that Jesus Is Jehovah as the 144,000 predestined Jews preach the salvation message. Sadly, this will be during the seven year great tribulation period and it will be a time of fiery judgments on the ungodly Gentiles, and yet during this fierce time, the entire House of Israel shall be saved. What a gracious, glorious, and wonderful Father-God.

We in America are blessed to have freedom of religion and the truth is preached in many churches, on the radio, via television, and now can be accessed by home computers. Through the Trinity Broadcasting Network, The Angel Network, The Inspiration Network, and The Word Network Christian television transmits "the truth" that the world is seeking. These truths are sent forth twenty four hours a day by satellite. Many around the world are hearing the good news of Jesus Christ for the first time. Much of the world has been in darkness and has not had the opportunity to accept the Covenant of Love. There will be little excuse for Americans who have had the advantage of both freedom of religion and opportunity to search out these immutable Christian truths for oneself!

L. Ron Hubbard began his adult life as a writer of Science Fiction stories. He eventually became the founder of Scientology. He cultivated his ideas into a religious philosophy, with the principle foundation of possessing a science of knowledge. It allows one to create a new reality which promotes survival, ethics and earned rights. Many Hollywood celebrities have turned to this cult of promotion through works. The Bible teaches that no man can attain heaven through works. Ephesians 2:8-9, "For by grace are ye saved through faith; and that not of yourselves: it is the gift of God: Not of works, lest any man should boast."

Jim Jones, an American and founder of The People's Temple, moved his misled and misinformed followers to Jonestown, Guyana. Jones, a maniacal false shepherd, led his victims to their deaths. California Congressman Leo J. Ryan and others in Ryan's investigative party flew to Guyana and were shot and killed as they boarded their plane to leave Guyana. Jim Jones prompted mass suicide and mass murder. In his treacherous wake he left over 900 people dead by administering cyanide in massive quantities of Kool-Aid. The ways of these cryptic cult leaders often lead to a physical death.

David Koresh, born Vernon Wayne Howell, became leader of The Branch Davidians, a religious sect based in Waco Texas. The self-proclaimed prophet barricaded himself and 75 of his deluded followers in their compound. The FBI and The U.S. Bureau of Alcohol, Tobacco, Firearms and Explosives, tried unsuccessfully to rescue the children away from Koresh. Koresh and all those who followed him, even the children, were burned to death in a tragic fire, as Koresh's compound burned to the ground.

Cult leader, Dwight York, founded the United Nuwaubian Nation and established their home base in Atlanta Georgia. York also known as Malachi, Doc, and Papa presented himself as King! York's ever-changing doctrine should have been a red flag to his followers. Originally they were indoctrinated into a mishmash of Muslim-Judeo-Christian doctrines. First they were required to wear traditional Muslim garb, but the ever-changing mind and beliefs of York soon had these same people observing Native-American traditions. Before long, York was espousing Ancient Egyptian Mysticism and UFO's. Despite all the chaos York was successful in secluding his stressed and undernourished people from the mainstream population. The most vulnerable of the group, the children, both boys and girls, were forced to endure sexual abuse and even rape by York. Unbelievably, this cult is still in existence today, even though York is serving a 135 year prison sentence after being found guilty of sex crimes perpetrated against the children.

James Ray, self-help guru, was charged by the state of Arizona with 3 counts of reckless manslaughter. These charges resulted from the death of three of his followers during a "spiritual rebirthing" exercise in a Sweat Lodge ceremony. Two died as a result of heatstroke and the third died from organ failure due to hyperthermia. Ray charged thousands of dollars for these "spiritual quests" or "spiritual enlightenments." Some of Ray's spiritual exercises involved the participants acting out different roles and during these events, not surprisingly; James Ray role played "God!"

Some people drift slowly, being brainwashed or conditioned into believing man-made, man-centered religions, while others rush unheeded into cults. Most are trusting people in search of answers, but instead find only pathetic and empty falsehoods. Sexual crimes against cult members is a recurring theme among members and almost without exception, the sexual perpetrator is the cult leader. These pathetic victims submit their minds and bodies to deceptive and lying teachers. Jeremiah 23:1, "Woe be unto the pastors that destroy and scatter the sheep of my pasture! saith the LORD" Again, we prove scripture with scripture. Jeremiah 50:6, "My people hath been lost sheep: their shepherds have caused them to go astray, they have turned them away (from the truth) on the mountains: they have gone from mountain to hill, they have forgotten their restingplace."

Some cults are easier to recognize than many of the "main-line churches," which preach deadly doctrines. The Mormons (Church of the Latter Day Saints) are a sincere people who follow Joseph Smith, who claimed an Angel named "Moroni" appeared to him. The Book of Mormon was supposedly written through the instruction of this "so-called" Angel Moroni. The book is a hodgepodge of confusion. Joseph Smith and his followers never read, or never applied, the warning found in the Bible. Galatians 1:6-9, "I marvel that ye are so soon removed from him (Jesus) that called you into the grace of Christ unto another gospel: Which is not another; but there be some that trouble you, and would pervert the Gospel of Christ. But though we, or an angel from heaven, preach any other gospel unto you than that which we have preached unto you, let him be accursed. As we said before, so say I now again, if any man preach any other gospel unto you than that ye have received, let him be accursed." The truth is so plain that we are not to receive anything other than our Old and New Testaments that make up our Holy Bible. By reading the scriptures carefully and prayerfully, we can see for ourselves, and know, which belief systems or religion lines up with the will and word of God!

Many sincere and nice people have fallen into the snare of being a Jehovah's Witness. They have been told that only 144,000 of their people will be found worthy, by works, to enter heaven. No one can work his way to heaven. In Revelation, the Bible clearly states the 144,000 evangelists are Jews. Revelation 7:4, "And I heard the number of them which were sealed: and there were sealed an hundred and forty and four thousand of all the tribes of the children of Israel." The following verses explain there will be 12,000 out of each of the twelve Hebrew tribes. These are going to be Jews preaching the salvation message of Jesus Christ during the seven-year tribulation at the end of Gentile world domination. The present age of grace we are now living in will soon come to completion. We must all avail ourselves of the plan of salvation, which God has so graciously and wonderfully provided for us through the blood covenant of Jesus Christ the Messiah, before it is forever too late.

The Jehovah's Witnesses have a bible very similar to the King James Version, except there are grievous errors in their "bible." The King James Version, which is to be taken literally, reads in John 1:1, "In the beginning was the Word, and the Word was with God, and the Word was God." In this reference the "Word" translates to "Jesus." A frightening example of how the Jehovah's Witness bible adds only one word and neglects to capitalize the 'G' in God results in the entire meaning of scripture being changed. Their bible erroneously reads, John 1:1, "In the beginning was the word, and the word was with God and the word was a god." Simply adding a one-letter word, 'a' and not capitalizing the G, changes the entire text, dismissing the Deity of Jesus. This deceitful declaration reduces Jesus to less than who He was and is, "God Incarnate." We know that Jesus is the Word, by John 1:14, "And the Word was made flesh, and dwelt among us, (and we beheld his glory, the glory as of the only begotten of the Father,) full of grace and truth." Jesus is the flesh and blood of God and He lived among us. One of the names of Jesus is Emmanuel, which literally translates, "God with us." Man is given a grave warning against changing or adding any words written in the Bible. Revelation 22:18, "For I testify unto every man that heareth the words of the prophecy of this book, If any man shall add unto these things, God shall add unto him the plagues that are written in this book."

The preceding is just another of many examples how Satan will take a lake of truth to mask a pint of poison. It's pulpit poison, and leads to the destruction of souls. Again, 2 Timothy 2:15, "Study to show thyself approved unto God." The Bible also states in John 12:48, "He that rejecteth me (Jesus), and receiveth not my words, hath one that judgeth him: the word (recorded in the Bible) that I have spoken, the same shall judge him in the last day." The last days of this age--the Church Age--or the End of Gentile Domination is upon us. Read and study The Holy Bible, carefully applying its truths to be approved of God. Be ever mindful that your immortal soul is at stake! You must purpose in your heart not to be misled. All must be determined not to compromise. Don't be complacent when it comes to the safety of your soul. Pray daily for a desire for the truth. God is faithful if we ask. Luke 21:8, "And he said, Take heed that ye be not deceived: for many shall come in my name, saying I am Christ; and the time draweth near: go ye not therefore after them."

An alliance of Christians and Muslims worshipping together is a relatively new phenomenon called Chrislam. These two diverse religions are in opposition one to the other. Amos 3:3, "Can two walk together, except they be agreed?" Absolutely not! Christianity is the New Covenant God made first to the Jews and then to the Gentiles (all humanity is welcome) through Jesus Christ. His willingness to shed His own sacrificial blood is the personification of love. This great love is presented to all mankind everywhere as the only avenue of salvation. Jesus The Christ is the chief cornerstone of the New Testament. The Muslim religion is built on falsehoods, misrepresentations of the truth, and its very foundation is built on the seat of Satan. Allah is a pseudo-god of hatred and vengeance. God was very clear in His direction to believers in 2 Corinthians 6:14, "Be ye not unequally yoked together with unbelievers: for what fellowship hath righteousness with unrighteousness? and what communion hath light with darkness?" Professing Christians uniting with Islam, whether through ignorance, fear, misplaced tolerance, or a pretense of fashion, will undoubtedly bring upon themselves swift destruction. We must not compromise our standing with God to please another.

To be a Muslim, and embrace the Islamic religion, is to follow the beliefs of Mohammad. Many have turned to this doctrine without realizing that in reality, they would not want to reap the consequences. On the surface it sounds good, peace through submission to Allah. Islam is, in actuality, a replacement theory for both Judaism and Christianity. This belief transfers the blessings belonging to Isaac to Ishmael. One must be warned that Islamic extremists have a doctrine of hate. If possible, radical Islam would annihilate Judaism and Christianity. This is possibly The Great Antichrist spirit of apocalyptic proportion of the last days Jesus forewarned in our Bible Scriptures. 2 Thessalonians 2:5-7, "Remember ye not, that, when I was yet with you, I told you these things? And now ye know what withholdeth (The Holy Spirit is the restraining force here on earth) that he (Antichrist or son of perdition) might be revealed in his time. For the mystery of iniquity (iniquitous Antichrist spirit) doth already work: only he (Holy Spirit) who now letteth will let, until he (Holy Spirit) be taken out of the way." At the time of the rapture of the Church, the Holy Spirit will be received back up into heaven with the Church. The Holy Spirit, prophesied by Old Testament Joel, was sent down from heaven on the day of Pentecost as to endow man with Godly abilities during the Church-Age. The believer is to be endued with wisdom, guidance, and Holy Ghost power. After the rapture of the Church, the absence of God's Holy Spirit - God's restraining force; Satan, and the great antichrist spirit, will be strengthened to carry out Satan's wicked plans. Continuing in 2 Thessalonians 2:9-12, "Even him (Antichrist), whose coming is after the working of Satan with all power and signs and lying wonders, And with all deceivableness of unrighteousness in them that perish; because they received not the love of the truth, that they might be saved. And for this cause God shall send them strong delusion, that they should believe a lie: That they all might be damned who believed not the truth, but had pleasure in unrighteousness." The Spirit of Antichrist is already at work, and it is very possible that the Great Antichrist Spirit described in these verses is the doctrine of the hatemongering Islamic Extremist.

Is it possible that the False Prophet will be the reigning supreme spiritual leader of Islam? The Ayatollah, as the false shepherd of doom, who professes he is chosen by Allah (their god) to bring about the end of the world through a Jihad. Islamic Extremists profess Islam to be the one true religion and that only a

Jihad (their holy war) against Jews and Christians will usher in their awaited Messiah, the Mahdi. The Antichrist will, at some future time, stand up and claim to be the Messiah, or perhaps this Mahdi. At this appointed time, Antichrist will enter the Jewish Temple, or perhaps The Dome of The Rock Mosque, and demand worship. Antichrist is going to be a counterfeit Christ. He will possess abilities to perform lying signs and wonders in the heavenly sky and on the earth. He will be satanically energized and will be the son of perdition. He will blasphemously profess himself to be God and set himself up to be worshipped. Revelation 14:9-12, "And the third angel followed them, saying with a loud voice, If any man worship the beast and his image, and receive his mark in his forehead, or his in his hand, The same shall drink of the wine of the wrath of God, which is poured out without mixture into the cup of his (God's) indignation; and he shall be tormented with fire and brimstone in the presence of the holy angels, and in the presence of the Lamb (Jesus): And the smoke of their torment ascendeth up for ever and ever: and they have no rest day nor night, who worship the beast and his image, and whosoever receiveth the mark (666 or symbolic of) of his name. Here is the patience of the saints: here are they that keep the commandments of God, and the faith of Jesus."

Denying Jesus' death on the cross makes His Holy Blood to no avail for those who deny it. Hebrews 9:22, "... without shedding of blood is no remission (of sins)." Everyone who is in the world needs to accept the new Blood Covenant Jesus Christ made for all. It was Jesus himself, and no substitute, who died on the Cross in our stead. Through Himself, and none other, can we obtain eternal life! Our God is the God of forgiveness and love. Our God is not vindictive, nor hateful. Neither is He a God of whims. That perfect plan is related in John 3:16-18, "For God so loved the world, that he gave his only begotten Son, that whosoever believeth in him should not perish, but have everlasting life. For God sent not his Son into the world to condemn the world; but that the world through him (Jesus) might be saved. He that believeth on him is not condemned: but he that believeth not is condemned already, because he hath not believed in the name of the only begotten Son of God." Our merciful and great God is: LOVE. He loves everyone! He loves the sinner, the Muslim, the Hindu, the Buddhist, the doubter, the agnostic, the atheist, the cultist, and the backslidden Christian. Jesus died that all people everywhere could accept Him, and are freely given the opportunity to repent of their sins, and remit them to Jesus' precious Blood and by doing so, obtain eternal life. 1 John 2:2, "And he (Jesus) is the propitiation for our sins: and not for ours only, but also for the sins of the whole world."

Jesus, himself, warned us of false doctrines and deceitful men. Luke 20:45-47, "Then in the audience of all the people he said unto his disciples, Beware of the scribes, which desire to walk in long robes, and love greetings in the markets, and the highest seats in the synagogues, and the chief rooms at feasts; Which devour widows' houses, and for a shew make long prayers: the same shall receive greater damnation." The call of God to man or woman is to walk a humble walk before our Holy God. Jesus himself was humble and meek. Don't be led astray through deceitfulness of self-exaltation, pomp and circumstance, or superfluous rituals. Matthew 23:8-10, "But be not ye called Rabbi: for (only) one is your Master, even Christ; and all ye are brethren. And call no man your father upon the earth (pertaining in a religious sense): for (only) one is your Father, which is in heaven. Neither be ye called masters: for (only) one is your master, even Christ." The title "Minister" means "to serve," to be a servant to a congregation or a group of people. The term "Pastor" is also a humble title pertinent to Shepherding God's sheep. Leaders who exalt themselves, "holier than thou," posturing themselves as self-righteous, is indicative of hypocrisy, displeasing the Living God. We are all brothers and sisters in God. Jesus is our mediator and none other. 1 Timothy 2:5, "For there is one God, and one mediator between God and men (all mankind), the man Christ Jesus." Same chapter verse 8, "I will therefore that men pray every where, lifting up holy hands, without wrath and doubting." We must seek the approval of God and be very sure we are not following vain rituals or practices that only men or churches have made. We must diligently search and seek God's desire for us by reading our Bibles and praying. God will lead us in the path of righteousness for His glory and our good. We need to pray to the Father in the name of Jesus. We need no other person or priest. Again, not following the orders of men, but rather obeying the commandments of God. For example, in Exodus 20:4-5, "Thou shalt not make unto thee any graven image (for worship), or any likeness of any thing that is in heaven above, or that is in the earth beneath, or that is in the water under the earth. Thou shalt not bow down thyself to them, nor serve them ..." So many people blindly obey the order of man, tradition, or church. Just because others may bow down before a graven image (statue), even one of Jesus, or Mary His Mother, does not give us an excuse to follow a man-made tradition, contrary to the second of the Ten Commandments of God. What would have been the fate of the three Hebrew children (Daniel chapter 3) if they had bowed down before the golden image (statue)? The answer is they would have been destroyed. The only reason anyone should bow down is to pray and worship, in the posture of humility, in a spirit of worship due the Almighty. Never are we to bow down to any man or statue! Only ONE, our Mighty God, deserves our reverential praise and worship, and only ONE can hear and answer our prayers.

If we serve Him here on earth we will reign with Him in eternity. He (Jesus) has gone to prepare a place for us that where He is, there we may be also at the appointed time. We have experienced a shakeup in the recent past among Christian leaders. No doubt some trials came as traps, which were set by Satan, the arch tempter and deceiver. Opposed to that, however, the Almighty God is continually sifting and separating the wheat from the chaff. God said, "My heart will not always strive with man." We must be careful to walk the narrow pathway described in Matthew 7:13-16, "Enter ye in at the strait gate: for wide is the gate, and broad is the way, that leadeth to destruction, and many there be which go in thereat: Because strait is the gate, and narrow is the way, which leadeth unto life, and few there be that find it. Beware of false prophets, which come to you in sheep's clothing, but inwardly they are ravening wolves. Ye shall know them by their fruits ..." Continuing with verses 21-23, "Not every one that sayeth unto me, Lord, Lord, shall enter into the kingdom of heaven; but (only) he that doeth the will of my Father which is in heaven. Many will say to me in that day, Lord, Lord, have we not prophesied in thy name? and in thy name have cast out devils? and in thy name done many wonderful works? And then will I profess unto them, I never knew you: depart from me, ye that work iniquity." God sifts to save the good wheat and to disperse the evil as chaff before the four winds. The unrepentant ones are the chaff, but the wheat are the ones who repent openly before God, and God Himself will forgive and restore that one to a right relationship to Him.

The atheist does not believe there is a God. Unless he softens his heart to let his mind be receptive to God's word, he will remain an atheist until he dies. Standing before the judgment seat of God, at that time he will become a believer. However, that will be forever too late. His fate was sealed by his self-centered lifestyle during his earthly life.

Agnosticism means "no knowledge." It is the belief that man can never answer his own ultimate questions about things pertaining to science or religion, such as matter, mind, or God. Many are "deluded" by their own conceit and vain wisdom. 1 Corinthians 3:18-21, "Let no man deceive himself. If any man among you seemeth to be wise in this world, let him become a fool, that he may be wise. For the wisdom of this world is foolishness with God. For it is written, He taketh the wise in their own craftiness. And again, The Lord knoweth the thoughts of the wise, that they are vain. Therefore, let no man glory in men, for all things are yours."

We must all beware of self-exaltation. If we make ourselves "the lord of our life" we leave no room for Lord Jesus to dwell within us through the infilling of his Holy Spirit. There is a philosophy called humanism. If this theory is embraced, it brings forth misery and ends with "man-most-wretched!" Jesus must be first in our lives, our own willfulness second to His perfect will. This philosophy of humanism, prevalent today, is vain and deceitful. It sets up the wants and wisdom of man against the will and wisdom of God. When we walk after our own desires, it hinders our faith. The humanists profess everything begins with man and ends with man. Its emphasis is on nature, not deity. Society has, sadly, devised its own standards of morals which violate the laws of God. 2 Timothy 3:1-4, "This know also, that in the last days perilous times shall come. For men shall be lovers of their own selves, covetous, boasters, proud, blasphemers, disobedient to parents, unthankful, unholy, Without natural affection, trucebreakers, false accusers, incontinent, fierce, despisers of those that are good, Traitors, heady, high-minded, lovers of pleasures more than lovers of God."

Obtaining peace and joy here on earth cannot be bought or obtained through earthly pursuits. The priceless treasure of inner peace is only acquired through a right relationship with God. Obedience to God brings its own rewards. The richest of men cannot buy the treasure of peace of mind, comfort in the time of sorrow, calmness in the midst of a storm or eternal life at the end of life's journey. A truly repentant heart and developing an intimacy with Jesus is the only avenue to this higher estate. Only empty alternatives and fleeting satisfaction is found temporarily in illicit sex, worldly pleasures or obtaining earthly treasures. There are many people turning to drugs and alcohol in an attempt to manipulate their emotions through chemical change. Chemicals enslave while ineffectively masking the original problem. There must be a genuine change within oneself. A person can get a new house, new job, new car, or even a new nose, but one is still the same person. The changes must come from righteous new principles, pure moral lifestyles, and Godly desires. There is a God-shaped void in every person's life, and Jesus is the only one that can satisfy that emptiness. Lying down at night knowing all is well within one's soul, and knowing "God is still on the throne," is the only avenue to true inner peace. All have problems and trials, for no one can lead a trouble-free life. To think otherwise is unrealistic. The word of God says, "It rains on the just and the unjust alike." But through all storms, we have the assurance that the Lord is on the throne and He is always our strength and stay.

This is an adulterous and wicked generation. We must not parley with temptation, or flirt with sin, for that puts us in greater danger of being overcome by evil.

The Unitarian-Universal Church has a foundation of liberalism. Freedom of belief and social justice are their basic principles, teaching every individual should develop his or her own personal philosophy of life. They erroneously teach "truth" is not absolute, that it changes from time to time. They do not believe in the virgin birth or the resurrection of Christ from the dead. Each Unitarian-Universal church can differ from its affiliates.

The Evangelical Lutheran Church in America previously allowed homosexuals to serve as ministers only if the minister professed celibacy. This church is estimated to have four and one half million members. In 2009 the largest of the Evangelical Lutheran Churches voted to allow non-celibate homosexuals to serve as clergy if they are in a "Committed relationship."

There are many "Gay Churches" comprised of homosexual-lesbian congregations, often led by ordained homosexual pastors. Those who practice these abominations have willfully disregarded God's Holy Scriptures, deceived by Satan, the seducer of men's souls. To wear this veil of wickedness as a cloak of Godly worship is abhorrent! The very word "gay," used for this warped, spiritual condition is also a cloak to disguise the truth. One of Oprah Winfrey's personal spiritual advisors stated on her television show, "being gay (homosexual) is a gift from God." That is an untruth and in complete opposition to God's word. God's word is the ultimate authority. Satan is the "gay" deceiver selling attitudes and altering values. Satan advocates homosexuality and other perversions, while society justifies and sanctions such acts. One must sincerely seek truth because the truth concerning sin, and sinful lifestyles, is being perverted. God is erroneously being presented as accepting of sin. Wrong! God can never, and would never, accept any sin. God DOES accept sinners when they repent of their sin and turn away, forsaking their sins. God forgives the homosexual sinner just as He forgives the sinner who has been a thief; the sinner who has been a murderer; or the sinner who has been a liar. God is holy and all sin is unacceptable. God does not accept homosexuality, murder, thievery, lying, or any other sin. One cannot remain in their sin and believe God condones their sins! He is merciful and loving and forgives everyone who is truly repentant and, through the indwelling of His Holy Spirit, gives one opportunity and strength to overcome the sin and live life victoriously. 1 John 3:7-8, "Little children, let no man deceive you: he that doeth righteousness is righteous, even as he (Jesus) is righteous. He that committeth sin is of the devil; for the devil sinneth from the beginning. For this purpose the Son of God (Jesus) was manifested, that he might destroy the works of the devil."

Obama's former "Safe Schools" Czar, Kevin Jennings, founder of the Gay, Lesbian and Straight Education Network has implemented his perverted lifestyle beliefs into our school systems. Children are now taught in our schools that alternative lifestyles are acceptable, and are subtly encouraged to explore sexual activities including homosexuality. God's word teaches any and all sexual activity outside the sanctity of marriage is in direct conflict with the Bible. Contrary to God's divine order, there has been a dangerous increase in homosexual behavior in the past few decades. The Bible condemns this in the Old Testament, Leviticus 18:22, "Thou shalt not lie with mankind, as with womankind: it is abomination." Despite numerous scriptures declaring God's displeasure with homosexual or lesbian activity, countless people indulge in this destructive lifestyle. The unsaved and unrepentant are prone to sin and oppose God. The New Testament confirms God's unchanging stance and condemnation in these practices, in Romans 1:24-28, "Wherefore God also gave them up to uncleanness through the lusts of their own hearts, to dishonor their own bodies between themselves: Who changed the truth of God into a lie, and worshipped and served the creature more than the Creator, who is blessed for ever. Amen. For this cause God gave them up unto vile affections: for even their women did change the natural use into that which is against nature (lesbianism): And likewise also the men, leaving the natural use of the woman, burned in their lust one toward another (homosexuality); men with men working that which is unseemly, and receiving in themselves that recompense of their error which was meet. And even as they did not like to retain God in their knowledge, God gave them over to a reprobate mind, to do those things which are not convenient." Neither man's will, nor the false doctrines of any church, can or will change God's immutable truths.

Redemption must be followed by sanctification. God did not save us to remain the same sin-laden people. There must be change. Satan has used the doctrine of "once-saved always-saved," to propagate the weak, sin-laden church of Laodicea. This is the Church of the end-time (Revelation 3:14-22): lukewarm and weakened by compromise with the world. America has become sin-laden and a thoroughly corrupt society, as people cultivate this untruth.

"Once-saved, always-saved," was first preached by John Calvin in the 1500s. He erroneously taught absolute predestination of souls by the election of God. Calvin believed that God had foreordained some people for salvation and some for eternal damnation. Careful study of scripture explains there is an ecclesia, this means "the called out ones." The ecclesia is the Church. This call is to everyone, and excludes no one. The call of repentance and salvation through Jesus Christ is to whosoever will-let him come! This call is to all, both Jew and Gentile. In the following scripture, we see God does have an election. He has predestined or foreordained some. However, this election only pertains to the Jews and is yet future. Revelation 7:4, "And I heard the number of them which were sealed (yet future during the seven-year tribulation time period appointed by God for the salvation of the Jews): and there were sealed an hundred and forty and four thousand of all the tribes of the children of Israel." The scriptures continue to explain that there will be 12,000 out of each of the 12 tribes of Israel. These are Jews who God predestined to preach the Gospel of Jesus Christ to their countrymen (the Jews) during the great tribulation period. These are the 144,000 Jews whom God has predestined. This prophecy is, as yet, unfulfilled. God has elected and predestined these elect to carry the salvation message during the great seven-year tribulation period. This prophecy will come to fruition after the rapture of the Church. At this time, the Holy Spirit will be taken back up into heaven closing the dispensation of Grace.

Calvin taught, to the detriment of souls that "saved ones" could not, in finality, fall from grace. Sad to say, this dogma, which misconstrues vital scriptures, is a stronghold of deception, flourishing in our world today. I strongly agree that if one is truly saved that one cannot lose their eternal salvation. If a person professes salvation yet is comfortable in sin I urge that one, with all sincerity to search their heart and determine whether that one is truly saved or merely "confessing salvation" rather than the obligation of "confessing sin." The key to maintaining a right-relationship with God is-OBEDIENCE! If we do sin, we do have an advocate with the Father who is Jesus Christ.

There are many who have turned the grace of God into an excuse to commit blatant sin. We still have these sinners in the midst of our churches today. Man can fall from grace, but not through any fault of God. In an effort to ease the guilt of their own sins, they proclaim "all men sin daily." These same ones even falsely indict the Apostle Paul as one who continued in sin. Now, man is not perfect and will not be perfected until we get to heaven. But those who remain in sin, exalting their own will over God's commandments, need to do some serious soul-searching. When one professes salvation, there must be a change in that one. If there is no evidence of change in one's behavior, habits, and friends, perhaps there has not been a heart change. We must develop a Godly, holy hatred of sin and all sinful activities.

1 Timothy 1:13, "Who (Paul) was before a blasphemer, and a persecutor, and injurious: but I obtained mercy, because I did it ignorantly in unbelief." It is evident by this, and many scriptures, Paul did not continue to "sin daily" as the sin-laden Church of Laodicea (our present-day Church) preaches. Paul clearly states "before" his conversion he was a sinner, but he obtained mercy because he did commit these sinful deeds in ignorance. Not one of us is yet perfected but everyone of us must be striving for perfection. 2 Corinthians 7:1, "Having therefore these promises, clearly beloved, let us cleanse ourselves from all filthiness of the flesh (not a physical bathing of the flesh but yield your body to a spiritual cleansing) and spirit, perfecting holiness in the fear of God." Those who practice or condone continued willful sin will be weighed in the balance and found sorely lacking

before the judgment seat of the righteous and Holy God. 1 Corinthians 9:27, "But I (Paul) keep under my body, and bring it into subjection: lest that by any means, when I have preached to others, I myself should be a castaway." Clearly, Paul lived an exemplary life before God and man. We must, as Paul, bring our bodies into subjection to line up with God's divine plan for mankind. There is a universal need for salvation of souls and every believer has direct access to God through Jesus Christ. Man is utterly incapable of saving or redeeming one's self. One's salvation cannot be earned, for it is a free gift. Once, having obtained salvation that one cannot carelessly continue in sin lest they also become a castaway. Man must recognize the Bible, as the inspired word of God, the only infallible authority of God's ways and God's will for mankind. If a person professes salvation, yet is comfortable in sin, that one should sincerely seek God's Truths and make sure they are, in fact, saved. If one does sin, Jesus forgives and blots out the transgression. We do always have with us a fallen sin nature, so we must guard against the temptations and war daily against our old sin nature. Our mantra should be, "The old man is dead; long-live the new creature." Once born again, we have become a new creature in Christ Jesus!

There are many religions abounding today but be warned for there is only one way that leads to everlasting life and that is through The Lord Jesus who is The Christ. John 14:6, "Jesus saith, unto him, 'I am (Jesus is the Great I AM) the way, the truth, and the life: no man cometh unto the Father, but by me."

Man must commit to an earnest self-examination. The Apostle Paul stated in 2 Corinthians 13:5 "Examine yourselves, whether ye be in the faith; prove your own selves. Know ye not your own selves, how that Jesus Christ is in you, except ye be reprobates?" Jesus Christ's love for you and for me is so great that He died for us while we were yet sinners. Justifiably, He will not allow us to "remain in sin." We cannot do anything of ourselves, but when we invite Jesus into our hearts, and become yielded to the Holy Spirit, we become endued with overcoming power. Through the baptism and indwelling of the Holy Ghost, we are afforded victory over the world, sin, and Satan. We, as Christians, must walk in love and the simplicity of holiness; yet remain strong, unmovable and unshakeable in our Christian stance. God's uncompromising Word is hammered on the anvil of TRUTH!

Chapter Seven

A New Name for an Old Game

"And when they shall say unto you, Seek unto them that have familiar spirits, and unto wizards that peep, and that mutter: should not a people seek unto their God? for the living to the dead?"

(Isaiah 8:19)

Film star, Shirley MacLaine has been instrumental in furthering a soul-searing and deadly cult. It propels one deeper and deeper into the occult. If Satan can control the mind, he can then control the soul, and one's eternal destiny. The New Age Movement is satanically energized and has lethal consequences. It takes one's mind and soul from reality, and openly exposes one to the dark side that is the realm of Satan. New Age leaders conjure up "entities" for communication purposes. It is a known fact that if one asks of the wrong source, that one would receive the wrong answer. All demons and demonic activity result in grim reaping. To enquire of a wizard, witch, or solitary spirit, is to invite misinformation and is a guarantee of an unfortunate ending, if that one has not repented.

All sorts of divining are condemned. Divining is infringing upon the rights belonging to God alone. "Spirit guides" are just one of the many forms of divining. Deuteronomy 18:10-12, "There shall not be found among you any one that maketh his son or his daughter to pass through the fire, or that useth divination, or an observer of times (astrology, horoscopes, and time periods of the Zodiac), or an enchanter, or a witch. Or a charmer, or a consulter with familiar spirits, or a wizard, or a necromancer (one who seeks to interrogate the dead for purposes of magically revealing the future or influencing the course of events). For all that do these things are an abomination unto the LORD: and because of these abominations the

LORD thy God doth drive them out from before thee." The very foundation of the New Age Movement is the use of "spirit guides." These spirit guides are merely lying demons, speaking forth from the person who is "channeling." As I was praying for greater insight into the tenets of the New Age Cult, God graciously gave me a word of knowledge by dropping into my mind the phrase, "A new name for an old game." God revealed that "New Age" is just that: "an old game."

This channeling is not new; it is in fact an ancient evil. Confirming this: Ecclesiastes 1:9-10, "The thing that hath been, it is that which shall be; and that which is done is that which shall be done: and there is no new thing under the sun. Is there any thing whereof it may be said, See, this is new? it hath been already of old time, which was before us." Therefore, the so-called "New Age" is an ancient evil of long ago. It was revived from Satan's cellar and claims a new name for a spiritually wicked old game. The Old Testament Prophet, Isaiah warns in 8:19-22, "And when they shall say unto you, Seek unto them that have familiar spirits, and unto wizards that peep, and that mutter: should not a people seek unto their God? for the living to the dead? To the law and to the testimony: if they speak not according to this word, it is because there is no light in them (here we see spiritual darkness devoid of truth and goodness). And they shall pass through it, hardly bestead and hungry (Spiritually lacking): and it shall come to pass, that when they shall be hungry, they shall fret themselves, and curse their king (leader) and their God, and look upward. And they shall look unto the earth; and behold trouble and darkness, dimness of anguish; and they shall be driven to darkness." This scripture clearly explains their fate. If one desires to know anything, seek humbly and sincerely of our holy God, in prayer. We must have a God-centered religion, anything less is to be self-centered, desiring one's own will and ways of the world instead of God's and His holy commandments. Practicing the occult is spiritual suicide and that one is settling for empty substitutes, which cannot satisfy, resulting in man most wretched!

Music pop star Madonna has taken up the practice of Kabbalah. It is an ancient evil and is a bastard derivative of Judaism. Kabbalah, with its occult practices of mysticism, was an affront to God in ancient times and is still an affront to God today!

Psychic-medium John Edward McGee Jr., from the television show, "Crossing over with John Edward" and "John Edward Cross Country" uses spirits to guide him in communicating with the dead. On his television show he relays messages to his audience with information reportedly obtained through persons who have died. We have just studied the word of God, and know that these practices are an abomination to God.

The Harry Potter book series is an interesting, end-time phenomenon. The series of books are works of fiction and have set records as the fastest selling books in history. The books chronicle the life of Harry Potter, an orphan boy who discovers that he is a wizard. He attends Hogwarts School of Witchcraft and Wizardry, and has flashbacks of the murder of his parents. The world of Harry Potter, with wizards and sorcerers, could be a stepping-stone for young minds to be lured into the dark side. These books have been used to pique children's interest into the occult. The Bible clearly denounces such practices as abominable and only worthy of death. Leviticus 20:27, "A man also or woman that hath a familiar spirit, or that is a wizard, shall surely be put to death: they shall stone them with stones: their blood shall be upon them."

The Bible gives an account of King Saul who enquired of the witch of Endor. Saul sought answers through a spiritualist and his fate was sealed. 1 Samuel 28:7, "Then said Saul unto his servants, Seek me a woman that hath a familiar spirit, that I may go to her, and enquire of her. And his servants said to him, Behold there is a woman that hath a familiar spirit at Endor." King Saul reaped the consequence of his offense against God. 1 Chronicles 10:13-14, "So Saul (first king of Israel) died for his transgression which he committed against the LORD, even against the word of the LORD, which he kept not, and also for asking counsel of one that had a familiar spirit, to enquire of it; And enquired not of the LORD: therefore he slew him, and turned the kingdom unto David the son of Jesse." The woman of whom Saul asked counsel was the witch of Endor and proved to be the wrong source. Consistent with God's word, Saul died for this sin and his sons and his entire family perished with him.

England's Princess Diana was called "The People's Princess." In many ways she was the world's princess. She was young, beautiful, and well-loved throughout the world. She mistakenly had confidence in Astrology and believed that the aligning of the stars held life's answers. She was tragically killed in an auto accident while vacationing in Paris, France. It was reported she would not leave for vacation until she had her Astrological chart done. If the stars held the answers to life that she was so desperately searching for, she would not have gone on the vacation in which she would lose her life.

Many believe Balaam, at one time, had been a mighty prophet of God. As he continually grew proud and covetous (both Satanic traits), God departed from him. As Balaam took up diabolical arts, his separation from God became greater. We have abundant proof Balaam lived and died a wicked man; an enemy of God and God's people. Balaam loved the rewards of divination and the wages of unrighteousness. 2 Peter 2:15, "Which have forsaken the right way, and are gone astray, following the way of Balaam the son of Bosor, who loved the wages of unrighteousness." Concerning the administration of the gospel, self-exaltation, loving the name, the fame, and or the money are characteristics of the wicked! Using God as a means to obtain riches can result in everlasting punishment. Jude 11-13, "Woe unto them! for they have gone in the way of Cain, and ran greedily after the error of Balaam for reward, and perished in the gainsaying of Core. These are spots in your feasts of charity, when they feast with you, feeding themselves without fear: clouds they are without water, carried about of winds; trees whose fruit withereth, without fruit, twice dead (they shall suffer the second death, hell), plucked up by the roots; Raging waves of the sea, foaming out their own shame; wandering stars, to whom is reserved the blackness of darkness forever."

When one thinks of witchcraft or a sorcerer, one may picture a witch stirring with a stick while brewing a potion in a black caldron. Illegal drug use is prevalent in our society today. America declared a war on drugs many years ago. It appears to be a losing battle, as more and more people become addicted to these illegal potions, purposed to alter minds, moods, and emotions. Those dealing street drugs are called pushers, because they thrust drugs into society often on the young and vulnerable school-age children. Those trafficking drugs are often called "drug lords." This is not a title to be sought after. Satan himself is referred to as "lord of the flies" in the Bible. The illegal uses of street drugs kill countless people every day. These pathetic users will often commit any crime to obtain the sought-after, expensive fix. Our prisons are overcrowded because of the makers, suppliers, and the recipients of these illegal substances. Tragically, drug use has destroyed people, families, homes, and neighborhoods. It has had a devastating effect on our society as a whole. It is not surprising that "street drugs" is also a new name for an old game.

The Bible teaches against the sin of witchcraft. The New Testament Book of Galatians chapter five lists sins of witchcraft, drunkenness, murders, and revellings and states those who commit these sins shall not inherit the kingdom of God. The word witchcraft in the Greek text is: *Pharmakeia*, medication by magic, literally or figuratively: sorcery or witchcraft. A variation of the word is pharmakeus from the root word, pharmakon, meaning a drug, i.e. spell giving potion, a magician-sorcerer. *Pharmakos* is the same as sorcerer. This drug-ravished society has fallen prey to one of Satan's oldest games - Potions that Destroy! Satan is the destroyer of lives, bodies, minds, and the souls of men. How sad that so many in our nation have followed the pied piper of doom! Jesus is the only answer to those who have fallen prey to addiction of alcohol, prescription drugs, or street drugs.

There is an account of a sorcerer named Simon in the New Testament. Acts 8:5-8, "Then Philip (one of Jesus' apostles) went down to the city of Samaria, and preached Christ unto them. And the people with one accord gave heed unto those things which Philip spake, hearing and seeing the miracles which he did (in Jesus' name). For unclean spirits, crying with loud voice, came out of many that were possessed with them: and many taken with palsies, and that were lame were healed. And there was great joy in that city." Miracles that are performed in the name of Jesus, authenticates the witness of God's messenger and God's message. These scriptures are given as an example of warning against the error of Simon the Sorcerer and all sorcery. Continuing in Acts 8:9-24, "But there was a certain man, called Simon, which beforetime in the same city used sorcery, and bewitched the people of Samaria, giving out that himself was some great one: To whom they all gave heed, from the least to the greatest, saying, This man is the great power of God. And to him they had regard, because that of long time he had bewitched them with sorceries. But when they believed Phillip preaching the things concerning the kingdom of God, and the name of Jesus Christ, they were baptized, both men and women. Then Simon himself believed also: and when he was baptized, he continued with Phillip, and wondered, beholding the miracles and signs which were done.

Now when the apostles which were at Jerusalem heard that Samaria had received the word of God, they sent unto them Peter and John: Who, when they were come down, prayed for them, that they might receive the Holy Ghost: (For as yet he--The Holy Ghost--was fallen upon none of them: only they were baptized in the name of the Lord Jesus.) Then laid they their hands on them, and they received the Holy Ghost. And when Simon saw that through laying on of the apostles' hands the Holy Ghost was given, he offered them money, Saying, Give me also this power, that on whomsoever I lay hands, he may receive the Holy Ghost. But Peter said unto him, Thy money perish with thee, because thou hast thought that the gift of God may be purchased with money. Thou hast neither part nor lot in this matter: for thy heart is not right in the sight of God. Repent therefore of this thy wickedness, and pray God, if perhaps the thought of thine heart may be forgiven thee. For I perceive that thou art in the gall of bitterness, and in the bond of iniquity. Then answered Simon (the sorcerer), and said, Pray ye to the Lord for me, that none of these things which ye have spoken come upon me." One must repent of sins upon realization of God's divinity and anyone or any action that has been in contraposition against God. Sin is destructive and must be remitted to the blood of Jesus. Commit to water baptism and pray for the baptism and power of the indwelling Holy Ghost and that one will be set free and delivered from destruction.

As a strong spiritual life is built on "line upon line, precept upon precept" of righteousness, so it is also with a declining spiritual state. Ever yielding one's self to sin results in spiritual ruin and is detrimental to one's soul by the reverse process. This process includes such seemingly mundane things as books on the occult, horoscopes, tarot cards, and Ouija boards, which "seem" an innocent game, but will lead deeper into a more soul-ravaging, sinful state. All these dark-side instruments are abominations in God's sight and must be destroyed. Acts 19:18-19, "And many that believed (after hearing of Jesus) came, and confessed, and shewed their deeds. Many of them also which used (before salvation) curious arts brought their books together, and burned them before all men: and counted the price of them, and found it fifty thousand pieces of silver."

Both white magic and black magic are evil and destructive forces. There are those who misguidedly differentiate between a "good" or "white witch" as opposed to a "bad" or "black witch." In truth, all witches belong to the realm of Satan. Wiccans incorporate witchcraft into their belief system and followers worship the horned god. Wicca includes forms of goddess-oriented neo-paganism, and is a nature-based cult.

Newly forming vampire cults across the nation show a frightening interest in blood and blood practices. This is not just a harmless trend, but is a doctrine of devils and demons with an iniquitous interest in blood. These cults are comprised mainly of young people. How sad that they have lost their way and will reap woeful consequences if they do not repent and turn to God. There is only one Supreme Blood Sacrifice, and that is The Blood Covenant of Jesus Christ. God's own Son, Jesus, shed His innocent atoning blood, once for all, while hanging on a cross at Calvary. It is the only remedy for sin.

God's majestic and unrivaled power cannot be reduced to mere magic, or trickery through deception! Potions, spells, incantations, witch doctors, voodoo, are all snares and were spawned by Satan.

Forty years ago people wouldn't even acknowledge that Satan existed. Now, many are following and worshiping him. Regretfully, many young people, for reasons of curiosity or a quest for power, have tragically followed the wicked one. Satan has no loyalties or lasting allegiances. After securing a soul he will then turn the flesh over for destruction. Satan has come to steal, kill, and destroy. The literal meaning of the name "Satan" is "destroyer."

Satanism is the ultimate force of destructive worship. If his followers continue on the path with Satan in their futile crusade for fame or power, their fate will be the same as his-doomed! If they serve him and do not repent of their evil deeds that are comprised of blood sacrifices, demonic rituals, and trinkets of the black arts, they will burn with him. Hell was created for Satan and his angels; however, all who follow him are condemned to eternal hell-fire. Matthew 13:41-43, "The Son of man (Jesus) shall send forth his angels, and they shall gather out of his kingdom all things that offend, and them which do iniquity; And shall cast them into a furnace of fire: there shall be wailing and gnashing of teeth (in torment). Then shall the righteous (ones obedient to God's word) shine forth as the sun in the kingdom of their Father (Jehovah-God). Who hath ears to hear, let him hear." Again, we have a warning, and a call to repentance from sin and sinful practices that offend a holy and righteous God. Our merciful Jesus extends his nail-scarred hands and reaches down to deliver all those who sincerely cry out for mercy and forgiveness.

John 10:10, "The thief (Satan) cometh not, but for to steal, and to kill, and to destroy: I (Jesus) am come that they might have life, and that they might have it more abundantly." Analysis of this scripture makes it is easy to understand why the name of "Jesus" is unmentionable in satanic worship. There is unparalleled power in the name of Jesus, for He alone has come to save and deliver, and in so doing, He triumphed over Satan.

Romans 16:20, "And the God of peace shall bruise Satan under your feet shortly. The grace of our Lord Jesus Christ be with you, Amen."

Chapter Eight

The Enemy Within

"There is a generation that are pure in their own eyes, and yet is not washed from their filthiness."

(Proverbs 30:12)

Understanding the deceit and treachery of false doctrines and false teachers we must now search our hearts to see if we are self-deceived.

The enemy within is self-deception! 2 Timothy 2:19-26, "Nevertheless the foundation of God standeth sure, having this seal, The Lord knoweth them that are his. And, let every one that nameth the name of Christ depart from iniquity. But in a great house there are not only vessels of gold and of silver, but also of wood and of earth; and some to honour and some to dishonour. If a man therefore purge himself from these, he shall be a vessel unto honour, sanctified, and meet (or fit) for the master's use, and prepared unto every good work. Flee also youthful lusts: but follow righteousness, faith, charity (love), peace, with them that call on the Lord out of a pure heart. but foolish and unlearned questions avoid, knowing that they do gender strifes. And the servant of the Lord must not strive; but be gentle unto all men, apt to teach, patient, In meekness instructing those that oppose themselves; if God peradventure (perhaps) will give them repentance to the acknowledging of the truth; And that they may recover themselves out of the snare of the devil, who are taken captive by him at his will." God is merciful, but warns us in the last days that apostasy would abound. If a professing Christian deliberately rejects, or falls away from, the truth, that one becomes apostate. We must guard our faith and always retain the knowledge that God has a standard of obedience. He expects us to obey!

Many people today have become so complacent in sin that they have become apostate. Satan has lulled Christian believers into a false sense of security while being mired down in sin. He deceived Eve and he will deceive us also, if he can. Deliberate sin is Satanic and must be recognized as such.

It is the deceitfulness of our own willful lusts and desires that war daily against our souls - flesh against Spirit. Galatians 5:16-17, "This I say then, Walk in the Spirit, and ye shall not fulfil the lust of the flesh. For the flesh lusteth against the Spirit, and the Spirit against the flesh: and these are contrary the one to the other: so that ye cannot do the things that ye would (desire to do)."

Sin manifests itself in two ways. First, it appears to be insignificant and harmless. Second, it becomes intoxicating, pleasurable, and desirable. Continued sin sears the conscience and brings forth destruction. Self-justification and excuse-making are characteristics of the wicked!

The weed of sin reaps woeful rewards. Galatians 6:7-8, "Be not deceived; God is not mocked: for whatsoever a man soweth, that shall he also reap. For he that soweth to his flesh shall of the flesh reap corruption; but he that soweth to the Spirit shall of the Spirit reap life everlasting." If a man plants a garden of corn he will harvest corn. Plant corn, one will reap corn. If one commits sin, that one will reap punishment. One cannot sow the bad seed of disobedience to God's word and expect to reap blessings and approval of God. 1 Corinthians 15:34, "Awake to righteousness, and sin not; for some have not the knowledge of God: I speak this to your shame." There are fatal consequences to sin. Proverbs 14:12, "There is a way which seemeth right unto a man, but the end thereof are the ways of death." If a man sows sin and corruption, he will reap death and hell. We must war against that old enemy within, self-delusion.

God has given fixed laws of blessing or cursing. You and I are not exceptions. We are free moral agents, knowing the difference between good and evil. Remember, Eve and her husband Adam both disobeyed God and ate of the forbidden tree of knowledge, consequently knowing good and evil. We, and we alone, are responsible for our conduct! We alone will stand before God and give an account of our deeds, not excuses.

The Bible is explicit in its description of sin. Galatians 5:19-21, "Now the works of the flesh are manifest, which are these; Adultery, fornication (unlawful lusts, harlotry, incest, etc...), uncleanness, lasciviousness (filthy wantonness), Idolatry, witchcraft (divination or rewards of divination, sorcery, magic, medications, potions), hatred, variance (quarreling, contention or strife), emulations (malice, envy, unfavorable jealousy), wrath, strife, seditions (rage), heresies (perverting the true meaning of God's word), Envyings, murders, drunkenness, revellings (partying), and such like: of the which I tell you before, as I have in time past, that they which do such things shall not inherit the kingdom of God."

Years ago, while in intercessory prayer, God spoke to me and told me, "His Jewish people missed the mark by their arrogant, stiff-necked ways." While I was thinking on this, He continued, "The failures of the Gentile people have exceeded the failures of the Jews." Gentiles have missed the mark by lackadaisical self-indulgence and self-justification, thus becoming an insipid, self-satisfied, foolish people.

Proverbs 30:12, "There is a generation that are pure in their own eyes, and yet is not washed from their filthiness." Woe to the Gentiles who accepted the crucifixion of Jesus Christ, yet are still spiritually filthy.

Galatians 3:1, "O foolish Galatians, who hath bewitched you, that ye should not obey the truth, before whose eyes Jesus Christ hath been evidently set forth, crucified among you?" Woe to the Jews who did not accept Jesus Christ because of the hardness of their hearts. Woe to the Gentile Nations, who believe that by casually accepting Jesus, they become holy and acceptable unto God. Wrong! Satan has been effective in his campaign to generate this malignant lie. The result is that weak, self-proclaimed Christians believe even though they are in this compromised sinful state, they are still saved and going to heaven. Wrong again!

We see the final state of compromising God's righteous laws in Revelation 3:16, "So then because thou art lukewarm, and neither cold nor hot, I will spue thee out of my mouth." There is no distinction between big sin and little sin. Sin is Sin. As stated in Revelation 21:8, "... all liars, shall have their part in the lake which burneth with fire and brimstone: which is the second death." Social liars, or those who tell white lies, are going to hell just as are habitual liars. All unrepented sin results in death and hell.

1 Corinthians 5:6-7, "... Know ye not that a little leaven (as yeast in bread) leaventh the whole lump? Purge out therefore the old leaven (sin), that ye may be a new lump (born again, not yielded to

sin), as ye are unleavened. For even Christ our passover (Lamb) is sacrificed for us." America needs revival. A great and mighty revival would come to America if her people would call out to God and repent. True repentance is to have a God-like, holy hatred for sin (Godly Sorrow). 2 Corinthians 7:10, "For godly sorrow worketh repentance to salvation not to be repented of: but the sorrow of the world worketh death." We must strive to be God-pleasers. God is not going to pour out His Holy Spirit upon a complacent, sin-sick society, who is content to remain deceived by the enemy within - SELF.

Man holds within his grasp the ability to choose his own destiny: heaven or hell! Remember, the soul is the part of man that never dies. Our birth makes us mortal, but our death makes us immortal. Sow a thought, reap an action; sow a habit, reap your destiny.

Chapter Nine

Sound the Alarm

"Blow the trumpet in Zion, sanctify a fast, call a solemn assembly: Gather the people, sanctify the congregation, assemble the elders, gather the children, and those that suck the breasts: let the bridegroom go forth of his chamber, and the bride out of her closet."

(Joel 2:15-16)

God has always forewarned His people through prophecy. Prophecy is threefold: being past, present, and future. Prophecy is history prewritten, foretelling something before it happens. This is the distinctive difference of our God-inspired Bible as opposed to the Qur'an or the Book of Mormon. God causes His word to be fulfilled and has kept the Holy Scriptures down through, literally, thousands of years and causes them to be fulfilled.

In 1947, the first group of the Dead Sea Scrolls was found in a Qumran Cave in Israel. The entire Old Testament, with the exception of the Book of Esther, was found in manuscripts of papyrus and leather. The Book of Isaiah, for example, was found word for word - perfect as it is still found today in the Bible. Our God is unchanging. We serve a God from whom we know what to expect, and likewise what He expects from us. He has proved himself trustworthy. His word is unalterable and sure. Isaiah 28:10, "For precept must be upon precept, precept upon precept; line upon line, line upon line; here a little, and there a little."

God is unchanging, steadfast, and totally predictable. God does not spring any surprises or traps on his own believers. He always warns and prepares, and actually goes before his children. Jeremiah 6:10, "To whom shall I speak, and give warning, that they may hear? ..." God's warnings are multiple. Joel 3:9, "Proclaim ye this among the Gentiles; Prepare war, wake up the mighty men, let all the men of war draw near; let them come up."

We see continuity in many warnings. Matthew 23:37, "O Jerusalem, Jerusalem, thou that killest the prophets, and stonest them which are sent unto thee, how often would I have gathered thy children together, even as a hen gathereth her chickens under her wings, and ye would not!" Scripture reveals a loving, protective, and caring Father. He warns of wars and dangers, while providing the protection from any adverse circumstance or evil.

By a study of the Scriptures we can know what is shortly to come. Joel 2:1-5, "Blow ye the trumpet of Zion, and sound an alarm in my holy mountain: let all the inhabitants of the land tremble: for the day of the LORD cometh, for it is nigh (close) at hand; A day of darkness and of gloominess, a day of clouds and of thick darkness, as the morning spread upon the mountains: a great people and a strong; there hath not been ever the like, neither shall be any more after it, even to the years of many generations. A fire devoureth before them; and behind them a flame burneth: the land is as the garden of Eden before them, and behind them a desolate wilderness (a result of their destructive force); yea, and nothing shall escape them. The appearance of them is as the appearance of horses; and as horsemen, so shall they run. Like the noise of chariots on the tops of mountains shall they leap, like the noise of a flame of fire that devoureth the stubble, as a strong people set in battle array."

The Book of Joel was written approximately three thousand years ago. He was trying to give explanation of nuclear war and weapons, in an ancient language. His message is truly a message of warning. He was a full-view prophet for that time and for today. Joel 2:5, "... on the tops of mountains shall they leap ..." At present, huge banks of missiles have been procured, poised and positioned against Israel. Iran (Ancient Persia), and other Arab Nations, in league with Russia, are seemingly gathering together against Israel. This recent alliance between Russia, Turkey, and Iran indicate with great portent, an ominous threat to Israel. North Korea and China are also hostile and the Bible describes the Kings of the East and their million-man army will march against Israel. Countries regarding prophet Ezekiel's warnings to Israel are Germany, Persia (Ancient Iran), Ethiopia, and Libya. Ezekiel conveys these countries will come as a storm. Joel 2:6-7, "Before their face the people shall be much pained: all faces shall gather blackness. They shall run like mighty men; they shall climb the wall like men of war; and they shall march everyone on his ways, and they shall not break their ranks."

The "they" in verse 7 above, are "missiles" programmed to specific targets, an ominous, end-time army of munitions. Joel 2:8-9, "Neither shall one thrust another; they shall walk everyone in his path (bulls-eye war with missiles keyed to their target): and when they fall upon the sword, they shall not be wounded (if a sword falls upon a sword or a missile upon another missile, it will not be harmed, but successful, in its destruction). They shall run to and fro in the city; they shall run upon the wall, they shall climb up upon the houses; they shall enter in at the windows like a thief." Could this be a nuclear flash? Could this possibly be nuclear fallout, or chemical and biological warfare? Continuing in Joel 2:10, "The earth shall quake before them; the heavens shall tremble: the sun and the moon shall be dark, and the stars shall withdraw their shining." Nuclear fallout causes a thick haze as tangible as a mighty machine grinding out death. Joel 2:11, "And the LORD shall utter his voice before his army: for his camp is very great: for he is strong that executeth his word: for the day of the LORD is great and very terrible; and who can abide it?" The phrase "day of the Lord" means "the day of God's wrath." This "day" is not just a "solar day" of twenty-four hours, but rather is a "period of time" in which the Lord's wrath will be poured out upon the earth and its inhabitants. These scriptures were not meant to scare us, but prepare us for what is soon to come. Joel 2:12-13, "Therefore also now, saith the LORD, Turn ye even to me with all your heart, and with fasting, and with weeping, and with mourning: And rend (rip or tear) your heart, and not your garments, and turn unto the LORD your God: for he is gracious and merciful, slow to anger, and of great kindness, and repenteth him of the evil."

We, living in the last days of this age, recognize all the mighty and sure signs surrounding us that these prophecies are for our near future! God is going to allow man to do his worst to man, then Jesus will end the battle of Armageddon at His second coming. God will no longer withhold His anger from a wicked and adulterous people who love their unrighteous deeds. Jeremiah 6:15, "Were they ashamed when they had committed abomination? nay, they were not at all ashamed, neither could they blush: therefore they shall fall among them that fall: at the time that I visit them they shall be cast down, sayeth the LORD."

Alas, the Creator of Heaven and Earth and all living, will surely weigh this generation in the balances of justice and righteousness and find it wanting - sorely lacking! Mark 13:7-8, "And when ye shall hear of wars and rumours of wars, be ye not troubled: for such things must needs be; but the end shall not be yet. For nation shall rise against nation, and kingdom against kingdom: and there shall be earthquakes in divers (widespread) places, and there shall be famines and troubles: these are the beginnings of sorrows."

No other time in all history of the earth has men seen the hand of an angry God moving in signs to warn men by elements. We are faced with the possibility of sudden destruction by earthquakes, volcanoes, fires, floods, tornados, hurricanes, or a tsunami. Man is vulnerable to catastrophic upheavals of nature. Mere mortals cannot devise safeguards from these disasters.

Man is mighty like a rose. Job 14:1-2, "Man that is born of a woman is of few days and full of trouble. He cometh forth like a flower, and is cut down: he fleeth also as a shadow, and continueth not." Who are we to think we can war against the Mighty God? How long does man think that God will allow sin to reign in the mortal bodies he created for his pleasure? God warned that His Spirit shall not always strive with man.

God compares these current days with the days of Noah. Matthew 24:37-39, "But as the days of Noe (same Noah, different spelling) were, so shall also the coming of the Son of man (Jesus) be. For as in the days that were before the flood they were eating and drinking, marrying and giving in marriage, until the day that Noe entered into the ark, And knew not until the flood came, and took them all away; so shall also the coming of the Son of man be."

Jesus is coming soon to rapture those who are readied and waiting. We must be prayed up, watching, and waiting for His imminent appearance. Matthew 24:40-42, "Then shall two be in the field; the one shall be taken, and the other left. Two women shall be grinding at the mill; the one shall be taken, and the other left. Watch therefore: for ye know not what hour your Lord doth come."

In light of these scriptures it is evident not everyone is going to be taken in the rapture with Jesus. Luke 21:34-36, "And take heed to yourselves, lest at any time your hearts be overcharged with surfeiting (indulging fleshly appetites), and drunkenness, and cares of this life, and so that day come upon you unawares. For as a snare shall it come on all them that dwell on the face of the whole earth.

Watch ye therefore, and pray always, that ye may be accounted worthy to escape all these things that shall come to pass, and stand before the Son of man."

One need not be afraid, only ready, for it will happen suddenly. Scripture proves scripture. There are two prior examples recorded of a "bodily translation into heaven." These men were Enoch and the prophet Elijah. Genesis 5:24, "And Enoch walked with God: and he was not; for God took him." Enoch's testimony was, "I have pleased the Lord." My heart's desire is to be able to have a testimony such as Enoch! God's ways are consistent, what has been before, will be again. The prophet Elijah was also taken alive into heaven in a whirlwind and a chariot of fire. 2 Kings 2:11, "And it came to pass, as they (Elijah and Elisha) still went on, and talked, that, behold, there appeared a chariot of fire, and horses of fire, and parted them both asunder; and Elijah went up by a whirlwind into heaven." Remember fire denotes God's presence and power! Neither Enoch nor Elijah experienced death. They were both, at separate times in history, supernaturally raptured or translated bodily into heaven by our immutable God.

Matthew chapter 25 explains a parable of ten virgins. "Virgins," in this parable, symbolizes all Christian believers and are representative of Jesus' waiting bride. However, in this account only five are found worthy to go with Christ. Five were wise, but five were foolish. While the bridegroom (Jesus) delayed his coming, the ten virgins slept. At midnight there was a cry made, "Behold the bridegroom cometh." The five foolish virgins had no oil (oil is representative of the Holy Spirit), for their lamps had gone out. These five foolish are an example of apostate Christendom. These will be found unacceptable to the bridegrooms' call. The five wise virgins, having their lamps filled with oil (Holy Spirit) were ready when Jesus came. The prepared bride had donned the wedding garments, representing the righteousness of Jesus through the Holy Spirit, and went to meet the bridegroom, before the door was shut. Reiterating Matthew 25:13, "Watch therefore, for ye know neither the day nor the hour wherein the Son of man cometh."

We must examine ourselves and see if Christ were to come this hour, would we be found worthy to escape the great tribulation period that is going to come upon the whole earth? Tragically, many Christians are not going to make it. Self-justification and excuses for sin are dangerous and deceptive. Our life must line up with the will of God, for He changes not.

2 Peter 2:4-8, "For if God spared not the angels that sinned, but cast them down to hell, and delivered them into chains of darkness, to be reserved unto judgment; And spared not the old world, but saved Noah the eighth person, a preacher of righteousness, bringing in the flood upon the world of the ungodly; And turning the cities of Sodom and Gomorrha into ashes, condemned them with an overthrow, making them an ensample unto those that after should live ungodly; And delivered just Lot, vexed (upset, bothered) with the filthy conversation of the wicked: For that righteous man dwelling among them, in seeing and hearing, vexed his righteous soul from day to day with their unlawful deeds." God punishes the wicked but will deliver the Godly. Continuing in verses 9-10, "The Lord knoweth how to deliver the godly out of temptations, and to reserve the unjust unto the day of judgment to be punished: But chiefly them that walk after the flesh in the lust of uncleanness, and despise government. Presumptuous are they, selfwilled, they are not afraid to speak evil of dignities." There are significant similarities of the lifestyles and ungodly conduct in our present day, and the behavior of those living in the sister cities of Sodom and Gomorrha. Homosexuality was unashamedly practiced there and God overthrew these inhabitants for their blatant, ungodly wicked sins. The United States and England are in direct contraposition to God's word as homosexuality is presented as acceptable and endorsed.

A resounding alarm gives warning through scriptures to the slumbering masses of apostate Christians, and the unbelievers, that the midnight hour is rapidly approaching in which the dispensation of grace will be ended. Giving warning that all must prepare to meet the Lord Jesus Christ. This dispensation of grace is drawing to a rapid close and there will be seven years of Great Tribulation for those who have not accepted Jesus as Messiah. It will be a grievous time of unparalleled suffering.

The Gospel of Christ has been, by many, preached for fame, gain, and self-exaltation. Wars have been fought because of doctrine, vain genealogy, and advantage. Many have misused and trampled underfoot the precious Cleansing Blood of our Lord and Savior. However, there has always been a nucleus of faithful ones who humbly seek the Lord and walk pleasing to Him. We must all aspire to have the testimony of Enoch: "I have pleased the Lord."

Revelation 3:19-22, "As many as I love, I rebuke and chasten: be zealous therefore, and repent. Behold, I stand at the door (door of salvation), and knock: if any man hear my voice (Jesus' voice), and open the door, I will come in to him, and will sup with him, and he with me. To him that overcometh (sin, temptations, and the lure of the world) will I grant to sit with me in my throne, even as I also overcame (the world, Satan, death, the grave, and hell), and am set down with my father in his throne. He that hath an ear, let him hear what the Spirit saith unto the churches." Heaven is a prepared place for a prepared people. In John chapter 14, Jesus said, "I go to prepare a place for you that where I am ye may be also."

I had a dream. In it, I was walking down a pathway in a lovely wooded area; it was night, yet it was not dark because there was a full moon. As I stood gazing at this beautiful harvest moon, suddenly, there appeared pure red blood as if some invisible, inexhaustible source was pouring red blood down over the moon. The pure red blood started flowing slowly down over the top and sides of the moon. Profuse amounts of blood was moving, deliberately, and utterly covering and obscuring with its irrevocable flow, that beautiful moon. When the commission of the blood was complete, and the moon had been turned to blood, it was an awesome sight and its adverse effect was profound. I believe through the dream, God was revealing that the time is close at hand, even at the door. As Noah and his family waited in the ark, God Himself shut the door (Genesis 7:16). God is warning all today, as in the days of Noah, men will be ungodly and when the days of this present Gentile Age is complete, God will shut the door.

Joel 2:27-32, "And ye shall know that I am in the midst of Israel, and that I am the LORD your God, and none else: and my people shall never be ashamed. And it shall come to pass afterward, that I will pour out my spirit upon all flesh; and your sons and your daughters shall prophesy, and your old men shall dream dreams, your young men shall see visions; And also upon the servants (of God) and upon the handmaids in those days will I will pour out my spirit. And I will shew wonders in the heavens and in the earth, blood, and fire, and pillars of smoke. The sun shall be turned into darkness, and the moon into blood, before the great and the terrible day of the LORD come. And it shall come to pass, that whosoever shall call on the name of the LORD shall be delivered: for in Mount Zion and in Jerusalem shall be deliverance, as the LORD hath said, and in the remnant whom the LORD shall call."

Blow the Trumpet in Zion and sound the alarm! God is warning by His word, and through many undeniable signs, that the rapture is imminent - even at the door. The Battle of Armageddon is near, and the day of the Lord is at hand. His impending judgment draws near. The second coming of Jesus Christ will be at the end of the seven-year tribulation period. Christ's kingdom will be set up here on earth for Jesus' Millennial Reign. Webster's Dictionary refers to this time period in this way: "the thousand years mentioned in Revelation 20, during which holiness is to prevail and Christ is to reign on earth." The world is being readied for these happenings. God's Word forges ahead irrefutable, and accomplishes His will by the Holy Spirit!

Chapter Ten

Fishers of Men

"And Jesus said unto them, Come ye after me, and I will make you to become fishers of men."

(Mark 1:17)

Many years ago, in the mid-seventies, I was given a night vision from God. In the vision I was standing on the seashore. In the water were approximately twelve to fifteen men forming a circle, and they were standing in just above waist deep water. They bent slightly; their hands and arms went down into the water, and as they lifted up their arms high above their heads, they held a fisher's net. The fishing net was laden with fish. It was a supernatural catch. The amount of fish was innumerable, and the size of these innumerable fish varied. Some were so large that, in the natural, just one fish would have been impossible for these men to lift. Everything concerning the catch was extraordinary. In the natural realm, men would have been physically incapable of lifting that many fish. The fish themselves would not have been able to be heaped that high without sliding off, down over the sides of the net. Even in the oceans' deep that amount of fish would be an impossible catch; moreover, the fishermen were few in number, and standing in relatively shallow water. The net itself would have broken under all the weight. The vision was not of our natural earthly realm, for all the laws of physics went unheeded, but was being viewed in the supernatural realm of God. The vision continued, and I was then standing a little further back from the sea, on the sand. There appeared in the sand an opening and the sand rapidly started funneling down through this opening. It was as if the sand was disappearing down into a vast hourglass. Next, and very suddenly, the earth started to shake with incredible violence. It shook with such intensity and force; I was amazed when the shaking subsided that I was still standing on my feet! I then looked down at the sand on which I was standing, and I saw a coin lying on the sand. As I stooped to pick it up, I realized I had never seen a coin like this before. As I was turning it over, to examine the coin, my attention was drawn back to the seashore. The night vision continued and I saw standing on the seashore, the Ancient of Days (Biblical name for Jesus). He stood magnificent, looking out over, as if calmly, surveying the sea. His back was to me and His hair was white in color and to His shoulders in length and He was wearing robes light in color, perhaps white. He had the appearance of strength, and I understood in this night vision, the Ancient of Days owns the eminence of serenity.

I believe the supernatural catch of fish is symbolic of a supernatural end-time harvest of souls. America is in great need of Spiritual revival. The demonstration of sin in America has become epidemic. In an attempt to exalt the lower, base nature of mankind over God's standards of righteousness, man has become combative against anyone who adheres to Biblical standards. Man has deemed grotesque sins of sexual immorality as acceptable to society and therefore whoever opposes these perversions, is portrayed as hostile and is ridiculed. Sin abounds. Not just sins of a sexual nature, but all types of sins are being manifested. Multitudes of crimes and cruelties are being unleashed into society. The need for repentance is evident. Personal guilt and confession that, sin is sin, and all sin is unacceptable to God is the foundation of salvation. God's holy hatred of sin, and His love for mankind, was proven at Calvary. God's love is so great that it took Him to the cross. He loved us while we were yet sinners and took the guilt, shame, and penalty of our sins onto himself.

Jesus is calling all to come to Him, just the way you are. It is impossible for man to change without Jesus. Man cannot wait until he is good enough or worthy enough to come to Jesus. The call is to all to come now, just as you are. Jesus' precious blood will cleanse you and then, and only then, will the necessary changes start to take place. The old sin-nature will be purged and then that one will be able to put off the old man, or sin nature, and put on the new creation in Christ Jesus! Romans 5:20-21, "... But where sin abounded, grace did much more abound: That as sin hath reigned unto death, even so might grace reign through righteousness unto eternal life by Jesus

Christ our Lord." Jesus has come to save even the worst of sinners among us and He is married to the backslider.

After salvation everyone is called to the ministry of furthering the salvation message of Jesus. Mark 1:15-17, "And (Jesus) saying, The time is fulfilled, and the kingdom of God is at hand: repent ye, and believe the gospel. Now as he (Jesus) walked by the sea of Galilee, he saw Simon and Andrew his brother casting a net into the sea: for they were fishers. And Jesus said unto them, Come ye after me, and I will make you to become fishers of men. And straightway (immediately) they forsook their nets, and followed him." There are multitudes in need of salvation, but too few are sharing the good news that Jesus has come to seek and save the lost. Matthew 9:35-38, "And Jesus went about all the cities and villages, teaching in their synagogues, and preaching the gospel of the kingdom, and healing every sickness and every disease among the people. But when he saw the multitudes, he was moved with compassion on them, because they fainted, and were scattered abroad, as sheep having no shepherd. Then saith he unto his disciples, The harvest truly is plenteous, but the laborers are few; Pray ye therefore the Lord of the harvest, that he will send forth laborers into his harvest." God is calling laborers, and the clarion call is to all.

1 Corinthians 12:4-11, "Now there are diversities of gifts, but the same Spirit. And there are differences of administrations, but the same Lord. And there are diversities of operations, but it is the same God which worketh all in all. But the manifestation of the Spirit is given to every man to profit withal. For to one is given by the Spirit the word of wisdom; to another the word of knowledge by the same Spirit; To another faith by the same Spirit; to another the gifts of healing by the same Spirit; To another the working of miracles; to another prophecy; to another discerning of spirits; to another divers kinds of tongues; to another the interpretation of tongues: But all these worketh that one and the selfsame Spirit, dividing to every man severally as he will." Jesus has called all and, through the Holy Spirit, gives to everyone who follows Him ability and power to be useful and valuable in the ministry. It is not one's ability, but one's availability. Ephesians 4:11-13, "And he (the Holy Spirit) gave some, apostles; and some prophets; and some, evangelists; and some pastors and teachers; For the perfecting of the saints, for the work of the ministry, for the edifying of the body of Christ: Till we all come in the unity (remembering we all are of the same Spirit and same

body) of the faith, and of the knowledge of the Son of God, unto a perfect man, unto the measure of the stature (importance) of the fullness of Christ." The time is short, and the laborers are few. John 4:35-36, "Say not ye, There are yet four months, and then cometh harvest? behold, I (Jesus) say unto you, Lift up your eyes, and look on the fields; for they are white already to harvest. And he that reapeth receiveth wages, and gathereth fruit unto life eternal: that both he that soweth and he that reapeth may rejoice together." With Jesus it is a win-win situation! There are no losers; both the presenters and recipients of God's salvation plan are rewarded with eternal life. What a deal!

Everyone must repent of their sins and be washed in the blood of the Lamb, and inherit the free gift of eternal life. Jesus' nail-scarred hand is reaching down, and His arms are open wide to receive all who will hear and obey. Luke 5:4-11, "Now when he had left speaking, he said unto Simon, Launch out into the deep, and let down your nets for a draught (draw). And Simon answering said unto him, Master (Lord Jesus), we have toiled all night, and have taken nothing: nevertheless at thy word I will let down the net. And when they had this done, they inclosed a great multitude of fishes: and their net brake. And they beckoned unto their partners, which were in the other ship, that they should come and help them. And they came, and filled both the ships, so that they began to sink. When Simon Peter saw it, he fell down at Jesus' knees, saying, Depart from me; for I am a sinful man, O Lord. For he was astonished, and all that were with him, at the draught of the fishes which they had taken: And so was also James, and John, the sons of Zebedee, which were partners with Simon. And Jesus said unto Simon, Fear not; from henceforth thou shalt catch men. And when they had brought their ships to land, they forsook all, and followed him." Just as Simon, James, and John forsook everything, simply taking Jesus at His word; they obeyed. We too, must trust, obey, and follow! Always bear in mind Jesus said, "Fear not," we also must not be in fear. One must understand it is His work and whom He calls, He also qualifies; we are called merely to follow Him.

The time is short. I believe the sand rapidly descending down through the hourglass was to serve as a warning that the time of the end is at hand! One must avail oneself now to this grand provision for salvation of one's soul for the midnight hour is soon approaching and then it will be too late. Revelation 3:3, "Remember therefore how thou hast received and heard, and hold fast, and repent. If therefore thou shalt not watch, I will come on thee as a thief, and thou shalt not know what hour I (Jesus) will come upon thee." God, through the word and by many signs and multiple warnings, has implored man to prepare for Jesus' imminent return. 1 Peter 1:5-9, "Who are kept by the power of God through faith unto salvation ready to be revealed in the last time. Wherein ye greatly rejoice, though now for a season, if need be, ye are in heaviness through manifold temptations: That the trial of your faith, being much more precious than of gold that perisheth, though it be tried with fire, might be found unto praise and honor and glory at the appearing of Jesus Christ: Whom having not seen, ye love; in whom, though now ye see him not, yet believing, ye rejoice with joy unspeakable and full of glory: Receiving the end of your faith, even the salvation of your souls."

I believe the incredible shaking of the ground that I experienced in my night vision warns of a great future earthquake. It could be a worldwide earthquake, of such a great magnitude, as to devastate and to propel the entire world into anarchy. Revelation 11:13, "And the same hour was there a great earthquake, and the tenth part of the city fell, and in the earthquake were slain of men seven thousand: and the remnant were affrighted, and gave glory to the God of heaven." Recorded further in the Book of Revelation is corroborating scripture. Understanding that the Book of Revelation is largely a prophetic book, yet to be fulfilled in the near future! Revelation 16:18, "And there were voices, and thunders, and lightnings; and there was a great earthquake, such as was not since men were upon the earth, so mighty an earthquake, and so great." The tribulations that are coming upon the earth will be so devastating as to cause men who have not sought refuge in Jesus to lament that they had been born because everything that can be shaken will be shaken.

In the vision, the coin I picked up from the sand and momentarily held was symbolic of the yet future "one world" currency. Many years later, and now many years in the past, I saw on television a coin that was reported to be a Euro dollar! It was round in shape and was astonishingly similar to the one I picked up from the sand. The decline in value of the American dollar and the global economic crisis will facilitate the acceptance of the one-world currency. Revelation 13:17, "And that no man might buy or sell, save (except) he that had the mark, or the name of the beast, or the number of his name." There will be in place at that time a system that will demand that one take a mark in order for one to buy, sell, or trade. This will be the mark of the beast and one must never accept this mark on one's hand or on one's forehead; for this will cause one to belong to the realm of Satan and will render that one's soul to be unsalvageable, or beyond salvation.

Seeing The Ancient of Days in my vision was one of the most awe-inspiring occurrences one could ever experience. It was a glimmer of heaven while still living on earth. I don't know if it will be Jesus as the Lion of the Tribe of Judah, or Jesus as the Ancient of Days, who will sit on the throne of David and rule and reign one-thousand years; for God has many names revealed and recorded throughout the Bible for He is a multifaceted God. The multiple names are indicative of His ability of refraction, or to change physical forces or conditions. I do know the Lord God is one Lord, and when Jesus returns will be revealed as The King of Kings and Lord of Lords. Our God possesses a triune nature consisting of a Body, Soul, and Spirit. Jesus and the Ancient of Days have to be interchangeable for they co-exist as one. Jesus has always been, and will always be. Recorded in Genesis, God created man while resurfacing the earth, and re-instituting the use of the sun and the moon. Genesis 1:26, "And God said, Let us make man in our image, after our likeness ..." Throughout eternity past, and throughout eternity future, our creator exists in the dimension of His own plurality, yet singular-One God!

Scripture proves scripture, and there are many examples of God appearing to man in bodily form, these are written and recorded in the Bible. Genesis 3:8, "And they (Adam and Eve) heard the voice of the LORD God walking in the garden in the cool of the day ..." God has, throughout time, revealed Himself to man. Genesis 18:1-3, "And the LORD appeared unto him (Abraham) in the plains of Mamre: and he sat in the tent door in the heat of the day; And he lift up his eyes and looked: and lo, three men stood by him: and when he saw them, he ran to meet them from the tent door, and bowed himself toward the ground, And said, My LORD (God present with Abraham in a physical body), if now I have found favor in thy sight, pass not away, I pray thee, from thy servant." What a merciful and loving Lord we serve. His unchanging love and concern for man has transcended down through the ages. It was God Himself who walked and talked with Adam and Eve in the cool of the day, just as it was

God Himself who, while accompanied by two angels, visited Abraham and Sarah in their tent during the heat of the day.

Hebrews 12:27-28, "And this word, Yet once more, signifieth the removing of those things that are shaken, as of things that are made, that those things which cannot be shaken may remain. Wherefore we receiving a kingdom which cannot be moved, let us have grace, whereby we may serve God acceptably with reverence and godly fear." We know with certainty and with clarity our God is from everlasting-to-everlasting. His ways are immutable and unchangeable. If there is something we do not understand, the problem is not with our God, or with His Word, the problem lies within our own understanding, or lack thereof. It is not necessary to understand everything, for this presents an opportunity to step out on faith and God is glorified through our unsighted trust in Him. This we know; God is THE GREAT I AM. It is in this great and mighty God that all things exist and consist and have their being.

Chapter Eleven
The Proficiency of Prophecy

> *"For I would not, brethren, that ye should be ignorant of this mystery, lest ye should be wise in your own conceits; that blindness in part is happened to Israel, until the fullness of the Gentiles be come in."*
>
> (Romans 11:25)

All of us living in these last days of the present Gentile age are seeing Bible prophecy fulfilled. It is an exciting, thrilling era. All, Jew and Gentile, have a rendezvous with prophecy. All prophecy is threefold: having primary, secondary, and ultimate fulfillments.

This threefold prophecy confirms Jesus is Messiah, the Savior of all peoples, nations, and tongues, and has its primary fulfillment in the Old Testament. Zechariah 12:10. "... and they shall look upon me (Jesus) whom they have pierced (on the cross), and they shall mourn for him ..." The prophet Zechariah was prophesying the crucifixion of Jesus and His death on the cross, approximately five hundred years before Jesus' birth. The secondary fulfillment is found in the New Testament in John 19:34, "But one of the soldiers with a spear pierced his side ..." This did, indeed, happen while Jesus hung on the cross at Calvary. The ultimate fulfillment of the prophecy is found in the Book of Revelation 1:7, "Behold, he (Jesus) cometh (second coming) with clouds; and every eye shall see him, and they also which pierced him ..." This is yet to come - yet in our future.

Another illustration of prophecy which is always threefold having past, present, and future accomplishments is one concerning the Hebrew Passover and its relationship to the redeeming Blood of Jesus Christ as The Passover Lamb. The Passover rite, to be carried out by the Hebrews, is found in Exodus chapter 12. The original Passover sacrament afforded protection from judgment. A lamb without blemish or fault had to be slain, and the blood had to be applied to their door posts for protection from judgment. This is prophetic of Christ's perfect work on the cross. Exodus 12:13, "And the blood (of the lamb) shall be to you for a token upon the houses where ye are: and when I (God) see the blood, I will pass over you, and the plague shall not be upon you to destroy you, when I smite the land of Egypt."

The second part of this prophecy is presented in John 1:29, "The next day John seeth Jesus coming unto him, and saith, 'Behold the Lamb of God, which taketh away the sin of the world." This scripture has a personal and spiritual application pertaining to our day, and one's individual salvation. We see in our future the ultimate fulfillment of this glorious prophecy proclaimed by angels in Revelation 5:12, "Saying with a loud voice, Worthy is the Lamb (Jesus) that was slain (at the cross) to receive power, and riches, and wisdom, and strength, and honour, and glory, and blessing."

The Book of Revelation is the last book in the New Testament and is the only book in the New Testament that is largely prophetic. The word "revelation" comes from the Greek word "*apokalupis*" and the English derivative is "apocalypse" meaning: to disclose what was hidden, and is now revealed or made known. The Book of Revelation is a study in eschatology. The word "eschatology" comes from two Greek words. The first word "eschatos" which means "last." The second word is "logos," and means "discourse" or "word." Thus, eschatology is the theology of the "end times."

John, who is called "John the Revelator," wrote the Book of Revelation. He reveals hidden mysteries as shown to him by Jesus Christ. Jesus revealed to John the great upheavals and the culmination of the end of Gentile world domination and Christ's millennial reign from Jerusalem. In effect, Jesus made known to us through John, events that will happen through the final judgment, the new heaven, the new earth, and the New Jerusalem.

John also wrote the Gospel of John and the Books of First John, Second John, and Third John. The Book of Revelation should be studied along with the Old Testament Book of Daniel. By divine inspiration from God, both Daniel and John were given the same message, which is "the message for our present day and time." God proclaimed Daniel to be "beloved of God," John was called the "Apostle that Jesus loved." In Revelation 1:19, John is told by Jesus, "Write the things which thou hast seen, and the things which are, and the things which shall be hereafter." John's message is to the seven churches. It states in Revelation 1:1-2,

"The Revelation of Jesus Christ, which God gave unto him, to shew unto his servants (us, today) things which must shortly come to pass; and he (Jesus) sent and signified it by his angel unto his servant John: Who bare record of the word of God, and of the testimony of Jesus Christ, and of all things that he (John) saw."

In all seven letters to the churches, Jesus states, "I know your works." Jesus also knows our works. Revelation 1:4 explains Jesus' message is to the seven churches which were in Asia (in John's day), but their counterparts are in our modern world today, making this the most relevant words of prophecy for our present-time churches.

Number One: The Church in Ephesus is commended for labor, patience, and hatred of evil, but reprimanded for leaving their first love (God).

Number Two: The Church in Smyrna is commended for works and tribulations, but reprimanded for saying they are Jews (they were not).

Number Three: The Church in Pergamos is commended for not denying the faith, but reprimanded for holding to the doctrine of Balaam and the doctrine of the Nicolaitanes (false religions) which God's word says He hates.

Number Four: The Church in Thyatira is commended for works, charity, service, faith, and patience. They are reprimanded because Jezebel (personification of idol worship) was allowed to teach and seduce the servants of God.

Number Five: The Church in Sardis is commended because there were a few who had not defiled their garments (representative of sin), but were reprimanded for not working.

Number Six: The Church in Philadelphia was commended because they kept the Word and did not deny the name of the Lord. This church is the only one of the seven churches that was not reprimanded. The word "Philadelphia" means "brotherly love."

Number Seven: The Church in Laodicea was the only church not to be commended, but was strongly reprimanded for being lukewarm. Revelation 3:15-16, "I know thy works, that thou art neither cold nor hot: I would thou wert cold or hot. So then because thou art lukewarm, and neither cold nor hot, I (God) will spue thee out of my mouth."

The majority of our modern-day churches are the remnant of the Church of Laodicea. They are complacent, lax, and guilty of misusing the Blood of Jesus. Lukewarm churches are guilty of the sin of compromising with the world, for ease and gratification of one's flesh. This is a fatal condition and results in total rejection (spit out) by God.

Revelation 21:8, "But the fearful, and unbelieving, and the abominable, and murderers, and whoremongers, and sorcerers, (drug distributors), and idolaters, and all liars, shall have their part in the lake which burneth with fire and brimstone: which is the second death." The first death is the physical death of the body. The second death is spiritual, an eternal state of dying, but never actually attaining death. It is a continual, never-ending torment of body and soul, forever, in conscious agony. This occurs in the "Lake of Fire" (hell).

Jesus Christ is our Paschal (Passover or Sacrificial) Lamb. He was not hurt by the second death, and became the first begotten of the dead. He was victorious over death and hell and the grave.

1 Corinthians 15:20-23, "But now is Christ risen from the dead, and become the firstfruits of them that slept. For since by man (Adam) came death, by man (Jesus) came also the resurrection of the dead. For as in Adam all die, even so in Christ shall all be made alive. But every man in his own order: Christ the firstfruits; afterward they that are Christ's at his coming." Jesus is coming again!

In Revelation 1:1, "Must shortly come to pass" is a phrase revealing Jesus' soon return and the fulfillment of the prophecies concerning the end of this age. Once again, scripture proves scripture. Revelation 1:4-5, "John to the seven churches which are in Asia: Grace be unto you, and peace, from him which is, and which was, and which is to come (Jesus); and from the seven Spirits which are before His throne; And (also) from Jesus Christ, who is the faithful witness, and the first begotten of the dead, and the prince of the kings of the earth. Unto him that loved us, and washed us from our sins in his own blood."

Jesus' return to the earth is imminent, even at the door. These mysteries have been made known to us through prophecy. 1 Thessalonians 4:13-18, "But I would not have you to be ignorant, brethren, concerning them which are asleep, that ye sorrow not, even as others which have no hope. For if we believe that Jesus died and rose again, even so them also which sleep in Jesus will God bring with him. For this we say unto you by the word of the Lord, that we which are alive and remain unto the coming of the Lord shall not prevent (preclude) them which are asleep. For the Lord himself shall descend from heaven with a shout, with the voice of the archangel, and with the trump of God: and the dead in Christ shall rise first: Then we which are alive and remain shall be caught up together with them in the clouds, to meet the Lord in the air: and so shall we ever be with the Lord. Wherefore comfort one another with these words."

We can discern this mystery by studying the scriptures. God does not want us to be ignorant of the events that He ordained to take place in our near future. Jesus was the first begotten of the dead, and at the time of His death on the cross, many graves were opened. Matthew 27:50-53, "Jesus, when he had cried again with a loud voice (from the cross), yielded up the ghost. And, behold, the veil of the temple was rent in twain from the top to the bottom; and the earth did quake, and the rocks rent; And the graves were opened; and many bodies of the saints which slept arose, And came out of the graves after his resurrection, and went into the holy city, and appeared unto many."

This was the first phase of the resurrection. Presently, at death, those who are righteous go to be with the Lord. These are the ones who have preceded us in death and they are already in heaven, with our Lord Jesus. This is the concurrent and secondary phase of the first resurrection, or a continuum of the resurrection of the dead in Christ. In one of the previous scriptures we read, "and the dead in Christ shall rise first." These are those who have preceded us in death, and they have already ascended into heaven. Jesus was the first begotten of the dead. There has been a continuum of the first resurrection.

Careful study of scripture reveals there is going to be a gathering of the righteous "living" to join the Lord and the righteous dead, those who have already preceded us in death. This future event is often referred to as the "rapture." Reiterating 1 Thessalonians 4:17, "Then we which are alive and remain shall be caught up together with them (already resurrected righteous dead) in the clouds, to meet the Lord in the air: and so shall we ever be with the Lord."

This great gathering into heaven at the appointed time, will be a bodily resurrection and translation of mortal flesh into glorified immortal bodies. It will be instantaneous and will happen without warning. 1 Corinthians 15:51-53, "Behold, I shew you a mystery; We shall not all sleep, but we shall all be changed, In a moment, in the twinkling of an eye, at the last trump: for the trumpet shall sound, and the dead shall be raised incorruptible, and we shall be changed. For this corruptible (flesh) must put on incorruption (glorified body), and this mortal must put on immortality."

It appears since the time of Christ's resurrection, those who have died in Jesus, or died a believer's death, have been immediately caught up to be with Jesus. In a sense the first resurrection has been continuing and ongoing. This has been the secondary phase of the prophecy concerning the first resurrection. The rapture, or the bodily translations into heaven, is a part of the first resurrection.

There will be a completion of the first resurrection. Revelation 20:4-6, "And I (John) saw thrones, and they sat upon them, and judgment was given unto them: and I saw the souls of them that were beheaded for the witness of Jesus, and for the word of God, and which had not worshipped the beast (the evil personage who causes people to take the Devil's mark – the Mark of the Beast), neither his image, neither had received his mark (Devil's mark) upon their foreheads, or in their hands; and they lived and reigned with Christ a thousand years. But the rest of the dead (unrighteous dead) lived not again until the thousand years (Jesus' millennial reign) were finished. This is the first resurrection. Blessed and holy is he that hath part in the first resurrection: on such the second death hath no power, but they shall be priests of God and of Christ, and shall reign with him a thousand years." This seems to be the ultimate fulfillment of the first resurrection.

The second resurrection will be a time of judgment for the wicked dead. The previous scripture explains that the unbelieving, morally corrupt, and those who took the mark of the beast, will not live again until the end of Christ's one-thousand year reign here on earth. Revelation 20:11-15, "And I (John) saw a great white throne, and him that sat on it, from whose face the earth and the heaven fled away; and there was found no place for them. And I saw the dead, small and great, stand before God; and the books were opened: and another book was opened, which is the book of life: and the dead were judged out of those things which were written in the books, according to their works. And the sea gave up the dead which were in it; and death and hell delivered up the dead which were in them: and they were judged every man according to their works. And death and hell were cast into the lake of fire. This is the second death. And whosoever was not found written in the book of life was cast into the lake of fire."

There are three hundred and eighteen references to the personal return of Jesus Christ in the New Testament. No one knows the day or the hour of his return, so we must be ever ready. 1 Thessalonians 5:1-2, "But of the times and seasons, brethren, ye have no need that I write unto you. For yourselves know perfectly that the day of the Lord so cometh as a thief in the night." This great gathering will be only to those who are living holy, sanctified lives, and have prepared themselves to meet our Lord face to face. Luke 21:36, "Watch ye therefore, and pray always, that ye may be accounted worthy to escape all these things (the seven years of punishment called the tribulation) that shall come to pass, and to stand before the Son of Man."

A revealing insight into the mystery of the events that will soon take place is written for our benefit and forewarning. In Revelation 4:1 a voice from heaven calls, "Come up hither, and I will shew thee things which must be hereafter." Could this be the rapture of the church, the catching away of God's saints? Could this be a prophetic look at "God's Church Triumphant" being bodily taken up into the heavens just before the Great Tribulation period begins? Those found worthy to escape the terrible woes coming upon the whole earth, will be raptured by Jesus! Believers will be mercifully rescued from this present world, and wondrously rewarded in heaven, all in one glorious nanosecond! The rapture of the church will include both Jew and Gentile believers in Jesus Christ.

To understand prophecy, we must remember God is the sovereign of the universe. God is the ultimate authority and has given man free will. At present, He is dealing with man through mercy and grace. God has dealt with man, precept upon precept, with line upon line, here a little, there a little. Everyone at some point in time finds themselves in the valley of decision. We all must decide our fate, for truly, we are free moral agents, to do our will, or God's will. To believe or not to believe is a choice. God's laws are not altered or hindered because of belief or non-belief. God's laws are still in effect and apply to everyone, and are applicable even to the non-believer. God <u>allows</u> man to be willful and suffer the consequences thereof. But God's desire is that everyone fully surrender to Him and receive the ultimate reward of eternal life and the joys of Heaven.

Careful study of the prophecies proves the Bible is a complete revelation of the sovereignty of God's proclamation to mankind. The Bible is unique in its contents. It is God's written revelation to man, and through the proficiency of prophecy foretells events before the events happen. God is infinite in all His ways, for God is Omniscient.

God is Alpha and Omega, the beginning and the end. God is Omnipresent and thus not confined by time. He was in eternity past and He is in eternity future! God will cause His prophecies to be brought to fulfillment. He is able to make his word accomplish what He has set it forth to do, and it will not return to God void. Every "i" will be dotted and every "t" will be crossed. Nothing is insignificant in the word of God. All scripture has deep and profound meaning and is multifaceted. A powerful example demonstrating God's ability to bring to fulfillment His every Word involves the nation Israel. God, Himself, divided the land of Israel among the twelve Hebrew tribes. As Moses pronounced the blessings to the twelve tribes and as he blessed the tribe of Asher, recorded for our insight and God's glory is a marvelous prophecy. Deuteronomy 33:24-25, "And of Asher he (Moses) said, Let Asher be blessed with children; let him be acceptable to his brethren, and let him dip his foot in oil. Thy shoes shall be iron and brass; and as thy days, so shall thy strength be." The Great International Iraq-Petroleum Enterprise was completed in 1935. It successfully laid one thousand miles of an oil pipeline made of iron and brass that stretches from Mesopotamia into Haifa Harbor. This modern-day oil pipeline runs across the bottom of the parcel of land given to Asher. His "foot" truly is in a literal sense, "dipped in oil and shod with iron and brass." God carefully watches over His word to perform it. It is not by accident or chance that this pipeline runs along the bottom of Asher's foot. Prophesied by God through Moses, and recorded in the Book of Deuteronomy, God foretold us this pipeline would go through this prophesied piece of land. Seemingly a very insignificant scripture comes alive with profound clarity, and with the sureness of God's wondrous working power.

God's plan and purpose for the nation of Israel, and God's plan for His church are made plain through prophecy and by the unmistakable signs all around us. There is nothing in prophecy that needs to be fulfilled before the event of the rapture of the church. This great gathering of righteous believers into glory is at hand. God has spent approximately two thousand years dealing with Jews and Gentiles, but we are coming to the consummation of time allotted for the "Gentile

Church Age." This has been a dispensation of mercy and grace. Fullness of this Gentile Age will culminate at the time of the rapture.

The last seven years of this age will be a time appointed to the Jews. The door has been opened wide to the Gentile nations. Salvation is not by election, but has always been free to all, first to the Jew and then to the Gentile, and to whosoever will believe and accept Jesus Christ. Romans 1:16, "For I am not ashamed of the Gospel of Christ: for it is the power of God unto salvation to every one that believeth; to the Jew first, and also to the Greek (Gentile)." Jesus died to make Jew and Gentile one.

Romans 11:1, "I (Paul) say then, Hath God cast away his people? God forbid ..." Same chapter, verses 20-21, "Well; because of unbelief they were broken off (God's natural branches, the Jews), and thou (believers, Jew and Gentile) standest by faith. Be not highminded (Gentile), but fear: For if God spared not the natural branches, take heed (be warned) lest he also spare not thee."

Paul explains it is because of unbelief that anyone, Jew or Gentile, is cut off from God. It is not by God's election, for then would God be unfair. God chooses those who choose Him. When one chooses God, that one becomes God's child. God does possess foreknowledge of those who choose Him. Romans 11:25, "For I would not, brethren, that ye should be ignorant of this mystery, lest ye should be wise in your own conceits; that blindness in part is happened to Israel, until the fullness of the Gentiles be come in." The fullness of the time allotted to the Gentiles will be complete at the time of the rapture of the Church.

The gospel has never converted all, but has always called out some. The prophet Amos foretells this in the Old Testament times. Amos 9:11-12, "In that day will I raise up the tabernacle of David that is fallen, and close up the breaches (Hebrew: broken hedge, or wall) thereof; and I will raise up his ruins, and will build it as in the days of old: That they may possess the remnant of Edom, and of all the heathen (Gentiles), which are called by my name (Christians), saith the LORD that doeth this."

In the New Testament recorded in Acts 15:14-18, "Simeon hath declared how God at the first did visit the Gentiles, to take out of them a people for his name (Christian). And to this agree the words of the prophets; as it is written, After this I will return (Jesus Christ is coming again), and will build again the tabernacle of David, which is fallen down; and I will build again the ruins thereof, and I will set it up: That the residue of men might seek after the Lord, and all the Gentiles, upon whom my name is called, saith the Lord, who doeth all these things. Known unto God are all his works from the beginning of the world."

Praise God! He re-gathered his people back to Jerusalem for the fulfillment of all prophecy. Jeremiah 23:5-7, "Behold, the days come, saith the LORD, that I will raise unto David a righteous Branch, and a King shall reign and prosper, and shall execute judgment and justice in the earth. In his days Judah shall be saved, and Israel shall dwell safely (Millennial Reign): and this is his name whereby he shall be called, THE LORD OUR RIGHTEOUSNESS (Hebrew: Jehovah-Tsidkenu). Therefore, behold, the days come, saith the LORD, that they shall no more say, The LORD liveth, which brought up the children of Israel out of the land of Egypt; But, (then they will say) The LORD liveth, which brought up and which led the seed of the house of Israel out of the north country (Russia), and from all countries whither I had driven them; and they shall dwell in their own land." As we have studied in previous chapters, God has re-gathered His Jewish people back to Israel from every corner of the world.

After the rapture, at His second advent, Jesus Christ's millennial reign will be here on earth. He will rule from the throne of David and He will build again the Tabernacle of David. Christ took the title of David's throne back to heaven with Him, assuring that David will never lack for one to sit on his throne. All things point toward the re-establishment of the Davidic ruler over Israel, Jesus Christ, God's anointed.

Luke 1:31-33, "And, behold, thou shalt conceive in thy womb, and bring forth a son, and shalt call his name JESUS. He shall be great, and shall be called the Son of the Highest: and the Lord God shall give unto him the throne of his father David: And he shall reign over the house of Jacob for ever; and of his kingdom there shall be no end."

At the fullness of time for the Gentiles, the Spirit of Grace will reveal to the Jews, Jesus Christ, Messiah. Zechariah 12:10, "And I will pour upon the house of David, and upon the inhabitants of Jerusalem, the spirit of grace and supplications (prayer and weeping): and they shall look upon me whom they have pierced, and they (the Jews) shall mourn for him (Jesus), as one mourneth for his only son, and shall be in bitterness for him, as one that is in bitterness for his firstborn."

There will be great sorrow when the eyes of the Jews are opened. Reiterating scripture, "blindness in part is happened to Israel, until the fullness of the Gentiles be come in." At this time they will recognize Jesus was, and is, the true Messiah-Y'shua.

America must awaken to righteousness. Many of us, Jew and Gentile, have already received Jesus as the Lord of our lives and the Savior of our souls. We must forsake sinful, and any and all, worldly ways. Those who have prepared themselves shall be ready to be received by him up into heaven. Those who are not prepared will have seven years of trouble, referred to as, "the time of Jacob's trouble." It will be a seven year period of great tribulation, full of woe and unthinkable suffering of every kind, beyond human imagination. I believe this time period will be a predominantly "Jewish" time. It appears the gentile age will be completed at the time of the rapture of the church.

Many scholars and theologians believe in a pre-tribulation rapture. If they are correct, all who have applied the blood of Jesus to their lives and have come out of sin will go to be with Jesus before, or at the very start of, the seven-year tribulation period. I personally believe this school of thought to be correct. This does not mean that believers will not suffer persecutions, for we are coming into an extremely dangerous time in history because the wicked are going to become even more wicked, and ungodliness will increase.

There are those who believe in a mid-tribulation rapture. This theory projects that those who are prepared to meet Jesus will be taken up into heaven after three and one-half years of punishment, at the middle of the seven year time period. Others theorize that there will only be a second coming of Jesus Christ, and this will happen at the end of the seven-year tribulation period. This theory teaches the "Rapture" will be simultaneous with the "Second Coming" of Christ and will not be separate events.

God's timing of these events is still a mystery and the timing of the following events is a mystery because scripture explains that no one knows the day or the hour of Christ's return. But we are to be wise and we are to know the season of His return. Luke 12:54-56, "And he (Jesus) said also to the people, When ye see a cloud rise out of the west, straightway ye say, There cometh a shower; and so it is. And when ye see the south wind blow, ye say, There will be heat; and it cometh to pass. Ye hypocrites, ye discern the face of the sky and of the earth; but how is it that ye do not discern this time?" We do not know the day or the hour. It is abundantly clear that the alarming speed with which all these signs and events surrounding us are coming into place that the time is at hand, even at the door. Revelation 10:7, "But in the days of the voice of the seventh angel, when he shall begin to sound, the mystery of God should be finished, as he hath declared to his servants the prophets." God has purposely obscured the day and the hour of these prophecies. We are cautioned to be ever watchful, and waiting for Jesus' soon return.

One example of the many prophecies that have been fulfilled in the last fifty years is recorded in the Old Testament. Isaiah 35:1, "The wilderness and the solitary place shall be glad for them; and the desert shall rejoice, and blossom as the rose." This scripture foretold Israel in this present time. The land is now lush and green, flourishing with fruits and flowers. Another fulfillment of prophecy, also recorded, in the Old Testament is Daniel 12:4, "But thou, O Daniel, shut up the words, and seal the book, even to the time of the end: many shall run to and fro, and knowledge shall be increased." John the Revelator and Daniel were both shown the same vision of these "end times." It was explained to Daniel that his prophecy was not for his day and time. He was told to "seal up the book" for the message was only relevant to these latter days. As told by Daniel, men will be running to and fro in that appointed time. Today there are trains, planes, and automobiles which are all playing a part in fulfilling this prophecy. Daniel also proclaimed through prophecy that "knowledge shall be increased." One hundred and fifty years ago, man was on horseback and riding in wooden wagons. In 1830 came the invention of "the Iron Horse." The first steam engine train was nicknamed the Iron Horse because it was used for transportation and as a conveyance of goods. Today, man is riding in space shuttles and walking on the moon. We are a fast-paced, sophisticated society. The fulfillment of these prophecies accompanied by many, many others should serve as a wakeup call to America, and to the world, that Jesus is coming again very soon. I personally have been privileged to be an eyewitness to the fulfillment of some of these ancient prophecies in my lifetime. At present, all the inhabitants of the world, Jew and Gentile, are living in the last days of Gentile world domination, and all have a rendezvous with prophecy!

Chapter Twelve

Mount of Slaughter

"And he gathered them together into a place called in the Hebrew tongue Armageddon."

(Revelation 16:16)

In a remarkable vision the Prophet Ezekiel tells of a vision of "dry bones" revived into an army of living men. This profound vision is symbolic of the restoration of Israel from their physical captivity and dispersion to their greater restoration: reconciling sinners to the Almighty God.

Ephesians 2:2, "Wherein in time past ye walked according to the course of this world, according to the prince of the power of the air, the spirit that now worketh in the children of disobedience." All who practice sin, and carelessly remain in an unredeemed spiritual state, are spiritually dead. Through the Spirit of grace, all Israel shall ultimately recognize Jesus Christ, The Righteous, as their Messiah and be saved.

Romans 10:1, "Brethren, my heart's desire and prayer to God for Israel is, that they might be saved." The apostle Paul, a Hebrew, had a love and concern for his people. Paul at one time persecuted the church and was even present when Stephen was martyred for a witness of the Gospel of Jesus Christ. Same chapter verses 11-14, "For the scripture saith, Whosoever believeth on him shall not be ashamed. For there is no difference between the Jew and the Greek: for the same Lord over all is rich unto all that call upon him. For whosoever shall call upon the name of the Lord shall be saved. How then shall they call on him in whom they have not believed? and how shall they believe in him of whom they have not heard? and how shall they hear without a preacher?" Continuing with verses 19-21, "But I say, Did not Israel know? First Moses saith, I will provoke you to jealousy by them that are no people (Gentiles), and by a foolish nation I will anger you. But Esaias (Greek for Isaiah), is very bold, and saith, I (Jesus) was found of them that sought me not (Gentiles); I was made manifest (known) unto them that asked not after me. But to Israel he (Jesus) saith, All day long I have stretched forth my hands unto a disobedient and gainsaying people."

Romans 11:1-3, "I say then, Hath God cast away his people? God forbid. For I (Paul speaking) also am an Israelite, of the seed of Abraham, of the tribe of Benjamin. God hath not cast away his people which he foreknew (Hebrew people are God's elect). Wot ye not what the scripture saith of Elias (Greek for Elijah)? how he maketh intercession to God against Israel saying, Lord, they have killed thy prophets, and digged down thine altars; and I am left alone, and they seek my life." Verse 5, "Even so then at this present time also there is a remnant according to the election (of Hebrews only) of grace." And verses 7-8 say, "What then? Israel hath not obtained that which he seeketh for; but the election hath obtained it, and the rest were blinded. (According as it is written, God hath given them the spirit of slumber, eyes that they should not see, and ears that they should not hear;) unto this day." Continuing on in Romans 11:20 "Well; because of unbelief they were broken off, and thou standest by faith. Be not highminded (Gentiles), but fear." In essence, Paul explains that God allowed this punishment to come upon His own natural children and he warns Gentile nations that God will not spare them, the children of adoption. Gentiles must not be high-minded, for God has given the adopted Gentiles an opportunity to be saved. This time period is often referred to as, "The Church Age" or "Age of Grace" which, according to Bible prophecy, is drawing to a close. God has always had a remnant of believing Jews. These are God's elect, and these are of whom He had foreknowledge. The 144,000 Jewish witnesses are predestined to preach the gospel during the seven years of great tribulation. God's word promises the whole house of Israel will be saved!

The Gentile nations have severely failed the patient and Holy God by using the Grace of God as a license to sin. We have failed God and have missed sharing in His divine fellowship. It was to be a means to provoke the Jewish children to jealousy. Oh what sorrow this heedlessness has been to God. This too, will bring heartrending sorrow to us Gentiles. God's great time clock will tick the last second allotted to the Gentiles and then it will start ticking out the last seven years appointed to the Jews. God is calling all, both Jew and Gentile, to call upon Him before the door is closed. God created man for His pleasure. He designed mankind to need and share sweet friendship, and He desires to bless us. It is not too late. The midnight hour is approaching and the enemies of God, and God's people, are gathering together against Israel. Romans 11:26-28, "And so all Israel shall be saved: as it is written, There shall come out of Sion the Deliverer, and shall turn away ungodliness from Jacob: For this is my covenant unto them, when I shall take away their sins. As concerning the gospel, they are enemies for your (Gentiles) sakes: but as touching the election, they are beloved for the father's sakes." In the preceding verses we feel Paul's sorrow for his own people, the Jews, for Jesus truly died to make Jew and Gentile one people-same Lord over all. I too have a sorrow for the Gentiles if we miss Jesus, we will have missed so much. As the storm clouds gather over the Land of Israel, Jesus is extending His nail-scarred hand to all, whosoever will come, come.

The year 1948 appears to have been a significant turning point in hastening the events of this age. In 1948, the state of Israel officially came into existence, a very notable event in the light of Biblical prophecy. God is gathering His Hebrew children back to their native land and their inheritance, Israel. Also, in that same year, the Hague Congress initiated the Council of Europe. In 1948, Communists overran Czechoslovakia and blockaded Berlin. These events spawned the North Atlantic Treaty Organization (NATO). Most likely this was the only thing that prevented Russia from a takeover of Western Europe at that time. The Space Age also began in 1948. Experiments in that year proved speculation that a rocket could be sent into the heavens, defying gravitational pull.

Israelis are now re-gathered in their own homeland. These events have all been prophesied. The world is being positioned and readied to accept the peace treaty brought into existence by Antichrist. He will eventually have nations sign a treaty that he, himself, does not intend to keep. Antichrist will break his own peace treaty. Be warned. This will only be a pseudo-peace treaty because only Christ can bring into existence true peace and safety. Be warned! This proclaimed improvement for world conditions through the proposed peace treaty by Antichrist should not, and must not, cause anyone to be reassured, for it will bring into existence a state of false worldly security. God warns us when they say "peace and safety," then sudden destruction. Ezekiel 38:7-8, "Be thou prepared, and prepare for thyself, thou, and all thy company that are assembled unto thee, and be thou a guard unto them. After many days thou shalt be visited: in the latter years thou shalt come into the land that is brought back from the sword, and is gathered out of many people, against (beside) the mountains of Israel, which have been always waste: but it is brought forth out of the nations, and they shall dwell safely all of them." The signs, proving the truth and fulfillment of this major prophecy, are happening all around us. These prophesied events are going to encompass and involve the entire world.

We are now living in revived Babylon, the last remnant of the fallen Roman Empire. "Babylon" symbolizes the totality of Gentile world power, which began with King Nebuchadnezzar, and will culminate with Antichrist as the one-world leader and will be the end of this fourth world-power. There is an illustration of the four world kingdoms in chapter thirteen, *The Daniel Determinant*. This fourth world power represented by the ten toes will not cling one to the other. It will be a confederation of ten countries, or perhaps 10 regional alliances, representing the New World Order. These ten will have a pact, but it will be broken during the seven years of tribulation that is coming upon the whole earth. The Antichrist will lead these countries, or alliances, against Israel and against all that is Holy.

Isaiah 34:1-2, "Come near, ye nations, to hear; and hearken, ye people: let the earth hear, and all that is therein; the world, and all things that come forth of it. For the indignation of the LORD is upon all nations, and his fury upon all their armies: he hath utterly destroyed them, he hath delivered them to the slaughter."

God's righteous indignation and judgments are going to be poured out on all those who have arrogantly refused Jesus. Those who rebelled against God's laws, who remained willingly ignorant of God's salvation plan, will follow the Beast. After three and one-half years, Antichrist will break the seven-year peace treaty. Jesus will finally step in and overthrow all evils at the Battle of Armageddon, which will be furiously raging. John the Revelator foretells that God will "allow" Antichrist to do his evils with the unbelieving and those wicked who have gathered together against Israel. Revelation 16:16, "And he gathered them together into a place called in the Hebrew tongue Armageddon." The meaning of Armageddon in Hebrew is "to gather" or "rendezvous."

God is going to allow man to do his worst to man, then God, with a mighty overthrow, will avenge Israel of all her enemies. No enemy of God, or Israel, will go unpunished. All have been forewarned. We all will be without excuse if we do not avail ourselves of the ark-of-safety, which is Jesus Christ.

It appears the prelude to this future battle may have already begun. Dessert Storm, "Shock and Awe," the Wars in Iraq and Afghanistan have already gathered a great army of men and munitions to that region. God's word declares this final battle will end Gentile world domination. The location of this war will be at Megiddo in the northern part of Israel, west of Jordan in the plains of Jezreel, which is between Samaria and Galilee. It will become a Mount of slaughter, because God will allow man to do evil against man at the battle of Armageddon. Jesus' sudden appearance of the second coming will then end this great slaughter. Scholars agree Iran (ancient Persia), Libya, Russia, Germany, China, North Korea, and a United Europe will all converge against Israel. All will assemble themselves together to take a great spoil.

Ending Satan's reign of evil, God Himself will supernaturally intervene. The wrath of our Holy God will be poured out upon the entire ungodly world. Armageddon will involve "God versus all Nations" at Jerusalem.

The Pharisees inquired of Jesus as to "when" the Kingdom of God should come to the earth, and Jesus gave many examples of the signs of the second coming. It will be at that time that Jesus will set up His kingdom here on earth and rule and reign from Jerusalem. The disciples then inquired of Jesus "where" would He return to earth. Luke 17:37, "And they answered and said unto him, Where Lord? And he (Jesus) said unto them, Wheresoever the body is, thither will the eagles be gathered together." Great flesh eating scavenger birds are going to eat the flesh of those who will die in the battle of Armageddon. Revelation 19:17-21, "And I saw an angel standing in the sun; and he cried with a loud voice, saying to all the fowls that fly in the midst of heaven, Come and gather yourselves together unto the supper of the great God; That ye may eat the flesh of kings, and the flesh of captains, and the flesh of mighty men, and the flesh of horses, and of them that sit on them, and the flesh of all men, both free and bond, both small (importance of rank) and great. And I saw the beast, and the kings of the earth, and their armies, gathered together to make war against him that sat on the horse, and against his army. And the beast was taken, and with him the false prophet that wrought miracles before him, with which he deceived them that had received the mark of the beast, and them that worshipped his image. These both were cast alive into a lake of fire burning with brimstone. And the remnant were slain with the sword (Word of God) of him (Jesus) that sat upon the horse, which sword proceeded out of his (Jesus') mouth: and all the fowls were filled with their flesh." At Jesus' second coming, the eastern sky will open and Jesus and all the saints accompanying Him, all riding upon white horses, armed with the Word of God that will destroy Satan because, IT IS WRITTEN!

God is allowing the stage to be set for the fulfillment of all the Bible's prophecies. Man, unaware of God's mighty plan to defeat Satan, has built a road allowing easy access to the site of this unrivaled war of wars. As God's judgments are being executed upon the earth, we learn in Revelation 16:12, "And the sixth angel poured out his vial upon the great river Euphrates; and the water thereof was dried up, that the way of the kings of the east might be prepared." This road has prepared a means for the "Kings of the East" with conquering powers, to converge against Israel. Russia, at present, is courting both Iran and China. Also, at present, there are ominous clouds gathering since North Korea has obtained nuclear weapons.

In 1959-1986 the governments of Pakistan and China built, and completed, the Karakoram Highway. This road links China's Sinkiang Province with Havelian, located sixty miles north of Islamabad, the capital of Pakistan. This highway is dubbed the "High Road to China" and the Ninth Wonder of the World. It is a five hundred mile, all-weather road. The kings of the east will unite with other leaders and, with evil intent, all converge on Israel. This Karakoram Highway will be the road that leads the enemies of Israel to her very door.

Revelation 6:15-17, "And the kings of the earth, and the great men, and the rich men, and the chief captains, and the mighty men, and every bondman and every free man, hid themselves in the dens and in the rocks of the mountains; And said to the mountains, and rocks, Fall on us, and hide us from the face of him that sitteth on the throne, and from the wrath of the Lamb (Jesus): For the great day of his wrath is come; and who shall be able to stand?"

Chapter Thirteen
The Daniel Determinant

"Seventy weeks are determined upon thy people and upon thy holy city, to finish the transgression, and to make an end of sins, and to make reconciliation for iniquity, and to bring in everlasting righteousness, and to seal up the vision and prophecy, and to anoint the most Holy."

(Daniel 9:24)

The date of the writing of the Book of Daniel is not actually known, but by historic events and the style of the written languages, Aramaic and Hebrew, it's estimated the book was written about six hundred years before Christ. Daniel was a Jewish captive, interpreting the dreams of a Gentile king. In chapters 2-7, Daniel used the Aramaic language to write concerning the fate of the Gentile nations. In chapters 8-12, Daniel used the Hebrew language, a possible indication that the Jewish clock will begin to tick again when we see these prophecies of Daniel being fulfilled.

Daniel, through careful study of Jeremiah's writings, understood the prophecy of the "Seventy Weeks" of the Jew's exile. Possibly no other prophet of the Old Testament had greater insight into the political future of governments, including the coming millennial Kingdom of Christ. The wide scope of future events covered in this writing, gives credit to Daniel as a "Full-View Prophet."

Daniel was taken captive in his youth and served in the palace of King Nebuchadnezzar of Babylon. Babylon was the first and greatest of the four world empires. Daniel excelled in wisdom, strength of character, and dedication to the one true God of Israel. So great was Daniel's faithfulness, God called him "Beloved of God" and rewarded his uncompromising dedication with a special gift of understanding of all visions and dreams. In a kingdom that was renowned for having the wisest of men, there was not one learned man found better than Daniel. He was found to be ten times wiser than all the astrologers (enchanters or sorcerers) and magicians in the entire Babylonian empire.

Despite what wise men or political figures of the world may think, the safety and endurance of kingdoms is decided according to the will and purpose of God. God is unchanging! He is the same sovereign God that allowed Daniel and the Israeli people to be taken captive into Babylon because of national sins. This same holy and righteous God is also going to judge America for her national sins. America has become a sanctuary for the spiritually unclean. God will remove His hand of blessing, protection, provision, and prosperity from America. We have become altogether spiritually unacceptable to this holy God. America has become an advocate for the sexually impure. Sexual sins of promiscuity, fornication, homosexuality, child molestation, and various sexual deviances are practiced and often condoned--at times flagrantly paraded in our streets! The spirit of greed and quest for power has permeated the government and big business. The abortion industry reveals the wickedness of the lawmakers, the corruption of a government, and the passiveness of a people that would allow blatant disregard for the sanctity of human life. America will be weighed in the balance and will be found guilty of gross national sins before a righteous and holy God!

This same holy God, who kept Daniel safe from harm and made a way of provision and blessing for him during national judgment, will also make a way of provision and blessing for those who will not bow their knee to the false gods of today.

In chapter two of the Book of Daniel, we see in the second year of the reign of Nebuchadnezzar, this spoiled monarch dreamed a dream that he could not remember, but it greatly disturbed him. Agitated and not able to sleep, he summoned all his astrologers, magicians, sorcerers, and the Chaldeans. Unreasonably, he demanded to know the dream's interpretation as well as the dream itself. Nebuchadnezzar had many men of wisdom surrounding him, but his need for Godly wisdom was made evident. He needed spiritual answers that neither man nor the world could give him. Evident also, is our need of the Creator and His Godly wisdom.

Daniel (whose name had been changed to Belteshazzar), fasted and prayed. After serious intercession before God, he requested to be brought before the king. The king inquired of Daniel, "Art thou able to make known unto me the dream which I have seen, and the interpretation thereof?" Daniel answered saying, "There is a God in heaven that revealeth secrets, and maketh known to the king Nebuchadnezzar what shall be in the latter days." Daniel said to King Nebuchadnezzar that God had shown him both the dream and its meaning.

The king had dreamed of a large and great image with a head of gold, breast and arms of silver, belly and thighs of brass, and legs of iron with feet part of iron and part of clay. He saw a stone that was cut out without hands, which crushed the feet of the image and broke them. This caused the fall of the entire image, which crushed to pieces as fine as dust, and the wind blew it away. No particle of it could be found. The stone that destroyed the image became a great mountain and filled the whole earth.

Daniel went on to tell Nebuchadnezzar God had also given him the interpretation of the dream. The image in the dream is symbolic of the four world empires. The king, himself, was, indeed, the head of gold on the image, which represented the first and greatest of the world empires, Babylon. King Nebuchadnezzar was the first sovereign ruler of the world. The second empire, represented by the breast and arms of silver, depicted a kingdom inferior to the first. This was the Medo-Persian Empire. The two arms are symbolic of the Meads and the Persians joining together to take over Babylon. The third empire, more inferior to the second, and represented by the belly and thighs of brass is symbolic of the third world power, the Greek, under Alexander the Great. The fourth world empire, even yet more inferior, is represented by the legs and feet of iron and clay and symbolic of the Roman Empire. The two legs illustrate the divided Roman Empire, east and west, weakened by the division.

The ten toes represent the alliance of ten nations, or perhaps regional alliances, forging a union in the latter days. Even as iron will not mix with clay, these ten nations or alliances shall not cleave (stay united) one to the other. Their demise will culminate with the defeat of the Antichrist and will end Gentile world rule. The smiting stone that broke the image is Jesus Christ. His sudden catastrophic judgment at Armageddon will lead to the destruction of this corrupt world system, and the beast of Revelation chapter 13 will be defeated. This man of sin, described as the beast along with the false prophet, will be thrown into the Lake of Fire. The Antichrist, who will be the embodiment of Satan, will be the one world leader of this last Gentile world empire that will be comprised of these ten nations or unions. Antichrist (Satan) will be thrown into the bottomless pit for one thousand years and the beast and the false prophet will be thrown into the Lake of Fire. Then Jesus will set up a kingdom (symbolized by the mountain), which will never be destroyed, and shall stand forever.

HEAD OF FINE GOLD
First world power: Neo-Babylonian Empire, 612-539 B.C.

BREAST AND ARMS OF SILVER
Second world power: Medo-Persian Empire, 539-331 B.C.

BELLY AND THIGHS OF BRASS
Third world power: Greek Empire, 331-63 B.C.

LEGS AND FEET OF IRON AND CLAY
Fourth world power: Roman Empire, 63 B.C.-476 A.D.

TEN TOES-PART IRON AND PART CLAY
Shall not cleave one to another. These represent ten future Regional Kingdoms or Regional Unions.

Gentiles have held world dominion for about twenty-six hundred years. It is interesting that this vast expanse of time started with a great image and will end with another great image. The first image, Daniel 3:10-11, "Thou, O king, (Nebuchadnezzar) hast made a decree, that every man that shall hear the sound of the cornet, flute, harp, sackbut, psaltery, and dulcimer, and all kinds of musick, shall fall down and worship the golden image: And whoso falleth not down and worshippeth, that he should be cast into the midst of a burning fiery furnace." The second image, yet future, which will be revealed is the Antichrist. Revelation 13:15, "And he (Antichrist) had power to give life unto the image of the beast, that the image of the beast should both speak, and cause that as many as would not worship the image of the beast should be killed." In Daniel's time there was forced false worship of an idol and once again there is going to be forced false worship of an idol.

Great was the image in Daniel's day and greater will be the future image foretold by John in the Book of Revelation. Today we see rapid changes taking place in our world's political arena. We, living today in these turbulent times, are seeing the fulfillment of prophesies foretold by Daniel from Nebuchadnezzar's dream. There are continual changes of every facet in world power. World economic collapse, an earthquake, or a nuclear strike, could pave the way for the Beast described in Revelation chapter 13. The Beast will lead the world into a one-world economic system. He will cause all to take his mark for all things necessary for economic survival, including medical treatment. It will be, in fact, Satan's mark. The acceptance and application of the Mark of the Beast will cause one to become unredeemable. This united system will present a one-world religion and the False Prophet will head this up. Antichrist, who will be the embodiment of Satan himself, will lead this New World Order.

The first six chapters of Daniel were relevant to his day and age. Chapters seven through twelve are parenthetical and largely prophetic. Remember, Daniel as the full-view-prophet of the entire Gentile Age, amplifies our understanding of these mysteries.

Daniel had a vision of the four winds, which troubled the waters. There were also, four beasts coming up out of the sea representing four diverse kingdoms. The Babylonian empire is first, represented by a lion. The second beast was seen as a bear and represented Medo-Persia, which became a joint government. The third beast was likened unto a leopard and was representative of the Grecian empire under Alexander the Great. The Roman Empire, symbolized by the fourth beast, was cruel, fierce and strongest of all. Daniel also saw a vision of ten horns, which are believed to represent ten kings of the ten nations or unions, forging the New World Order. Daniel saw, superimposed, one kingdom lifted up above the other. One represented what was, and the other represented what is to come. Daniel saw our present age, which is revived from the ancient Roman Empire, which fell.

This world system will become so evil and decadent that it too will fall, and at its fall the cry of an angel from Heaven will go forth. Revelation 18:2, "And he cried mightily with a strong voice, saying, Babylon the great is fallen, is fallen, and is become the habitation of devils, and the hold of every foul spirit, and a cage of every unclean and hateful bird." This scripture gives us insight to the wickedness of the revived Roman Empire, that we are living in today.

We see through Daniel the demise of the fourth beast, as it was and is yet to come: a dreaded enemy to God, the Christian Church and God's people. Antichrist is described in Daniel 8:23, "... a king of fierce countenance, and understanding dark sentences, shall stand up." Satan will head up this federated empire in our very near future. He shall come against God's order and speak blasphemies against even the Most High.

Daniel was then encouraged as his vision turned to the kingdom of God. The coming judgment of God Almighty, the righteous Judge, was seen as the Ancient of Days. Through Daniel's vision we also have a heavenly view of the Son of Man (Jesus) coming with the clouds of heaven (the second coming). Next there was a glorious view of Jesus' kingdom set up on earth, which will be an everlasting kingdom. The eighth chapter of Daniel is written in Hebrew, as are the continuing chapters of the book.

Daniel had yet another vision, one of a great "he-goat." The he-goat is Satan and out of the he-goat comes a "little horn," which will do all the works of Satan with deceptive signs and lying wonders. Daniel 8:9-10, "And out of one of them came forth a little horn (Antichrist), which waxed exceeding great, toward the south, and toward the east, and toward the pleasant land (Israel). And it waxed great, even to the host of heaven; and it cast down some of the host (one-third of heaven's angels) and of the stars to the ground, and stamped upon them." Lucifer, now renamed Satan, persuaded one third of the angels in heaven to obey and follow him in rebellion against God Almighty. This was an attempted coup in heaven, led by Lucifer while he was in his original created state. Lucifer and one third of heaven's angels were cast out of Heaven. Satan was cast to the earth and those angels who followed him are still reserved in chains of darkness to await the Judgment. This is a type and foreshadow of a future event when Satan, as Antichrist, will once again bring a revolution against God. This time Satan will deceive mankind instead of angels into following him in rebellion against God. Satan was defeated by God then, and will be defeated once again as he embodies Antichrist to accomplish his evil intent! Satan, envious of God, has always sought to be worshipped. He brought one third of the angels of heaven against God and was defeated. Satan will be a counterfeit Christ.

He will, at some future time, set himself up as God and demand all to bow down and worship him. It is feasible that he will present himself for worship in The Dome of The Rock Mosque. Scripture proves scripture. Mark 13:14, "But when ye shall see the abomination of desolation, spoken of by Daniel the prophet, standing where it ought not, let him that readeth understand, then let them that be in Judea flee to the mountains." The Jewish Temple was destroyed by Titus in A.D. 70. God instructs us to apply Godly wisdom and understanding to these mysteries. There are additional insights and warnings into the visions given to Daniel by God. Our loving Father God does not want us to be ignorant of Satan's devices. He has forewarned us of all that will happen because He does not want us to fall prey to this evil plan and this evil being. Matthew 24:15, "When ye therefore shall see the abomination of desolation, spoken of by Daniel the prophet, stand in the holy place (perhaps the Muslim's Dome of The Rock Mosque which at present time sits on the original Jewish Temple site in Jerusalem, would explain the terminology "holy place"), (whoso readeth, let him understand.)" Satan will once again suffer defeat by God, and those who follow his malignant lies, take his mark, or prostrate themselves before him in worship will be eternally lost, just as those angels are eternally lost to this very day. The epistle of Jude was written in A.D. 68 and substantiates the fate of these rebellious angels. Jude verse 6, "And the angels which kept not their first estate, but left their own habitation, he (God) hath reserved in everlasting chains under darkness unto the judgment of the great day."

Daniel sought the meaning of these visions with sincere prayer and fasting. The Lord rewarded Daniel with a most wondrous visitation of Jesus. This personage of Christ ordered the Angel Gabriel to cause Daniel to understand the visions. However, before Gabriel could appear to Daniel, he needed the help of Michael the archangel to fight the Prince of Persia (Satanic spirit of Ancient Persia which today is Iran) who resisted them as a hindering spirit to prevent the understanding of the visions, and the answer to Daniel's prayer. Daniel 10:14, "Now I (Gabriel) am come to make thee understand what shall befall thy people (the Jews) in the latter days: for yet the vision is for many days (end times)." Daniel 8:17, "... Understand, O son of man: for at the time of the end shall be the vision." The time of the end will be at the culmination of Gentile world dominion!

Daniel, who understood the timetable of the prophecy of the seventy weeks of captivity, is now commissioned by our Lord to make known to the Church the meaning of the last "week," or the last "seven years," which are relevant to the times in which we live today. Daniel 9:2, "In the first year of his reign I Daniel understood by books the number of the years, whereof the word of the Lord came to Jeremiah the prophet, that he would accomplish seventy years in the desolations of Jerusalem."

The Angel Gabriel told Daniel to understand these mysteries. God provided understanding for us through Daniel's revelations and study of scriptures. All of this was shown to Daniel, making him the prophet of prophets for the entire Gentile Age. His profound revelations give us insights into our near future. Looking into our future through Daniel's understanding of visions, dreams, and prophesies, and of the mystery of the seventy weeks, we can see with profound clarity, what must shortly come to pass. Through careful study and prayer we, too, can have insights into God's great deliverance plan.

The splendor of a more glorious redemption plan was divinely revealed to Daniel concerning God's greater fulfillment of "The Church" in these latter days.

Daniel 9:24-27, "Seventy weeks are determined upon thy people (Jews) and upon thy holy city (Jerusalem), to finish the transgression, and to make an end of sins, and to make reconciliation for iniquity, and to bring in everlasting righteousness, and to seal up the vision and prophecy, and to anoint the most Holy (Jesus). Know therefore and understand, that from the going forth of the commandment to restore and to build Jerusalem unto the Messiah the Prince shall be seven weeks, and threescore and two weeks: the street shall be built again, and the wall, even in troublous times. And after threescore and two weeks shall Messiah be cut off, but not for himself: and the people of the prince that shall come shall destroy the city and the sanctuary; and the end thereof shall be with a flood, and unto the end of the war desolations are determined. And he shall confirm the covenant with many for one week (seven years of tribulation): and in the midst of the week he shall cause the sacrifice and the oblation to cease, and for the overspreading of abominations he shall make it desolate ..." Messiah was cut off, but not for Himself. The supreme sacrifice of God was embodied in the flesh-and-blood body of Jesus the Christ! Jesus was God's sacrificial Lamb, and His atoning blood was the necessary element for the remission of sins. The Romans destroyed Jerusalem in A.D. 70. God allowed the destruction, and foretold these events before they happened.

Scholars believe this "seventy weeks" to be weeks of years. The prophecy of Daniel's seventy weeks should be recognized as pertaining to the Jews and to the holy city Jerusalem. The principle of "seventy weeks" is explained in Numbers 14:34, "After the number of the days in which ye searched the land, even forty days, each day for a year, shall ye bear your iniquities, even forty years, and ye shall know my breach of promise." God pronounces the concept of one year for every day. This pattern is repeated in Leviticus chapter 26:18-28, proving God's consistent way of dealing with His people. Scripture is proved and confirmed by other scriptures. God's punishment of Israel is sustained and lengthened seven times more. God judged Israel "guilty" and pronounced a sentence of seven times seventy years of punishment on her. The extended sentence was to be 490 years of punishment. This period of time began when the Jews came out of Babylonian captivity, spoken by Jeremiah and understood by Daniel. They were brought out of their harsh servitude in 445 B.C.

These events are based on the Jewish calendar which differs slightly from our Gregorian calendar. Dates before Jesus' birth are known as B.C. which is "Before Christ" and A.D. stands for the Latin phrase "anno domini" which means "in the year of our Lord."

The inaccuracy of the preceding Julian calendar prompted a Catholic monk to work a new calendar system in A.D. 532 which was established in the 1580s by Pope Gregory XIII. It began with the year he believed Christ was born. However, there is a discrepancy of as much as five years in the calculation to arrive at the year of Christ's birth. Affording credence to this error would put Christ's birth at around 5 B.C., but the exact year is unknown. The correct date of Jesus' death by crucifixion is believed to be A.D. 29.

The time count began in 445 B.C. Adding five years for the time discrepancy, brings us to 450 years, and then adding 33 years for Christ's life, brings us to 483 years. Just seven years short of the 490 year sentence imposed by God on the Jews. Daniel prophesied that after 69 weeks Messiah would be cut off, leaving one week (yet to come) to finish the transgression. This one-week, or seven remaining years, will be for the Great Tribulation period and unfulfilled prophecy yet for the Jewish nation and judgment on the wicked. No one can say with 100 percent accuracy these exact timeframes because we are not to know the day or the hour of Jesus' return or when the end shall be. We are to discern the season of His return!

This time period, referenced as the Great Tribulation, will bring untold terrors and sorrows. Revelation 16:13-15, "And I saw three unclean spirits (the un-holy trinity) like frogs come out of the mouth of the dragon (Satan), and out of the mouth of the beast (the one who causes all to take the mark), and out of the mouth of the false prophet (possibly, Islamic Fundamentalist spiritual leader falsely declaring "the beast" as the Mahdi). For they are the spirits of devils, working miracles, which go forth unto the kings of the earth and of the whole world, to gather them to the battle (Armageddon) of that great day of God Almighty. Behold, I (Jesus) come as a thief (unannounced). Blessed is he that watcheth, and keepeth his garments (we are to be clothed with the righteousness of Jesus the Christ), lest he walk naked, and they see his shame."

This "nakedness" is best explained as not a physical nakedness, but rather a spiritual nakedness of un-repented, and therefore uncovered sins. An analogous example is recorded in the Old Testament and pertains to King David. It is often said King David danced naked in the streets. He did not! Careful study of scripture reveals David, while rejoicing in the streets and glorifying God, merely took off his regal kingly robes and underneath he was clothed in royal priestly garments. His wife was enraged, because she did not esteem the priestly garments suitable to be worn by a king and she regarded David, without his regal kingly robe, as naked. We must wear Jesus' righteousness as a garment. When God sees us, we are covered with Jesus' righteousness.

God's mighty Jewish clock stopped seven years short of the 490 years, and God's grace was turned to the Gentiles for their grafting in. The Book of Revelation, written by John, in the New Testament, corroborates the Book of Daniel in the Old Testament. Daniel of the Old Testament times is the key to understanding these New Testament times. After Daniel received the weighty mysteries of these matters, he states in Daniel 12:8, "And I heard, but I understood not: then said I, O my Lord, what shall be the end of these things?" The Lord answered Daniel in 12:9, "And he (The Lord) said, Go thy way, Daniel: for the words are closed up and sealed till the time of the end."

In contrast to Daniel, who was told by Jesus to "seal up" the mysteries, John was told by Jesus in The Revelation to "not seal up" the mysteries. Revelation 22:10, "And he (Jesus) saith unto me (John), Seal not the sayings of the prophecy of this book: for the time is at hand."

We are shown these future events through prophecy, and one must remember pure prophecy is history pre-written! It was written, Jerusalem would be trodden down by the Gentiles and become desolate, then re-gathered and restored, but there is left one week yet to be completed of the prophesied seventy weeks.

Most beautifully clear is the pronouncement of Jesus the Christ and His Gospel of love and grace. Daniel recognized the need of this Savior when he acknowledged the sins of his people. He proclaimed a miracle of reconciliation unto everlasting righteousness would eventually prevail through Jesus Christ.

In a previous chapter, we studied the impact the events of the year 1948 had on the nation of Israel and on the entire world. It is evident that the year 1967 was yet another significant date of utmost importance. These pure and perfect prophecies prove there is no other God other than our Mighty Jehovah God. He is God of all the Israeli armies and will defeat Satan at Armageddon, in his malignant plan to once again try to overthrow God.

The 1948 Arab-Israeli war left the oldest part of Jerusalem known as the "Old City" in ruins. In June of 1967, another military victory for Israel allowed them to regain Jerusalem, long held by the Arabs. Israel, at this vital time, not only began to rebuild their city, but regained access to their holy site, the Wailing Wall. The Six-Day War in 1967 was most significant. Israel became a nation in May of 1948, but it was not until 1967 that Israel gained freedom from Gentile Rule. This was a major victory over all Gentiles. Romans 11:25, "For I would not, brethren, that ye should be ignorant of this mystery, lest ye should be wise in your own conceits; that blindness in part is happened to Israel, until the fullness of the Gentiles be come in."

Truly, the Jews did miss the Messiah through their stiff-necked ways, but the Gentiles have failed Messiah through weak, lukewarm compromise and indifference. Both the Jews and the Gentiles are guilty of misusing the Blood of Jesus! The Jews have denied His deity, and the Gentiles who accepted Jesus as Messiah yet have trodden His Blood underfoot, through willful sin and compromise.

We foresee a time approaching in the near future when we, Jew and Gentile, will all jointly fit together, flourishing in the good Olive Tree. The Jews are God's natural branches, which were cut off for a season. The Gentiles, a wild branch, were only grafted in to make Jew and Gentile one. Israel is now being readied to bud spiritually. Promises, which were once afar off, are now at the door. Matthew 24:32-34, "Now learn a parable of the fig tree; When his branch is yet tender, and putteth forth leaves, ye know that summer is nigh: So likewise ye, when ye shall see all these things, know that it is near, even at the doors. Verily I say unto you, This generation shall not pass, till all these things be fulfilled."

Knowing with certainty, Jesus is coming again and this is the season of His return, we must prepare, for the prophesied events are undoubtedly going to present themselves just as the scriptures have warned! Matthew 24:44, "Therefore be ye also ready: for in such an hour as ye think not the Son of man cometh." Woe to all of us, Jew or Gentile, who do not revere God and take heed to these warnings. Our Omniscient God miraculously revealed to us the interpretation of these ancient hidden mysteries. The living God of Israel, who is the God of all the Israeli Armies, has made known to Daniel, and now to us, their truths. Woe to us if we continue taking our ease, lulled into passivity, living carelessly in our ignorance and obstinate unbelief.

Chapter Fourteen
The Sting

"And the third angel followed them, saying with a loud voice, If any man worship the beast and his image, and receive his mark in his forehead, or in his hand, The same shall drink of the wine of the wrath of God, which is poured out without mixture into the cup of his indignation; and he shall be tormented with fire and brimstone in the presence of the holy angels, and in the presence of the Lamb."

(Revelation 14:9-10)

We've studied prophecy! It has a primary, secondary, and has an ultimate fulfillment. What is past is also prologue; what was, is yet to come. As scripture proves other scripture, prophecy likewise proves other prophecy. It's complex, yet simplistic.

John, the Revelator, describes a man yet to come and he gives mankind warnings. 1 John 2:18, "Little children, it is the last time: and as ye have heard that antichrist shall come, even now are there many antichrists; whereby we know that it is the last time." Satan, as Antichrist, will embody a man who will head up a great and terrible end-time army. There has been an ongoing battle between good and evil since iniquity was found in Lucifer's heart. He exercises maliciousness through pride, self-will, and covetousness. Unequalled in wickedness, Satan has always tried to seduce the souls of mankind. On a massive scale, he will once again attempt to usurp God and procure that which belongs to God. Satan is devious and cunning for he is the master of deceit. Satan is full of subtlety and must delude his followers. If exposed as the shepherd of destruction and death, no one would follow! Careful study of scriptures exposes this evil personage, who will rise up, propagating every facet of his malignant self-will. Cloaked in duplicity and all untruths he will try to outwit man since he cannot outdo our Lord.

Satan's name was Lucifer, which means "light bearer," before he was thrown down from heaven. He misled one-third of heaven's angels in rebellion against God. The angels were also expelled from heaven and to this day are reserved in chains of darkness awaiting the judgment. He was, and is, envious of God and has wickedness in his heart. After his fall from grace, the Lord God then changed his name to "Satan" meaning "destroyer." In Isaiah 14:12, "How art thou fallen from heaven, O Lucifer, son of the morning! how art thou cut down to the ground, which didst weaken the nations!"

Recorded in Isaiah, Satan proclaims his five "I wills." Isaiah 14:13-15, "For thou hast said in thine heart, I will ascend into heaven, I will exalt my throne above the stars of God: I will sit also upon the mount of the congregation, in the sides of north: I will ascend above the heights of the clouds; I will be like the most High. Yet thou shalt be brought down to hell to the sides of the pit." Lucifer, now Satan, presumptuously tries to exalt himself above God and all that is holy. It is Satan's prime desire to be the lone object of worship.

Satan, in the embodiment of the serpent, beguiled Eve into obeying him instead of obeying God. Satan hated Adam and Eve for they fellowshipped, communed, and worshiped the Father God. Because of his complicity, the serpent was cursed. Genesis 3:14, "And the LORD God said unto the serpent, Because thou hast done this, thou art cursed above all cattle, and above every beast of the field; upon thy belly shalt thou go, and dust shalt thou eat all the days of thy life." Mankind also received consequences and curses for disobeying God and obeying Satan. Same chapter verse 23, "Therefore the LORD God sent him forth from the Garden of Eden, to till the ground from whence he was taken." All man's sorrows and woes came into being at this time. Man had been created to live eternally in a heavenly place, enjoying his friendship with God, before Satan, through self-will and lawlessness, introduced sin into the world. The definition of sin is simply disobedience to God's commands. God's Word unmistakably states that one cannot serve two masters! It is clearly a choice. Everyone must decide to follow God, or to follow the Devil. Satan's attempt to overthrow God's authority, and his perverted desire to be commander over mankind, has been ongoing since Lucifer introduced rebellion and lawlessness. Satan emulates God to enhance his abilities to deceive mankind.

There has been a pattern of deception since the dawn of time. Satan led one-third of heaven's angels astray and, through temptation, caused Eve to obey him instead of obeying God. He has always enticed man to do evil exploits. King Herod made a decree at the time of Jesus' birth to have all the babies two years and under killed. God's ways are just and good. Satan's counter plans are wicked and vile. Revelation 12:4, "And his tail drew the third part of the stars (one-third of the angels) of heaven, and did cast them to earth: and the dragon (Satan) stood before the woman (Israel) which was ready to be delivered, for to devour her child (Jesus) as soon as it was born." This was a Satan inspired attempt to destroy God's plan of salvation that would come through Jesus the Christ. Satan also embodied Judas Iscariot, who betrayed Jesus to those who sought to kill the Lord of glory, for thirty pieces of silver. Jesus predicted that Judas was going to betray Him. John 13:21-27, "When Jesus had thus said, he was troubled in spirit, and testified, and said, Verily, verily, I (Jesus) say unto you, that one of you shall betray me. Then the disciples looked one on another, doubting of whom he spake. Now there was leaning on Jesus' bosom (chest) one of his disciples, whom Jesus loved. Simon Peter therefore beckoned to him, that he should ask who it should be of whom he spake. He then lying on Jesus' breast (chest) saith unto him, Lord who is it? Jesus answered, He it is, to whom I shall give a sop (probably unleavened bread dipped in a bitter liquid having great symbolism, used in the Passover Seder), when I have dipped it. And when he (Jesus) had dipped the sop, he gave it to Judas Iscariot, the son of Simon. And after the sop Satan entered into him (Judas). Then said Jesus unto him, That thou doest, do quickly."

God is omniscient, but Satan was confused by this mystery, thus confident he was destroying the Son of God on the Cross of Calvary. In actuality, Jesus was the Lamb of God, a worthy blood sacrifice. Through the shedding of Jesus' pure and holy blood, He bought back the souls of mankind from Satan! Imagine Satan's rage when he realized he had unwittingly played a major part in bringing God's plan of redemption to completion. 1 Corinthians 2:7-8, "But we speak the wisdom of God in a mystery, even the hidden wisdom, which God ordained before the world unto our glory: Which none of the princes of this world knew: for had they known it, they would not have crucified the Lord of Glory." Satan, embodied in Judas, betrayed Jesus unto death. Satan thought he was the victor as Jesus submitted to crucifixion on the Cross of Calvary.

The Hebrew people were the first Monotheists, recognizing and serving the one true Jehovah God. Judaism is the foundation of Christianity. Christians believe and worship the same one and only Jehovah God. Deuteronomy 6:4, "Hear, O Israel: the LORD our God is one LORD." New Testament scripture reference: Colossians 2:9, "For in him (Jesus the Christ) dwelleth all the fullness of the Godhead bodily." The foundation of understanding God is "One" is of paramount importance! Jesus Christ is the flesh and blood of Jehovah God. God's grand plan to redeem mankind back from Satan's snare is that Jesus Christ was "the body" of the one true God of Israel. It was God's own blood that became the supreme sacrifice for the remission of sins. Jehovah is one God, revealed in different names and aspects of His Being. All names encompass personified perfection of solidarity in plurality. Matthew 27:46, "And about the ninth hour Jesus cried with a loud voice, saying, Eli, Eli, lama sabachthani? that is to say, My God, my God, why hast thou forsaken me?" As Jesus cried out on the cross many witnesses mistakenly thought he was calling on, or referring to, Elijah. Jesus was speaking Aramaic and was calling on Elohim, which means God. Elohim is "God" as a plural noun with a singular meaning. Jesus was revealed as God in flesh-and-blood of the Godhead. Plural in the Hebrew or Aramaic language one would add "im," in the English language one would add an "s" to indicate plural. Jesus, as The Christ, was calling on Elohim in the evidenced plurality of His own Being!

Before his rebellion and subsequent expulsion, Satan, as Lucifer, dwelt in heaven. Satan knows and understands monotheism. He once dwelt in heaven and has firsthand knowledge that Jehovah is The One God in Whom all worship and adoration is due. Christians share the Hebrew Monotheistic Truth that Jehovah is one God. Satan has set forth to destroy those who follow God and eliminate God's people. The difference being, Christians understand the mystery of God in Christ! God is TRUTH and Satan is deception! They are in contraposition one to the other. It would be beneficial to Satan if he could wipe both Hebrews and Christians off the map. Satan has purposed to war against, and destroy, those who know the "Truth" and, through deception and fear, mislead the unknowing masses into obedience and eventual worship! Satan hates Christians and the Israeli people.

Under Adolph Hitler's vile regime, Satan's hatred against God's people was evidenced and demonstrated. Evil Hitler was satanically energized in his attempt to eradicate all Jewish people. Hitler was a type and foreshadow of Antichrist who will cause all people to take the mark of the beast. Hitler caused the Jews to wear the symbol of "the star of David" on an armband as a way of identifying them for community control, segregation, and eventual elimination. He caused millions to be murdered in numerous concentration camps situated throughout Europe during World War II. He also ordered the Jews to be tattooed with a number on their forearm. The armbands and the tattoos were a type and foreshadow of "the mark" of the beast, yet in the near future. This proves another example and substantiates Satan's pattern of irreligious hatred towards God's people and God's righteous love and superior plans.

Satan is gathering his forces and is planning an all-out attack against the human race. Satan is planning on killing those who know the "truth" and oppose him. His plan is to steal the souls of the uninformed, unbelieving masses by persuasive powers, trickery, and deceit. The Bible warns us that it will be a time of unrivaled cruelty. Satan is even now in his war room with all his minions plotting out the destruction and misery.

Satan is getting ready for a massive military coup d'état: The Sting! This duplicitous being, full of all guile and subtlety, has engineered a deadly, two-fold plan which, when unleashed and executed, will have both literal and spiritual results.

Webster's Dictionary defines "sting" as both a verb and a noun:

1. To prick painfully with a sharp pointed organ often bearing a poisonous fluid; to affect with a sharp quick pain; to cause to suffer acutely, to feel a keen, burning pain or smart; the thrusting of a stinger in the flesh.

2. An elaborate confidence game-or swindle.

Satan is planning a lethal game of wits. We also know his weaponry is powers of persuasion, deception, trickery, intimidation, and fear with lying signs and wonders. Satan's greatest advantage is that man is uninformed, resulting in a lack of caution and vulnerability. We must purpose in our hearts to guard our immortal souls and ourselves. We must not let Satan swindle us out of eternal salvation by taking "the mark." Once snared, there will be no reprieve. Vigilantly follow Bible scriptures. Leviticus 19:28, "Ye shall not make any cuttings in your flesh for the dead, nor print (tattoo) any marks upon you: I am the LORD." We are NOT to fear, our wondrous God has made a way of escape for those who believe! Satan was defeated; he is even now defeated and will be ultimately defeated! Friends, stand fast in the love and faith of our Lord Jesus Christ.

Prophecy proves prophecy just as scripture proves scripture. That which is past is also prologue. We have established Satan's pattern of warring against God and God's people. In the near future, Satan, as Antichrist, will once again try to deceive mankind into following him. Satan will embody Antichrist, and through his strong persuasive powers and lying wonders, this evil personage will deceive the peoples of the earth and eventually claim to be God and demand worship. Jesus' triumphal appearance at His second coming will overthrow Antichrist and his evil army at the battle of Armageddon.

Despite the Devil's deceitful declarations, he is only a created being, thus he cannot become God. He will closely emulate God, but there will probably be three evil personages on the scene -- an unholy trinity. Revelation 16:13-16, "And I saw three unclean spirits like frogs come out of the mouth of the dragon (Satan as Antichrist), and out of the mouth of the beast (head of economic system), and out of the mouth of the false prophet (who promotes false worship). For they are the spirits of devils, working miracles, which go forth unto the kings of the earth and of the whole world, to gather them to the battle of that great day of God Almighty. Behold, I (Jesus) come as a thief, Blessed is he that watcheth, and keepeth his garments (Jesus' righteousness covers us as a garment), lest he walk naked, and they see his shame (sins revealed and not covered). And he gathered them together into a place called in the Hebrew tongue Armageddon."

Antichrist will lead the New World Order comprised of ten nations or perhaps ten confederated regional unions that will be the last Gentile world power. The word Antichrist comes from the Greek word *anti-christos* meaning against, or instead of, Christ. He will be the last king of the last Gentile world power and therefore will be the last "king" of Gentile World Domination. He will incite hatred against God, and God's people, and all that is holy. He will lead the

Confederated Northern Army, and the whole world, against Israel to the Battle of Armageddon.

The Beast will head up the New World Order's economic system. Revelation chapter 13 reveals, "The Beast" will demand and cause everyone to receive a mark in their hand or on their forehead. It will be a requirement to get food, clothing, medical needs, shelter, or any and all of life's necessities. These supplies will only be distributed, and available, to the ones who have received Satan's mark. His plan is to cause all people to take the mark and by doing so, gain control over mankind. He will present himself as being the much sought-after solution. The contrary is true. The scriptures describe this end-time leader as the culmination of the evil of the ages. I believe this man is on the world scene today and will be a Muslim, or embrace Muslim ideologies. I believe he will be strategically placed in a powerful political position. Possibly this evil powerhouse will emerge from America or the future North American Alliance or Union. Revelation 13:16-18, "And he (the beast, probably, one third of the unholy trinity) causeth all, both small and great, rich and poor, free and bond (prisoners), to receive a mark in their right hand, or in their foreheads: And that no man might buy or sell, save (except) he that have the mark, or the name of the beast, or the number of his name. Here is wisdom. Let him that hath understanding count the number of the beast: for it is the number of a man; and his number is Six hundred threescore and six." Scripture tells us that he who has wisdom let him understand. We should all pray daily for Godly wisdom. Wisdom and understanding are gifts of the Holy Spirit. Could it be that each six is only symbolic or representative of this unholy trinity of men resulting in 6 6 6?

The False Prophet will head up the One-World Religion and propagate the Great Antichrist Spirit. 2 Thessalonians 2:3-12, "Let no man deceive you by any means: for that day (Day of the Lord) shall not come, except there come a falling away first (apostate Christendom), and that man of sin be revealed (Antichrist), the son of perdition; Who opposeth and exalteth himself above all that is called God, or that is worshipped; so that he (Antichrist) as God sitteth in the temple of God, shewing himself (Satan as Antichrist falsely claiming deity) that he is God. Remember ye not, that, when I was yet with you, I told you these things? And now ye know what withholdeth (restraining power) that he (Antichrist) might be revealed in his time. For the mystery of iniquity doth already work:

only he who now letteth (the Holy Ghost is the restraining power) will let (God will allow Antichrist to do his evil), until he (Holy Ghost) be taken out of the way (probably at the time of the rapture of the church). And then (probably immediately after the rapture) shalt that Wicked (capitalized denoting person) be revealed, whom the Lord shall consume with the spirit (Holy Spirit) of his mouth (The Word of God), and shall destroy with the brightness of his (Jesus' powerful appearance) coming (second coming): Even him (Antichrist), whose coming is after the working of Satan with all power and signs and lying wonders, And with all deceivableness of unrighteousness in them that perish (all who follow Satan); because they received not the love of the truth (Jesus is love and truth), that they might be saved. And for this cause God shall send them strong delusion, that they should believe a lie: That they all might be damned who believed not the truth, but had pleasure in unrighteousness."

The scriptures explain that this evil Antichrist spirit of iniquity is <u>already</u> working in the world. The power of the Holy Ghost is holding back these forces of evil until the exact moment God is ready to rapture the church. I believe at that time, the Holy Ghost will be taken back up into heaven with the Blood-Bought Church of the redeemed.

The "Islamic Extremists" thrive on a culture of hate. Their call for a jihad, or "holy war," will bring onto the world stage a merciless militia seeking to gain world power. The prophet Mohammad taught that the greatest blessing is Ishmael's instead of Isaac. Islamic belief transfers the blessings rightfully belonging to Isaac to Ishmael. Factually, Isaac was a type and foreshadow of Christ because Isaac was obedient to his father even when faced with death. Islam is a replacement theology for both Judaism and Christianity. 1 John 4:3, "And every spirit that confesseth not that Jesus Christ is come in the flesh is not of God: and this is that spirit of antichrist, whereof ye have heard that it should come; and even now already is it in the world." I believe the false Prophet will be spawned from this radical Islamic cult, which possesses all the necessary elements of the "great Antichrist spirit," prophesied in the Bible! This Islamic apocalyptic cult hates all Hebrew people and all Christians. They boast anti-Christian philosophy as well as anti-Semitic philosophy. The supreme spiritual leader of Iran, the Ayatollah, currently Ali Khamenei and the current President of Iran, Mahmoud Ahmadinejad project their cryptic ideologies of a jihad (holy war) which will bring about the end of the world. Their belief is that their Messiah, the Mahdi, will only return to earth after the entire world has converted to Islam. Their mantra will be: "Accept Allah or die by the sword." President Ahmadinejad has brazenly proclaimed they will drive Israel into the sea and that the blood of Americans (Christians) will run in the streets of our cities.

The sequence of events is most interesting because the timeframe of the rebuilding of the temple is still obscured. The Jew's Temple was destroyed by Titus in A.D. 70. There are scriptures that indicate <u>Jesus himself</u> will rebuild the Tabernacle at the time of His second coming. Old Testament prophet Amos 9:11, "In that day I (Lord Jesus) will raise up the tabernacle of David that is fallen, and close up the breaches thereof; and I will build it (the new Temple) as in the days of old." Correlating Old Testament prophesies is found in Zechariah 6:12-13, "And speak unto him saying, Thus speaketh the LORD of hosts, saying, Behold, the man whose name is The BRANCH (Jesus); and he shall grow up out of his place, and he (Jesus) shall build the temple of the LORD: Even he (Jesus) shall build the temple of the LORD; and he shall bear the glory, and he shall sit and rule upon his throne; and he shall be a priest upon his throne: and the counsel of peace shall be between them both." New Testament scripture: Acts 15:15-16, "And to this agree the words of the <u>prophets</u>; as it is written, After this I (Lord Jesus) will return (second advent), and will build again the tabernacle of David, which is fallen down; and I will build again the ruins thereof, and I will set it up (the Messianic Kingdom)."

Many believe, and perhaps correctly, that the Jews will rebuild before Christ's return, and it will be in the Jews' rebuilt Temple that Antichrist will enter, and blasphemously demand worship. This is possible. Perhaps war, or an earthquake, will cause the Dome of The Rock Mosque to come down and the Jews would then rebuild their Temple. Perhaps the rebuilding of the Temple will be negotiated as part of a peace agreement between the Arabs and the Jews allowing the Dome of the Rock Mosque to come down. But by other scriptures it does seem possible the Antichrist will enter <u>this</u> Mosque and blasphemously proclaim he (Antichrist) is God and arrogantly demand worship! The Dome of the Rock Mosque at present, sits on the old Jewish Temple site in Jerusalem. Matthew 24:15, "When ye therefore shall see the abomination of desolation, spoken of by

Daniel the prophet, stand in the holy place, (whoso readeth, let him understand.)" The Muslim's Dome of The Rock Mosque was built, and is still situated on, or near the old Temple site in Jerusalem. The previous scripture states that we can have understanding. Could this Mosque be "the abomination of desolation" spoken of by the prophet Daniel? At present it is standing on the holy place, the old Temple site. Mark 13:14, "But when ye shall see the abomination of desolation, spoken of by Daniel the prophet, standing where it ("it" denotes a thing or place rather than a person) ought not, (let him that readeth understand,) then let them that be in Judaea flee to the mountains." It appears that the Dome of The Rock Mosque <u>is an abomination, and it is standing on the Holy site at this present time!</u>

Through Old Testament prophecy, Daniel described the last king of the last Gentile World Dominion. Daniel was mighty in prayer and was given visions pertinent to our day and the end of this age! As we just read, Daniel's prophecy was of such great importance Jesus himself, warned and reiterated this prophecy. Daniel foretold the Antichrist's blasphemous declaration of deity, and that he will present himself to be worshipped. Prophet Daniel also described the ten toes of this last phase of the revived Roman Empire. There is an illustration in chapter thirteen: *The Daniel Determinant*, for reference. Daniel foretold that there would be ten kings to head up these ten countries (perhaps 10 regional alliances or unions) that will forge a union in the near future. They will form an alliance in the last days of this Gentile Age. This confederated empire, foretold by the prophets, will be short in duration. Ten countries (or regional unions) will unite and lead the world into war against Israel in the valley of Megiddo. This federation will be controlled by a supernatural force, which will commit unparalleled atrocities with relentless cruelty. Revelation 9:10, "And they had tails like unto scorpions, and there were stings in their tails: and their power was to hurt men five months." A preceding scripture reveals the origin of these demonic, locust-like creatures, which have stingers in their tails as scorpions. Revelation 9:3, "And there came out of the smoke (from the pit) locusts (Greek: pointed as lightning) upon the earth: and unto them was given power, as the scorpions of the earth have power." Revelation 9:11, "And they had a king over them, which is the angel of the bottomless pit, whose name in the Hebrew tongue is Abaddon, but the Greek tongue hath his name Apollyon." Both names mean "destroyer." Satan's plans for destruction of souls through Antichrist adversely emulates God's perfect plan for salvation of souls through Jesus Christ. Could this possibly be mankind being "marked" or branded, possibly even a subcutaneous microchip implanted under the skin? Though we are unsure of their literal meaning, we know with certainty their deeds and purpose: "to hurt men five months." We know also their leader shall be Antichrist.

Many years ago I was praying in my bedroom and was very much awake; I asked the Lord if it were possible for me to know what the mark of the beast was going to be because I felt in my spirit that Satan was going to deceive people, and that multitudes would receive this mark through deception. 2 Corinthians 2:11, "Lest Satan should get an advantage of us: for we are not ignorant of his devices." Unexpectedly and instantaneously, during my humble, sincere prayer, I was no longer in my bedroom. It was as though I was in a vast dimension with no limitation or boundaries involving space. The limitless space of the heavens opened before me. There appeared two mountains, identical and positioned side by side, quickly the mountains became two men, and just as quickly they merged into one man.

Immediately, the one man was not there, but before me was an imposing figure. The image was supernaturally huge and towering upward into the heavens. My eyes continued moving upward as to take it all in. A similarity of the statue of Liberty was forming in my mind, but as my eyes continued moving skyward I saw this great figure had wondrous wings. It was a stationary figure and my eyes continued to move upward in wonderment. Awestruck, I continued to wonder at this immense and impressive figure. At that time, I was given understanding that I was going to see the mark of the beast! Frightened, I momentarily turned away covering my eyes, I instantly looked back and it was gone. I was in my bedroom and the vision was gone! I felt or had a "knowing" or "understanding" that there was a star. I did not "see" a star, but I had an inner knowledge that there was a star, or stars. I still do not know, to this day, what the mark of the beast is. I have, at many times in my life, researched stars in the Bible and related subjects and scriptures thoroughly in the Hebrew or Greek words even to their root meanings.

New Testament scripture 1 Corinthians 15:41, "There is one glory of the sun, and another glory of the moon, and another glory of the stars: for one star differeth from another star in glory." Jesus, as he was instructing the seventy during His ministry on earth, explained He had witnessed Lucifer's expulsion from heaven when Satan led the rebellion against God. Luke 10:18, "And he (Jesus) said unto them, I beheld Satan as lightning fall from heaven." It is not known for certainty what Lucifer did in heaven. He is described as having "pipes," some believe that he had something to do with music. Could it be that these "pipes" have more to do with oil pipes supplying light? Revelation 8:10-11, "And the third angel sounded, and there fell a great star from heaven, burning as it were a lamp (lit or torch), and it fell upon the third part of the rivers, and upon the fountains of waters; And the name of the star is called Wormwood (capitalized): and the third part of the waters became wormwood (Hebrew root word: to curse, regarding as poisonous and therefore accursed-hemlock, wormwood); and many men died of the waters, because they were made bitter." It is interesting that a third of the angels fell and a third of the waters will be made poisonous. The curse of false doctrines, false teachers, and false leaders are as poisonous to our minds and souls as a serpents' sting. It is also relevant that Jesus Christ is the Fountain of Living Water, the complete opposite of Wormwood! Revelation 7:17, "For the Lamb (Jesus) which is in the midst of the throne shall feed them, and shall lead them unto living fountains of waters: and God shall wipe away all tears from their eyes."

If Lucifer (now Satan) was perhaps a type of light-bringer while in heaven and was perhaps instrumental in worship, it would correlate with his ability to feed men of the earth false doctrines. Genesis 2:1, "Thus the heavens and the earth were finished, and all the host of them." It would appear that this was the time Lucifer and all the angels were created. I believe Satan to be the ancient author of all false doctrines, all false religions, all heathen deities, and this would correlate and substantiate his desire to be worshipped. Satan, from the beginning, has misinformed, misrepresented, and misdirected angels and mankind. He did not succeed in heaven, and he will not succeed here on earth. He has been the author of confusion and, stemming from envy and pride, has infringed into God's domain and God's authority. Trying to appear benign, Satan insinuates sin and the consequences of sin as non-consequential. His schemes are always subtle, and have deadly, devastating results. I believe, once again, he is going to pull off "The Sting" of the ages and try to swindle mankind out of their immortal souls. Satan cannot be wholly responsible; men have played a part, just as Adam and Eve played a part and made a decision to yield to temptation, instead of remaining faithful and obedient to God Almighty.

Mankind has a proclivity to sin and is inclined to be self-willed. Amos 5:25-27, "Have ye offered unto me sacrifices and offerings in the wilderness forty years, O house of Israel? But ye have borne the tabernacle of your Moloch and Chiun your images, the star of your god, which ye have made to yourselves. Therefore will I cause you to go into captivity beyond Damascus, saith the LORD, whose name is The God of hosts." The scripture in Genesis 2:1 suggests that at the time Lucifer was created, he was among the hosts of heaven, and possibly <u>was</u> the host of heaven, but God was, and is, the <u>God of the hosts of heaven</u>. Jehovah God warns Judah also through yet another Old Testament prophet. Zephaniah 1:4-7, "I will also stretch out my hand upon Judah and upon all the inhabitants of Jerusalem; and I cut off the remnant of Baal from this place, and the name of the Chemarims (idolatrous priests) with the priests; And them that worship <u>the host of heaven</u> upon housetops; and them that worship and that swear by the Lord, and that swear by Malcham (Molech, Moloch, or Malcham--all same false god); And them that are turned back from the Lord; and those who have not sought the Lord, nor enquired of him. Hold thy peace at the presence of the Lord God: for the day of the Lord is at hand: for the Lord hath prepared a sacrifice (Jesus's Blood: The Sacrificial Lamb of God), he hath bid his guests." These are serious end-time warnings for every man is responsible and accountable for his own soul. Amos chapter 5:14-15, "Seek good, and not evil, that ye may live: and so the LORD, the God of hosts, shall be with you, as ye have spoken. Hate the evil, and love the good, and establish judgment in the gate: it may be that the LORD God of hosts will be gracious unto the remnant of Joseph." Since Israel's great offense was taking up the star, symbolic of a false god, one must diligently search for truth, for all truth is parallel and imperative to life. While researching the Hebrew word Moloch: (king) the chief deity of the Amorites--primitive root to reign, to ascend to a throne, rule, set up to; and the Hebrew word: Chiun, a statue, idol by euphemism (substitution) for some heathen deity, corresponding to Priapus or Baal-peor, gave me great insight. This was such a great offense to God that it was reiterated in the New Testament. Acts 7:42-43, "Then God turned, and gave them (Hebrews) up to worship the host of heaven; as it is written in the book of the prophets, O ye house of Israel, have ye offered to me slain beasts and sacrifices by the space of forty years in the wilderness? Yea, ye took up the tabernacle of Moloch and <u>the star of your god Remphan,</u> figures which ye made to worship them: and I will carry you away beyond Babylon." Remphan, in Hebrew, is a statue or idol, a euphemism (a substitution) for some heathen deity and corresponding Priapus or Baal-peor. Baal is a Phoenician deity meaning master, owner, lord, or to have dominion over. One of Satan's chief endeavors is to be Lord over mankind. From Baal we get Beelzebub, a name derived from Baalzebub which literally means "Lord of the Flies." How fitting that is; Satan, Lord of the Flies.

What is the "star of their false god Remphan or Moloch" that the Israelites took up, as spoken of in the Book of Amos, chapter 5:26? If this isn't known, one must diligently seek and search truth. By blindly following tradition, one might fall prey to Satan's plan. Matthew 24:24, "For there shall arise false Christs, and false prophets, and shall shew great signs and wonders; insomuch that, if it were possible, they shall deceive the very elect." The Jewish people are God's elect. The Star of David is lauded as a holy symbol. Could it, in actuality, be the symbol of the false god Remphan? Since we do not "know" what the actual mark will be, we must all pray for discernment concerning all the mysteries of the Bible.

What the actual "mark" is still remains obscured. It's possible this mark could be a literal 666. Pertinent data on a microchip can now be implanted under the skin to be instantly evaluated by a scanner. Could it be a mark, tattoo, social security number, or symbol of esteemed significance that people would freely welcome and receive? For example, could it possibly be a symbol regarded as spiritual and patriotic, lauded and accepted by man as holy? We must NEVER take any mark on our forehead or in our hand, or have any type of microchip implanted. We know Satan is full of deceit and trickery; he is going to try and pull off "The Sting" of the ages in an attempt to procure the souls of men. One must not "blindly" follow ancient tradition. Everyone must pray and diligently seek answers to one of the mysteries of the ages! Prayerfully consider the Hebrew emblem, called the Star of David. What is its origin? If we are not sure-Pray!

2 Peter 1:19-21, "We have also a more sure word of prophecy; whereunto ye do well that ye take heed, as unto a light that shineth in

a dark place, until the day dawn, and the day star (Jesus) arise in your hearts: Knowing this first, that no prophecy of the scripture is of any private interpretation. For the prophecy came not in old time by the will of man: but holy men of God spake as they were moved by the Holy Ghost." Let's turn our attention once again to the demonic, end-time army. Revelation 9:10, "... and there were stings in their tails: and their power was to hurt men five months."

The "mark of the beast" will have meaning of both literal and spiritual significance. This "star" mentioned in Amos in the Hebrew language means, "sense of blazing;" figuratively, a prince stargazer; a primitive root to prick or penetrate, hence to blister (as a smarting or eating into) as to burn, as a branding or burning, such as a tattoo. A "tattoo" is a burning or a wounding, as to penetrate or burn into flesh. It is a literal type of "branding."

When we accept Jesus Christ as our Lord and Savior and are baptized, we are sealed unto the day of redemption with the Holy Spirit of Promise. It is an invisible yet all-powerful, all-encompassing, absolute shield. In dire contrast, if one should accept the mark of the beast, that one would be forever lost--beyond redemption. Revelation 14:9-12, "And the third angel followed them, saying with a loud voice, If any man worship the beast and his image, and receive his mark in his forehead, or in his hand, The same shall drink of the wine of the wrath of God, which is poured out without mixture (undiluted) into the cup of his indignation; and he shall be tormented with fire and brimstone in the presence of the holy angels, and in the presence of the Lamb: And the smoke of their torment ascendeth up for ever and ever: and they have no rest day nor night, who worship the beast and his image, and whosoever receiveth the mark of his name. Here is the patience of the saints: here are they that keep the commandments of God, and the faith of Jesus."

When Antichrist presents himself on the world-scene, Satan will be ready with his mark to brand upon the unbelieving, uninformed, and complacent masses. It will be a time of unrivaled fiery trials because all will be lost or taken away. Gone will be physical comforts, worldly securities, jobs, shelter, and food. Let no need, no, not even for the saving of your own life, seduce you into receiving the mark. Revelation 13:17, "And that no man might buy or sell, save he that had the mark ..." Obtaining mortal needs in exchange for our immortal souls is the ultimate "Sting!" Revelation

19:20, "And the beast was taken, and with him the false prophet that wrought miracles before him, with which he deceived them that had received the mark of the beast, and them that worshipped his image. These both were cast alive into a lake of fire burning with brimstone."

<u>Nothing</u> is worth being excluded for all eternity from the presence of our Creator, the Heavenly Father, and being cast into the fires of hell - <u>forever!</u>

John, the Apostle, reveals in Revelation 20:4, "And I (John) saw thrones, and they sat upon them, and judgment was given unto them: and I saw the souls of them that were beheaded for the witness of Jesus, and for the word of God, and which had <u>not</u> worshipped the beast, neither his image, neither had received his mark upon their foreheads, or in their hands; and they lived and reigned with Christ a thousand years."

Serious, dedicated study shows the diversity of these two spiritual entities. "Jesus Christ the Righteous," is the full embodiment of all that is pure and holy. "Satan the Destroyer," is the epitome of evil. This is a remarkable portrayal of "absolutes"--good versus evil.

An apocalyptic view of Satan's final doom is declared in Isaiah 14:15-16, "Yet thou shalt be brought down to hell, to the sides of the pit (a sharp contrast to his five "<u>I wills</u>"). They that see thee shall narrowly look upon thee, and consider thee, saying, Is this the man that made the earth to tremble, that did shake kingdoms." Our God is always true to His word. God has ordained that He is going to confine Satan in the bottomless pit for the one-thousand-year reign of Jesus Christ from Jerusalem.

Satan, the interloper, is a wily substitute for Jesus The Christ. Satan is the Prince of Darkness, symbolized by the wormwood and the gall. He only begets misery and his ways lead to destruction and death. In contraposition, we have Jesus The Messiah who will be the light of the Holy City, New Jerusalem and His ways lead to everlasting life. Revelation 21:6, "And he said unto me, It is done. I am Alpha and Omega, the beginning and the end. I will give unto him that is athirst of the fountain of water of life freely."

Chapter Fifteen

The Black Horse and Rider

And when he had opened the third seal, I heard the third beast say, Come and see. And I beheld, and lo a black horse; and he that sat on him had a pair of balances in his hand."

(Revelation 6:5)

In the mid-1970s I was given a night vision from God. In the vision, I was standing in the middle of a broad, wide street at the integral part of the intersecting of three streets. It was a very large progressive American city. Suddenly, I heard behind me loud crashing and crushing sounds and a great disturbance. I instantly turned to determine the cause of the commotion. I was astounded for there was an enormous black horse and rider crushing cars and trucks and everything in its direct path. People were running and screaming, terrified as they perished beneath the horses' purposeful galloping and unimpeded strides. It was a supernatural destructive force encompassing an immense, vast swath. In its wake it left everything trampled and demolished. It was so large and powerful; in its path all things were diminished in size and became subject to certain death and annihilation. It crushed everything in its straightforward, oncoming path and without effort! It was nearing the intersection in which I stood amazed and transfixed by the sight of this phenomenal black horse and rider. I was in its direct path, but I was not in fear, just absorbing this awesome sight that was rapidly approaching the place where I stood. Its hoofbeats sounded as thunder as it approached where I was standing, it shied and took smaller steps, dancing sideways as a spirited horse will often do. I looked up to try and take in all of its magnificence. The horse had a definite beauty that should have been a contradiction, because its mission was one of destruction and death, but it was truly a frighteningly beautiful sight. The horse that was now before me shied and danced sideways, its gait slowed and it paused, but its feet never stilled. The horse and rider were of such immense proportions that I had to look up in an effort to take in the sight before my eyes, for the horse's underbelly was exceedingly high, far above my head. The horse and rider were both formed of the same substance, and both were all black in color. Their outward appearance was of a substance that I cannot explain. They were both made of a type of iron or metal, an indestructible, impenetrable substance, yet they appeared to be perfect in proportion and the movement was perfection and naturally fluid. They were of supernatural proportions, and possessed supernatural capabilities. The sight was fierce and I was awestruck. In another split-second they were gone.

Simultaneously, I turned as my attention was drawn in another direction. A woman of mid-life age was wearing a modest dress and was standing at a gasoline pump; aggravated because the man attending the gasoline station would not accept her five-dollar bill. He had a pen-like object in his hand that had a light on the end of this object. At the woman's frustration and insistence, the attendant once again ran this object across the five-dollar bill end-to-end, or lengthwise. It reminded me of a pencil or a pen that had a small light on the end. In my mind, I referred to this object as a "zipper" because as he quickly ran it across the money, it appeared that the light just "zipped" over the U.S. currency made of paper. At the conclusion of this second try, the man handed the woman back her money; the woman's financial transaction was unacceptable to the man.

At that moment I turned, as once again, my attention was drawn in another direction. There, before me was a church. It was a medium sized structure, white in color, and possessed white columns across the entire front. Immediately, an oblong shape started to become visible across the top front of the church building. It was as if twinkling and flashing lights of a theater marquee were manifesting to create the outside framework of a sign. Then letters started appearing that were being formed out of the same supernatural lights. I thought, in my natural mind, the letters were going to reveal the name of the church of God's choosing, but as the beautiful flashing bright and sparkling letters appeared, it was a message of instruction to the church. The supernatural sparkling letters formed two words: *Friends Study*.

It would be several decades later, that I understood the black horse and rider represented judgment. Judgment is an unwelcome and largely unaccepted message. It brings to mind the old adage of a king who had the messenger boy killed because the king did not like the content of the message that the boy simply delivered.

I had, for many years, held to a vague and erroneous ideology that the black horse and rider of Revelation, and of my night vision, was representative of an agent crying for equality. The rider on the black horse carries a balancing scale and this predetermined view seemed logical.

On September 11, 2001, I was driving my daily 35-40 minute commute to work. It was my usual custom to pray during this early morning drive. My prayer language, or gift of tongues, is a large part of my daily prayers, appreciation-worship of God, and prayers of intercession for others. The gift of tongues is the Holy Spirit of God that dwells within the yielded believer praying directly to God on high. Our omnipresent God sent down to mere man the working-operational force of God, to aid and fortify believers. The indwelling of the Holy Ghost is a very necessary and central part of our Christian service to God.

On this fateful September morning, I was alone in my car and praying out loud when a powerful Godly warfare Spirit rose up in me. In the forty years of praying in the Spirit I had never experienced such a powerful, strong, warring force. My natural body could hardly contain the power and strength of this warring Spirit! It was a spirit of combat! I wondered in my natural mind what was going on in the Spiritual realm. Shortly before 8:30 am I clocked in and hurried into work. At approximately 8:45 am I was in an inner office with about ten other people and we heard "awes" of exclamations emanating from the larger outer office that was equipped with a television. The supervisor went out to inquire what was happening and soon solemnly returned. He briefly stated a plane had hit one of the Twin Towers of The World Trade Center. Approximately 15 minutes later, we once again heard the gasps of those in the larger outer office; the supervisor again went out for an update. He again returned, obviously shaken by the subsequent event, and announced a second plane hit the second of the Twin Towers. We all sat in silence a moment just trying to absorb the devastating soul-shaking news. I instantly knew this was the origin of the unusual warring intercession of Spiritual combat I had experienced approximately 45 minutes earlier while driving to work in my car.

I knew the supervisor was a retired military man, and I felt confident that he was a knowledgeable source for inquiry. I asked, "You are a military man; is there any way this could have happened accidentally?" He solemnly answered, "No, this could not have been an accident." It was announced that the office would be closed for the day and we could leave. At home, I sat watching the unfolding horror that was being televised, through live feed, from New York City. The third plane crashed into The Pentagon, which is the seat of our military headquarters. The fourth plane's target is believed to have been the White House in Washington D.C., but crashed into a field in Pennsylvania as the heroic passengers thwarted the evil plans of the plane's hijackers. I became heart-sick at the similarities of the destruction I was witnessing, via television, that were taking place, and the destruction that I had been shown in the night vision, many years past. It is not a popular assertion, but I know, and now understand, that the black horse and rider represent judgment.

In light of this, an initial judgment was visited upon America. I realize thousands of innocent people were hideously murdered that tragic day by ungodly terrorists! It breaks my heart to convey this message. Mankind abandons and blames our merciful God; accusing God of injustices, not understanding it is not God who is responsible for judgment being visited on man, but sinful man. Un-repented sin must be judged. Sin's issue is destruction. Sin is the cause of all heartaches, woes, and man's miseries. The Bible instructs us to submit to a Godly, Spiritual self-examination or "self-judgment" so we can escape harsher future judgments. 1 Corinthians 11:31-32, "For if we would judge ourselves, we should not be judged. But when we are judged, we are chastened (corrected) of the Lord, that we should not be condemned with the world." I know in my Spirit God has great sorrow because America has become so wicked and perverse.

The Pilgrims, who founded America in 1620, made a radical departure from the Church of England; their goal was to purify the church, not to renounce it. These brave men founded America on righteous principles of purity, and established standards pleasing to our Holy God and the propagation of the Gospel of Jesus Christ. God blessed America and strengthened it because of this righteous Judeo-

Christian foundation. I believe God foreordained and prospered America to be a future defender of Israel. Sadly, and to our detriment, America is failing to properly aide Israel.

Moral decline in America has plummeted in recent decades and we are spiritually and morally deficient. 2 Samuel 7:14, "I will be his father, and he shall be my son. If he commits iniquity, I will chasten him with the rod of men, and with the stripes of the children of men." Just as a just father corrects an errant son, our heavenly Father corrects those He loves. Judgment being visited upon mankind is not the fault of God, but mankind, we being sinful. During Jesus' ministry here on earth, He was presented with a similar inquiry concerning two separate incidences that occurred during that timeframe. He was asked that if those who were killed were greater sinners and Jesus answered, absolutely not, but to avoid judgment men must repent. Luke 13:1-5, "There were present at that season some that told him of the Galilaeans, whose blood Pilate had mingled with their sacrifices. And Jesus answering said unto them, Suppose ye that these Galilaeans were sinners above all the Galilaeans, because they suffered such things? I tell you, Nay (no, not so): but, except ye repent, ye shall all likewise perish. Or those eighteen, upon whom the tower in Siloam fell, and slew (killed) them, think ye that they were sinners above all men that dwelt in Jerusalem? I (Jesus) tell you, Nay (not so): but, except ye repent, ye shall all likewise perish."

The sins, or shortcomings, of the Americans who died on September 11, 2001, in the four separate terrorist attacks, did not exceed those of any other American citizens. Many were in fact, commendable and exemplary people. While en-route to Washington D.C., a handful of heroic passengers aboard the fourth hijacked plane diverted the plane from the White House (which is believed to have been the hijacker's intended target) and the plane was crashed into a field in Pennsylvania. These must be credited with saving many other American lives, and as defenders of the White House. These are to be lauded as heroes for they thwarted the efforts of the evil Al-Qaeda operatives.

America must have repentance and revival, turning back to the foundation of Godly principles before widespread, unrestrained catastrophic judgments are unleashed upon us. One cannot be angry with our righteous God, for He is long-suffering that none should perish but that all come to the saving knowledge of Jesus Christ. Old

Testament prophet Habakkuk was bowed low by the knowledge that God allowed wicked men to prosper. God showed Habakkuk that He was going to allow the wicked Chaldeans to be used as a chastisement rod, or as a means of correction against Judah. Habakkuk 1:12-13, "Art thou not from everlasting O, LORD my God, mine Holy One? we shall not die. O LORD, thou hast ordained them for judgment; and, O mighty God, thou hast established them for correction. Thou (God) art of purer eyes than to behold evil, and canst not look on iniquity: wherefore lookest thou upon them that deal treacherously, and holdest thy tongue when the wicked devoureth the man that is more righteous than he?" Just as in Habakkuk's day, wicked, evil men took these innocent lives from us. Heartless beasts carried out these murders and unthinkable cruelties while full of vile hatred against the United States and Israel. Old Testament prophet Habakkuk sincerely sought God. He wondered why the evil Chaldeans were successful in their wickedness against Israel. God's unchanging, and consistent ways of dealing with His people are set and foundational. God has established from old, His righteous decrees and oversees their completion and accomplishments.

Scripture proves scripture. Old Testament Prophet Isaiah was shown the doom of Babylon at the hands of the Medes. In Isaiah 13:17-19, "Behold, I (God) will stir up the Medes against them, which shall not regard silver; and as for gold, they shall not delight in it. Their bows shall also dash the young men to pieces; and they shall have no pity on the fruit of the womb (babies); their eye shall not spare children. And Babylon, the glory of kingdoms, the beauty of the Chaldees' excellency, shall be as when God overthrew Sodom and Gomorrah." The prophet Isaiah was shown, and understood, that judgment of Babylon was for that time period, but was also a foreshadow of the totality, even to the completion of the Gentile world power or dominion, that extends to this very day. This began with King Nebuchadnezzar and will end with Jesus Christ as the Smiting Stone (as in the king's dream) when Jesus returns to earth to set up His millennial reign. Luke 21:24, "And they shall fall by the edge of the sword, and shall be led away captive into all nations: and Jerusalem shall be trodden down of the Gentiles, until the times of the Gentiles be fulfilled." Judgment is visited upon a nation when they have been warned time and time again, yet have failed to heed God's warnings.

We, in America, must repent and turn back to the Godly principles our great country was founded upon. This radical Islamic Jihadist Cult has set forth to destroy America and our people. The September 2001 attack involved 19 terrorists, and was a marker of the beginning of our economic crisis in America, and should serve as a wakeup call. Many Americans have turned to the false god of mammon, or wealth. Sadly, America has become greedy and corrupt, focusing on material gain, position, and personal power. God and civility has taken a back seat to entertainment and worldly pleasures! We have become thoroughly corrupt, forgetting God our creator, and forgetting it was He who caused our nation to become great. It is also a message of warning that this once great nation must turn back to God and the Godly principles on which it was founded. I believe this vicious attack serves as an ominous foreshadow of coming future judgments to America by vile, evil men. Revelation 6:5-6, "And when he had opened the third seal, I heard the third beast say, Come and see. And I beheld, and lo a black horse; and he that sat on him had a pair of balances (scales) in his hand. And I heard a voice in the midst of the four beasts say, A measure of wheat for a penny, and three measures of barley for a penny; and see thou hurt not the oil and the wine."

The destruction of the twin towers of The World Trade Center acted as a gateway for the start of the decline of America's economy. The World Trade Center was a symbol of America's prosperity. The New York Stock Exchange temporarily suspended trading, and the future of our economy became as cloudy as the haze covering New York City's area of destruction. The Pentagon is headquarters of our U.S. Military, and is symbolic of our military might. The White House is where The United States President resides while in office, and is symbolic of the American people! My heart grieves for the loss of all the innocent lives of women, children, and good men lost on that grievous day in September. One needs to learn the heart of God. He is a God of love, but He is a well-balanced Holy God, and abhors sin. Through His unfathomable love, He satisfied His wrath and judgment and applied the penalty of sin to Jesus Christ in our stead at Calvary.

The time of the Gentiles is rapidly drawing to a close. Everyone should avail oneself to the eternal security through Jesus Christ the Righteous, before the door of this present Gentile dispensation closes, and the last seven years of great tribulation begins. This invitation of salvation includes both Jew and Gentile. This great and loving plan does not exclude the Muslims. The Muslims make up a large part of the Gentile Nations. The invitation of forgiveness of sins through Lord Jesus' redemptive blood was offered once, for all. His love and concern for mankind is foundational for the tender mercies offered to whosoever will believe. The Qur'an mentions "Jesus the son of Mary and His many miracles." But be warned, the Qur'an does not give an accurate account of Jesus, or an accurate account of the events of His return. It denigrates His deity and contains gross misrepresentations of Jesus' truths! Jesus' love, His plan of eternal salvation for souls, and His miracles are available to all people everywhere who are in search of, and accepting of, Truth!

The next portion of the vision pertains to the end of our United States currency, or bartering system, as we know it. We are being propelled into a one-world monetary system. Years later, I would see for the first time an electronic scanner. Today, scanners are commonly used in most stores and places of business. An electronic scanner was the device the station attendant slid, or zipped, across the U.S. currency I was shown in my night vision. An electronic scanner is what I, in my ignorance, referred to as a zipper. I was using an adjective to describe a noun, because I was trying to explain the object by what it did. To my knowledge, the scanner had not been invented at that time in history. Perhaps, yet future, the scanner will also be used to scan and recover pertinent data contained in a subcutaneous microchip implanted under the skin of our hands or foreheads (the Mark of the Beast) perhaps for civil control, and will be mandatory to buy or sell after the New One-World currency has come into place. Revelation 13:17, "And that no man might buy or sell, save (except) he that had the mark, or the name of the beast, or the number of his name." One must never trade ones' eternal soul to purchase a temporal need!

The third part of my night vision is "a commission" which reveals the very heart and nature of our loving and merciful God. God does not want His people to be lacking any good thing. The preeminent advice to anyone is to study God's Word for oneself. 2 Timothy 2:15, "Study to shew thyself approved unto God, a workman that needeth not to be ashamed, rightly dividing the word of truth."

The Word is a lamp unto our feet, and the supernatural marquee theater lights encompassing the phrase *FRIENDS STUDY* seemed peculiar forty years ago. Today we are witnessing an end-time phenomenon best described as, Cultural Evangelism. A new venue of faith-based movies and videos influence millions of people, not only in America, but around the world. Matt and Laurie Crouch have been instrumental in the promotion of this genre of Christian based movies that emphasize positive faith building messages on "the Silver Screen." It is inspirational to see movie stars take a stance and use their talent to glorify the Lord. Mel Gibson's movie *The Passion of The Christ* was awe-inspiring. Mr. Gibson came under extreme criticism, concerning the movie, but I feel this great work fulfilled a God ordained call on his life. I personally think it to be an excellent film. It was said, among other things, that the film was too graphic as it detailed Jesus' agony while being beaten and bloodied as He was lashed with a whip, and graphically portrayed his subsequent, merciless crucifixion on the cross. Truth being, we could never duplicate or reenact the untold sufferings Jesus submitted Himself to for our sakes, and in our stead. John 15:13-15, "Greater love hath no man than this, that a man lay down his life for his friends. Ye are my friends, if ye do whatsoever I command you. Henceforth I (JESUS) call you not servants; for the servant knoweth not what his lord doeth: but I have called you friends; for all things that I have heard of my Father I have made known unto you."

Abraham's exemplary faith in God was recorded in the Old Testament book of Genesis. God and Abraham's faith-based friendship was reiterated in the New Testament. James 2:23, "And the scripture was fulfilled which saith, Abraham believed God, and it was imputed unto him for righteousness: and he was called the Friend of God." Jesus desires to be your personal friend and there are nine Spiritual gifts (recap in chapter ten: *Fishers of Men*) that He desires to impart to believers through faith. Another wonderful scripture is recorded in 2 Timothy 3:16-17, "All scripture is given by inspiration of God, and is profitable for doctrine, for reproof, for correction, for instruction in righteousness: That the man of God may be perfect, thoroughly furnished unto all good works." Continuing in 2 Timothy 4:1, "I charge thee therefore before God, and the Lord Jesus Christ, who shall judge the quick (alive) and the dead at his (Jesus') appearing and his kingdom (millennial reign)."

God is warning all of the manifold judgments coming to the earth. He is bidding all to seek shelter and everlasting life in The Blood of The Covenant. I believe the judgments have already begun.

Revelation chapter six, reveals Jesus as the Lamb, and these scriptures describe the seven sealed judgments coming to the earth. The first four of these judgments are presented as the Four Horsemen of the Apocalypse and forewarns of the horrendous world events that accompany these riders. The first: The White Horse; represents the emergence of the Antichrist. I believe this man of sin is already on the world scene today, but he will not be revealed in his true identity, as the willful king (he will try to usurp Jesus' throne), until the rapture of the Church. The Second: The Red Horse; representing "Gentile" war. This war, will be unrivaled in cruelty, and will result in the end of the Gentile World Power. The Third: The Black Horse; represents future economic judgments, eventually resulting in a world famine. The terrorist attack, on September 11, 2001, was the catalyst that started the U.S. economic decline that will end in a total and complete economic collapse not just in America, but for the world economies. The Fourth: The Pale Horse; represents death, and hell will follow. These fiery trials are foreordained for the unbeliever, and will be unprecedented in World and Biblical history. I believe we are in a transitional period that the Bible refers to as "the beginning of sorrows." If we were driving a car to the mountains we aren't just "BAM" in the mountains. It is a gradual progression because outlying the mountains are the foothills. It is difficult to determine when one has actually started into the foothills because it is a slow continuing progression; so it is with determining "the beginning of" these end-time judgments or "sorrows."

To the benefit of all, both Jew and Gentile, Jesus stood before "the judgment seat" in our stead. His unfathomable sufferings, sacrificial death, and triumphal resurrection from the dead, offers all men everywhere the opportunity of eternal salvation and safety. He made a way of escape for all who believe. Jesus is our ever-present friend, the defender of the faith, and our personal bravery!

Chapter Sixteen
Day of Preparation

"But, beloved, be not ignorant of this one thing, that one day is with the Lord as a thousand years, and a thousand years as one day."

(2 Peter 3:8)

In Genesis 1:1-5, "In the beginning God created the heaven and the earth. And the earth was without form, and void; and darkness was upon the face of the deep. And the Spirit of God (the Holy Spirit is the working-power force of our God, who has a triune nature), moved upon the face of the waters. And God said, Let there be light: and there was light. And God saw the light, that it was good: and God divided the light from the darkness. And God called the light Day, and the darkness he called Night. And the evening and the morning were the first day." Verse 14, "And God said, Let there be lights in the firmament of the heaven to divide the day from the night; and let them be for signs, and for seasons, and for days, and years." 2:1-4, "Thus the heavens and the earth were finished, and all the host of them. And on the seventh day God ended his work which he had made; and he rested on the seventh day from all his work which he had made. And God blessed the seventh day, and sanctified it: because that in it he had rested from all his work which God created and made. These are the generations of the heavens and of the earth when they were created, in the day that the LORD God made the earth and the heavens."

In the beginning of this current age, and recorded in our Bible, God re-instituted the use of the earth, sun, moon, and stars as explained in Genesis 1:14-19. There is no discrepancy in God's Word. In a previous beginning God had made the earth, sun, moon, and stars. In "our beginning," as recorded in Genesis 1:1-2, the earth was, for reasons known only to God, without form and was void. It had been covered with water and obscured by darkness, which was upon the waters (deep), substantiated by artifacts and fossils, which are found over many parts of our present world. This proves there were different types of prehistoric peoples (pre-Adamic, not our ancestors) and great animals (now extinct), on this earth, before we were created.

As we read in Genesis chapter one, we see God reshaping the existing earth as we know it, as a new creation for man and animals. We are Adamic man created by God in His own image. Adam was the first human being fashioned after the likeness of our Creator God. If there are questions concerning anything pertaining to the Bible, there is no error with God, or His Word. The fault lies within our own understanding. Man's wisdom is foolishness to God. Some scientists and scholars are confounded by their own wisdom. 1 Corinthians 3:19, "For the wisdom of this world is foolishness with God. For it is written, He taketh the wise in their own craftiness." Man cannot limit God to our own meager understanding, or our ceaseless misinterpretations, because God's limitless abilities and knowledge are immeasurable.

God is fair and just. He honors the order which He set up. After He created the earth, He rested on His seventh (Sabbath) day. On the principle of a seven-thousand-year week, we are preparing for another Sabbath Millennium.

Describing, through symbolism, four dispensations; the first three are representative of two-thousand-year periods, totaling six thousand years and the fourth is representative of a one-thousand-year period, or God's seventh day of Millennial Sabbath Rest--yet future.

1. The Father: "WATER"--Cleansing as related to washing by the word of God. Ultimately the literal flood of water was used to cleanse the world of wickedness and end the first dispensation.

2. The Son: "BLOOD"--Sacrifices of animal's blood for covering of sin, culminating with Jesus' ultimate atoning Blood sacrifice, once for all, because Jesus

was The Sacrificial Lamb of God. Jesus' physical death ended the second dispensation.

3. The Holy Spirit: "FIRE"--The Holy Spirit is evidence of God's divine presence on earth these last two thousand years. Our God chose to tabernacle with man through the indwelling Holy Ghost. When the Holy Ghost descended onto mankind, the event was evidenced as tongues of fire. He is God's earthly cleansing agent, or righteous representative, and abides within us. Literal fires will cleanse the earth of wickedness, at the end of this dispensation.

4. King of Kings and Lord of Lords: "PEACE"--God's day of rest will be a one-thousand-year period of peace, yet future. Jesus Christ, the flesh-and-blood body of God, will be revealed as The Lion of the Tribe of Judah. It is God's Sabbath Day of Rest, and He will rule and reign with peace; sitting on the throne of David from Jerusalem. The Lion will indeed lay down with The Lamb!

It is then, that Jesus Christ will set up His kingdom on earth. Zechariah 14:9, "And the LORD shall be king over all the earth: in that day shall there be one LORD, and his name one." Once again, in this scripture, we have yet another example of the interchange of a solar day for God's millennial day.

With the help of the following chart, God's great timetable presents another example of God's consistent ways of measure. God understands our human limitations and the shortness of mortal life. To help us comprehend, God scaled down His own big calendar using a thousand-year-day to one of our twenty-four hour solar days.

DISPENSATIONS COVERING SEVEN THOUSAND YEARS

FATHER	SON	HOLY SPIRIT	LORD
THE LORD	JESUS	CHRIST	LORD OF THE SABBATH MILLENNIUM
WATER	BLOOD	FIRE	PEACE
FIRST DAY / SECOND DAY	THIRD DAY / FOURTH DAY	FIFTH DAY / SIXTH DAY	SEVENTH DAY
TWO THOUSAND YEARS	TWO THOUSAND YEARS	TWO THOUSAND YEARS	ONE THOUS. YEARS

Arrows/events along the top:
- THE FLOOD; NOAH'S ARK
- THE CROSS; CHRIST'S DEATH
- SECOND COMING OF CHRIST AS KING JESUS

2 Peter 3:8, "But, beloved, be not ignorant of this one thing, that one day is with the Lord as a thousand years, and a thousand years as one day." Approximately six thousand years have passed since God reestablished the earth, and we, who are alive today, are to understand that God is preparing for His millennial rest! Continuing on in 2 Peter 3:9, "The Lord is not slack concerning his promise, as some men count slackness; but is long suffering to us-ward, not willing that any should perish, but that all should come to repentance." The times for the sun and the moon, the night and day are part of God's order and decree. He has provided us with boundaries for the land and even the times for the tides for His vast seas! God has a set time for the completion of this Church age in which we live today. He will accomplish what He has decreed!

Hosea 6:2, "After two days will he revive us: in the third day he will raise us up, and we shall live in his sight." Understanding is amplified through the prophet Hosea's writings. The progression of time, as shown on the preceding chart, substantiates God's pattern of one-thousand-year days. Jesus' plan of salvation has been available to mankind for two thousand years, or God's fifth and sixth millennial days. The approaching day will be God's seventh millennial day of rest. We will live in Jesus' sight during His one-thousand-year reign on earth, on the throne of David, in Jerusalem.

Revelation 20:6, "Blessed and holy is he that hath part in the first resurrection: on such the second death hath no power, but they shall be priests of God and of Christ, and shall reign with him (Jesus) a thousand years." The word "millennium" is a Latin word, which means "thousand." The world will go into great tribulation for seven years, the likes of which has never been on the earth before, and will never be on the earth again. This great tribulation period is imminent. It will be at the completion of the sixth thousand-year-day, preceding the millennial day of God's rest.

At the end of the seven years of tribulation, Jesus will appear again at His second coming. He will set His feet down upon the Mount of Olives at the spot from which He ascended up into heaven. He will establish His kingdom on earth, after this earth has been cleansed by fire.

There have been three dispensations, consisting of two thousand years in each dispensation. The first, God cleansed the earth with water, by the flood. Noah, and seven family members were saved. The second two-thousand-year period, God cleansed the earth by blood, culminating with Jesus Christ's ultimate atoning Blood sacrifice. The third dispensation, in which we live today, man is being cleansed by God's presence through the indwelling of The Holy Ghost. God's holiness, as fire, burns off the dross of sin and impurities of mankind. Ultimately, fire shall cleanse the earth at the time of the end. Nuclear bombs and possibly catastrophic upheavals in nature will likely start the fires. As an example, God rained fire and brimstone down from heaven onto the twin cities of Sodom and Gomorrah, because they were inundated with homosexuality and irreverence.

Jesus' words recorded in Luke 12:49, "I (Jesus) am come to send fire on the earth; and what will I, if it be already kindled?" If one has not accepted God's righteous cleansing power through the Holy Ghost, as evidenced and witnessed as tongues of fire on the Day of Pentecost, one could suffer the coming fires on earth and also in hell-fire to come. The Holy Ghost is a fore type, or foreshadow, of God's righteous presence dwelling within mankind, cleansing man from sin. God's holy presence has often been manifested, or symbolized, by fire. One must remember Moses witnessed God's holy presence in the burning bush.

Jesus will rule from Jerusalem during the coming millennium. Isaiah 9:7, "… the zeal of the LORD of hosts will perform this." When we carefully and prayerfully study the Word, we see Jesus Christ will establish His kingdom upon the earth. During this time, Satan will be bound (chained) for God's Day of Rest (one thousand years). No more warring! Good is warring at present against evil, and good is always victorious. God is going to restrain Satan in chains of darkness. Revelation 20:1-3, "And I saw an angel come down from heaven, having the key of the bottomless pit and a great chain in his hand. And he laid hold on the dragon, that old serpent, which is the Devil, and Satan, and bound him a thousand years, And cast him into the bottomless pit, and shut him up, and set a seal upon him, that he should deceive the nations no more, till the thousand years should be fulfilled."

The pattern of time established by God ordains a week of six days for work and the seventh day for rest. Exodus 20:8-11, "Remember the sabbath day, to keep it holy. Six days shalt thou labour, and do all thy work: But the seventh day is the sabbath of the LORD thy God: In it thou shalt not do any work, thou, nor thy son, nor thy daughter, thy manservant, nor thy maidservant, nor thy cattle, nor thy stranger that is within thy gates: For in six days the LORD made heaven and earth, the sea, and all that in them is, and rested the seventh day: wherefore the LORD blessed the sabbath day, and hallowed it (made it holy)."

God is fair and just. Since days of old, God ordained by His word, and has established laws, boundaries, precepts and judgments. He, Himself honors and abides by these and expects us to obey and honor them also.

The Ten Commandments are holy and not grievous to keep. We're no longer under the law, however, the Ten Commandments have never been diminished or revoked and continue to be in full effect today.

Leviticus 20:7-8, "Sanctify yourselves therefore, and be ye holy: for I am the LORD your God. And ye shall keep my statutes, and do them: I am the LORD which sanctify you (make holy)." It was so important to our mighty Holy God, that we should do no work on the Sabbath, that He instituted a "Day of Preparation." It was the day before the Jews' Sabbath. All the preparation of foods, cleaning the house, and any or all manner of work, either inside or outside had to be done the preceding day. They had to get their house, their fields, and themselves prepared for the Sabbath day of rest.

Preparation Day was exceedingly important to God, as all His ways are significant. We cannot comprehend the seriousness and holiness of the Lord and His order. It is written, Hebrews 12:14, "Follow peace with all men, and holiness, without which no man shall see the Lord." All must take warning; we must all seek after righteousness and yield ourselves to God's provision of sanctification, for without holiness no man shall see the Lord.

The importance of honoring the Sabbath and the importance of the preparation day is made clear during the Exodus, when God was delivering the Hebrew children out of Egyptian bondage. He provided all their needs; the manna was food from heaven and was angel's food. It was rained down during the night and when they awoke, they all gathered enough for that one day. Exodus 16:22-31, "And it came to pass, that on the sixth day they gathered twice as much bread (manna), two omers for one man: and all the rulers of the congregation came and told Moses. And he said unto them, This is that which the LORD hath said, To morrow is the rest of the holy sabbath unto the LORD: bake that which ye will bake to day, and seethe that ye will seethe: and that which remaineth over lay up for you to be kept until the morning. And they laid it up till the morning, as Moses bade: and it did not stink, neither was there any worm therein. And Moses said, Eat that to day; for to day is a sabbath unto the LORD: to day ye shall not find it in the field. Six days ye shall gather it; but on the seventh day, which is the sabbath, in it there shall be none. And it came to pass, that there went out some of the people on the seventh day for to gather, and they found none. And the LORD said unto Moses, How long refuse ye to keep my commandments and my laws? See, for that the LORD hath given you the sabbath, therefore he giveth you on the sixth day the bread of two days; abide ye every man in his place, let no man go out of his place on the seventh day. So the people rested on the seventh day. And the house of Israel called the name thereof Manna: and it was like coriander seed, white; and the taste of it was like wafers made with honey." God's ways are immutable! God rained down angel's food from heaven, five days a week, but on the sixth (day of preparation), there was rained down a double portion. This double portion was provision for the seventh day.

This is our day of preparation. Just as the Jews had their sixth day for preparation of the Sabbath, God is calling us to prepare for His millennial Sabbath. Presently we are in transition; we are witnessing the Gentiles gathering together against Israel. The One-World Order will facilitate the culmination of Gentile rule, and the second coming of Jesus. At that time, He will rule and reign from Jerusalem.

It is at this time, the Beast and the False Prophet will be thrown into the Lake of Fire, and Satan will be bound. Satan will not be able to influence mankind, and there will be war no more during God's Day of Sabbath Rest. What a glorious time to look forward to.

Isaiah 11:6-10, "The wolf also shall dwell with the lamb, and the leopard shall lie down with the kid; and the calf and the young lion and the fatling together; and a little child shall lead them. And the cow and the bear shall feed; their young ones shall lie down together: and the lion shall eat straw like the ox. And the sucking child shall play on the hole of the asp (deadly snake), and the weaned child shall put his hand on the cockatrice' (adder's) den. They shall not hurt nor destroy in all my holy mountain: for the earth shall be full of the knowledge of the LORD, as the waters cover the sea (saturated with knowledge). And in that day there shall be a root of

Jesse (Jesus), which shall stand for an ensign of the people; to it shall the Gentiles seek: and his rest shall be glorious." At that time deliverance will be complete as Jesus (Yeshua), will be renowned as Messiah, and revealed as the Ancient of Days! All glory to the Lamb of God that was slain.

Isaiah 53:1-12, "Who hath believed our report? and to whom is the arm of the LORD revealed? For he shall grow up before him as a tender plant, and as a root out of a dry ground: he hath no form nor comeliness; and when we shall see him, there is no beauty that we should desire him. He is despised and rejected of men; a man of sorrows, and acquainted with grief: and we hid as it were our faces from him; he was despised, and we esteemed him not. Surely he hath borne our griefs, and carried our sorrows: yet we did esteem him stricken, smitten of God, and afflicted. But he was wounded for our transgressions (sins), he was bruised for our iniquities: the chastisement of our peace was upon him; and with his stripes we are healed. All we like sheep have gone astray; we have turned everyone to his one way; and the LORD hath laid on him the iniquity of us all. He was oppressed, and he was afflicted, yet he opened not his mouth: he is brought as a lamb to the slaughter, and as a sheep before her shearers is dumb (silent), so he openeth not his mouth. He was taken from prison and from judgement: and who shall declare his generation? for he was cut off out of the land of the living: for the transgression of my people was he stricken. And he made his grave with the wicked, and with the rich in his death (a rich man donated his tomb); because he had done no violence, neither was any deceit in his mouth. Yet it pleased the LORD to bruise him; he hath put him to grief: when thou shalt make his soul an offering for sin, he shall see his seed, he shall prolong his days, and the pleasure of the LORD shall prosper in his hand. He shall see of the travail of his soul, and shall be satisfied: by his knowledge shall my righteous servant justify many; for he shall bear their iniquities. Therefore will I divide him a portion with the great, and he shall divide the spoil with the strong; because he hath poured out his soul unto death: and he was numbered with the transgressors (the two thieves on the crosses beside him); and he bare the sin of many, and made intercession for the transgressors (saying, Father, forgive them for they know not what they do)."

This prophecy in Isaiah foretold Jesus' mission in life, and He is still making intersession for us. Old Testament prophet Isaiah warns us in 55:6-7, "Seek ye the LORD while he may be found, call ye upon him while he is near: Let the wicked forsake his way, and the unrighteous man his thoughts: and let him return unto the LORD, and he will have mercy upon him; and to our God, for he will abundantly pardon."

The Lord is preparing for His second coming and we also should be prepared. Isaiah 62:10-12, "Go through, go through the gates; prepare ye the way of the people; cast up, cast up the highway; gather out the stones; lift up a standard for the people. Behold, the LORD hath proclaimed unto the end of the world, Say ye to the daughter of Zion, Behold thy salvation cometh; behold, his reward is with him, and his work before him. And they shall call them, The holy people, The redeemed of the LORD: and thou shalt be called, Sought out, A city (Jerusalem) not forsaken."

Jesus as the "Son of Man" walked among us and His life was an example of love and humility. His meekness, gentleness, and sweet spirit of servitude fulfilled scriptures. Reiterating Isaiah 53:3, "He is despised and rejected of men; a man of sorrows, and acquainted with grief: and we hid as it were our faces from him; he was despised, and we esteemed him not."

Again, for it is line upon line, percept upon precept. Jesus, as the Son of Man, rode into Jerusalem on a lowly ass. Matthew 21:5, "Tell ye the daughter of Sion, Behold thy King cometh unto thee, meek, and sitting upon an ass, and a colt the foal of an ass." Jesus rode through the Eastern Gate, into Jerusalem, humbly riding upon a lowly ass. As we studied scriptures in previous chapters, we concluded the ass or donkey was a beast of burden, and Jesus was carrying the burden of redeeming mankind back from Satan. The ass, and the foal of the ass, was symbolic of the Old and New Testaments. Jesus was bringing to conclusion the Old Testament, and ushering in the New Testament, knowing the New Covenant would be signed with His own Holy Blood.

Matthew 23:37, "O Jerusalem, Jerusalem, thou that killest the prophets, and stonest them which are sent unto thee, how often would I have gathered thy children together, even as a hen gathereth her chickens under her wings, and ye would not!"

Everyone should read the 24th chapter of Matthew. It concerns the day of Jesus' return. Again, "Study to shew thyself approved." It is the Word of God that is going to judge us. No excuse will do. There will be a time when every unbeliever's rejection of Jesus

Christ will be final. To be eternally denied access to the Holy presence of God for any sin, lifestyle, or worldly possession is futile. The world, and the things of this world, are going to pass away. The trappings of this world become unimportant compared to one's eternal soul. Hell is a literal place. God originally created the lake of fire for the Devil and his angels. Matthew 25:41, "Then shall he say also unto them on the left hand, Depart from me, ye cursed, into everlasting fire, prepared for the devil and his angels." God's salvation message is to whosoever will come, come! Everyone must be prepared to stand before, and in the presence, of our Holy and righteous God!

Old Testament prophet Joel foretold that God is going to pour out His Holy Spirit in these last days. Prepare yourself, for the day of the Lord, and His judgments, is near. We read in the Book of Exodus, God rained down a double portion of manna from heaven for the Jews' day of preparation. Pray for a double portion of the Holy Spirit (as food and strength for our souls), Who will infuse us with wisdom and guidance in this, our Day of Preparation. It is the time to repent, and ask Jesus to cleanse our souls and expurgate our sins. The soul is the part of mankind that never dies. I believe the greatest task a man has in his life is to prepare for his death.

Don't think this a doomsday message, for the Gospel means "good news!" Jesus Christ has brought salvation for souls, and He has gone to prepare a heavenly place for us. We must prepare to make ourselves ready for God's Millennial Day of Rest. Hebrews 9:27-28, "And as it is appointed unto men once to die, but after this the judgement: So Christ was once offered to bear the sins of many; and unto them that look for him shall he appear the second time without sin unto salvation." If we abide in Christ we cannot be hurt by the second death; at which time the unrepented sinner will spend eternity in hell.

Isaiah 35:8 is one of my favorite Bible scriptures, "And an highway shall be there, and a way, and it shall be called The Way of Holiness; the unclean shall not pass over it; but it shall be for those: the wayfaring men, though fools, shall not err therein." One does not stumble onto "The Way of Holiness" but one must predetermine and prepare daily to walk holy and pleasing before Jehovah God.

The greatest deliverance is yet to come. Jesus made His humble, yet triumphant entry into Jerusalem. He is coming again; but at His second coming Jesus will appear in clouds of glory with ten thousands of His saints. Jesus will sit on the throne of David and rule and reign from Jerusalem. The approaching dispensation will be "The Kingdom Age." It will be a glorious dispensation of peace and safety for one thousand years.

Revelation 19:11-16, "And I (John) saw heaven opened, and behold a white horse; and he that sat upon him was called Faithful and True (Jesus), and in righteousness he doth judge and make war. His eyes were as a flame of fire, and on his head were many crowns; and he had a name written, that no man knew, but he himself. And he was clothed with a vesture (garment of holiness) dipped in blood (the Sacrificial, Holy Blood Jesus shed while hanging on the cross): and his name is called The Word of God. And the armies which were in heaven followed him upon white horses, clothed in fine linen, white and clean. And out of his mouth goeth a sharp sword (His Word), that with it he should smite the nations (ungodly nations that will converge against Israel): and he shall rule (one thousand years) them with a rod (Shepherd's instrument) of iron: and he treadeth the winepress of the fierceness and wrath of Almighty God. And he hath on his vesture and on his thigh a name written, KING OF KINGS, AND LORD OF LORDS." Jesus The Christ: Glorious Savior!

Chapter Seventeen
The Defeat of Satan

"And I saw an angel come down from heaven, having the key of the bottomless pit and a great chain in his hand. And he laid hold on the dragon, that old serpent, which is the Devil, and Satan, and bound him a thousand years."

(Revelation 20:1-2)

Since the dawn of sin, on that dreadful day in the Garden of Eden, man has faced a choice as where to place his allegiance. Wars have been fought since the beginning of time for gold, wealth, empires, fame, and power. There was even a Civil War fought in our very own America. That war pitted brother against brother. In World War II, one could not have fought under the evil Hitler regime while fighting for the armed forces of the United States and her allies. The much sought-after prize in this great and mighty battle between good and evil is not being fought for any of the above reasons. This warfare is for the souls of men -- yours and mine! This battle is very personal. Our souls are our utmost valuable possession. There can be no price put on a human soul. You may ask, "What is my soul?" Your soul is YOU. It's the conscious, living, thinking part of you that will never die: it is ETERNAL.

Our daily conduct is most relevant in our inter-relationship with others and affects our inter-relationship with God. Our conduct must conform to obedience to God's commandments. Our souls are rewarded with eternal salvation to live forever in Heaven or consigned to suffer eternal damnation in the Lake of Fire in hell. We must consider what is the right choice in our personal morals, business ethics, and spiritual convictions. Even our thought life must conform to be in obedience to God.

Man has a choice! All mankind must choose to serve our old sin nature, resulting in our soul becoming a pawn of Satan, or one can choose not to sin, and receive the priceless reward of eternal life. When we repent of sins, submit to water baptism, and pray for, and receive, the baptism in the Holy Ghost, our lives will line up with the Word of God. We will develop a God-like holy hatred of sin and the cheap and tawdry rewards of sin! We are then also endowed with power to resist the enemy of our souls. Upon receiving the complete infilling of the Holy Ghost with signs following, we defeat Satan daily on a person level. Resolve to resist temptations. Prayer is a weapon. Pray even for a desire to pray and a desire to read the Bible. As we become sanctified, and set apart for God's service, we have won a battle. At the completion of our life here on earth, whether via the rapture or the grave, we will have won the war and through personal rank defeated Satan.

We cannot just "hope" that our good outweighs our bad on the Day of Judgment. Satan's stratagem is deception. Satan always misquotes, misapplies, and misuses the scriptures. He clouds our minds and beguiles us into complacency and easy lifestyles. The road that leads to everlasting life is not easy. It is an ongoing spiritual war. Ephesians 6:11-12, "Put on the whole armour of God, that ye may be able to stand against the wiles of the devil. For we wrestle not against flesh and blood, but against principalities, against powers, against the rulers of the darkness of this world, against spiritual wickedness in high places."

You cannot serve two masters, just as you cannot serve on opposite sides of any declared war. Matthew 6:24, "No man can serve two masters: for either he will hate the one, and love the other; or else he will hold to the one, and despise the other. Ye cannot serve God and mammon (wealth and greed deified)."

In war there are always heroes. Some can be found behind pulpits, others ministering in jails, on the streets, in hospitals, and on the missionary fields. A true seasoned prayer warrior would be found alone on his knees interceding to God for others. The Bible states, "The effectual, fervent prayer of a righteous man availeth much." We must be resolute and courageous soldiers, fighting in different theaters of this war, nevertheless united in the cause of the Cross. There is a saying: "No Cross-No Crown." It is imperative to be stalwart in obedience to God's leadership and serve with conviction. We, as mortal men, cannot fully understand what God will do, for, through, by, or because of one person who believes and does not doubt. In order to comprehend this ancient ongoing battle, we must realize Satan has already lost. The Word declares Satan's final doom; it is the Lake of Fire. Now we must decide to follow this shepherd of doom and destruction and suffer his fate, or we place our allegiance with Jesus Christ The Righteous and receive the reward of everlasting life. Man has been presented with a clear and simplistic choice. Joshua 24:15, "And if it seem evil unto you to serve the LORD, choose you this day whom ye will serve; whether the gods (false gods) which your fathers served that were on the other side of the flood, or the gods (false gods) of the Amorites, in whose land ye dwell: but as for me and my house, we will serve the LORD." It is the same age-old question Joshua asked that is being asked today. Who will you serve? It is getting in. or it is getting out: it is either hot, or it is cold, but we are without excuse!

We can do nothing of ourselves. Philippians 4:13, "I can do all things through Christ which strengtheneth me." Glory to God! Be a good soldier and then fight for the right. There is a saying: "I'm a blood-bought soldier, Lord knows I've come to fight. I live by the Holy Bible, that's how I know I'm right!"

Paul said in Ephesians 6:13-19, "Wherefore take unto you the whole armour of God, that ye may be able to withstand in the evil day, and having done all, to stand. Stand therefore, having your loins girt about with truth, and having on the breastplate of righteousness; And your feet shod with the preparation of the gospel of peace; Above all, taking the shield of faith, wherewith ye shall be able to quench all the fiery darts of the wicked. And take the helmet of salvation, and the sword of the Spirit, which is the word of God: Praying always with all prayer and supplication in the Spirit, and watching thereunto with all perseverance and supplication for all saints; And for me, that utterance may be given unto me, that I may open my mouth boldly, to make known the mystery of the gospel."

Through the powerful indwelling Holy Ghost we can serve notice on the wicked one: "Satan I am going to pull your kingdom down!" Luke 10:13-20, "Woe unto thee, Chorazin! woe unto thee, Bethsaida! for if the mighty works had been done in Tyre and Sidon, which have been done in you, they had a great while ago repented, sitting in sackcloth and ashes. But it shall be more tolerable for Tyre and Sidon (who were indifferent to God and all that is holy), at the judgement, than you. And thou, Capernaum, which art exalted to heaven, shalt be thrust down to hell. He that heareth you heareth me (Jesus); and he that despiseth you despiseth me; and he that despiseth me despiseth him (God) that sent me. And the seventy (Jesus' appointed) returned again with joy, saying, Lord, even the devils are subject unto us through thy name. And he (Jesus) said unto them, I beheld Satan as lightning fall from heaven. Behold, I (Jesus) give unto you power to tread on serpents and scorpions, and over all the power of the enemy: and nothing shall by any means hurt you. Notwithstanding in this rejoice not, that the spirits (evil spirits) are subject unto you; but rather rejoice, because your names are written in heaven"

As we sound the battle cry, watch how the Lord intercedes against our enemies, for even Satan will fall as Goliath fell. David went out to meet that powerful giant, Goliath. To the natural eye, David appeared to have only one slingshot and five smooth stones. However, spiritually he was wearing the invisible armor of God. Goliath is symbolic of the world; big, powerful, bold, corrupt, and a master warrior by experience. David, a shepherd boy, was a young man of God and was fighting for the side of right. He was not a seasoned warrior, but David stood in the power of God's might. Goliath roared against David and said, "Who am I, a dog, that you send a boy out to fight against me?" Goliath proceeded to roar against David and David's Jehovah God. Scripture is marvelous and reiterating what may appear as insignificant or superfluous is filled with symbolism. 1 Samuel 6:16, "And when the five lords of the Philistines ..." It is most glorious and symbolic that David picked up five smooth stones. Goliath was a Philistine and there were five provinces in Philistia. The five provinces of the Philistines were spiritually defeated that day. God gave David the victory. David threw a stone from his slingshot, and it hit Goliath on the forehead and the giant fell. David picked up Goliaths' own sword and took his head that very day! That notable, mature warrior was roaring against God and God's own, and Goliath was defeated. This is another example of how we are blessed with all the necessary components to triumph over our enemies and even the Devil himself!

We must always remember the battle is God's. Isaiah 54:17 promises, "No weapon that is formed against thee shall prosper." Glory to the God in Whom we can trust! We can face any Goliath with God on our side. One man plus God equals an army. Remember, we have overcoming power through the word of God.

Speak forth in faith, knowing our God carefully watches over His word to perform it!

Our assurance is declared in Leviticus 26:7-8, "And ye shall chase your enemies, and they shall fall before you by the sword. And five of you shall chase an hundred, and an hundred of you shall put ten thousand to flight: and your enemies shall fall before you by the sword." The sword is the word of God. With the indwelling power of the Holy Spirit, we have necessary weapons to fight battles against sin, fear, an unsound mind, sickness, disease, drugs, alcoholism, pride, selfish attitude, lust, or a broken heart and loneliness. We can, through God's strength and the Word, overcome all the traps Satan has set for us. We are more than conquerors through Christ.

The human mind is a battleground. One must guard one's thought life. Sin starts with a thought, just a seed of wrong that is planted. The Bible gives warning in 2 Corinthians 10:5, "Casting down imaginations, and every high thing that exalteth itself against the knowledge of God, and bringing into captivity every thought to the obedience of Christ." It is critical that Satan not be given any ground or place. Our minds cannot dwell on the weak and errant things of this world without risk of being given over to them. Ephesians 4:23-29, "And be renewed in the spirit of your mind; And that ye put on the new man, which after God is created in righteousness and true holiness. Wherefore putting away lying, speak every man truth with his neighbor: for we are members one of another (in Christ). Be ye angry, and sin not: let not the sun go down upon your wrath: Neither give place to the devil. Let him that stole steal no more: but rather let him labour, working with his hands the thing which is good, that he may have to give to him that needeth. Let no corrupt communication proceed out of your mouth, but that which is good to the use of edifying, that it may minister grace unto the hearers."

Our enemy can gain considerable ground through unrestrained thoughts. We can't prevent a bad thought from coming into our minds, but we must not keep them or dwell on them. Dwelling on evil thoughts will eventually lead to temptation, resulting in unrestrained self-will, and eventually the commission of the evil deeds. Philippians 4:8, "Finally, brethren, whatsoever things are true, whatsoever things are honest, whatsoever things are just, whatsoever things are pure, whatsoever things are lovely, whatsoever things are of good report; if there be any virtue, and if there be any praise, think on these things."

We must not concern ourselves with what the world may think of us. Many people are more concerned of garnering the world's displeasure than God's! Proverbs 1:7, "The fear of the LORD is the beginning of knowledge: but fools despise wisdom and instruction." Psalm 51:10, "Create in me a clean heart, O God; and renew a right spirit within me." Psalm 37:27, "Depart from evil and do good."

Unrighteousness cannot triumph in the end, and the end of something is more important than the beginning. The attributes of Christianity are love, forgiveness, righteousness, meekness, gentleness, humility, and faith. These Christ-like characteristics become strategic weapons against our mortal enemy, Satan. He has no understanding of these because they are in direct contraposition of his nature. Satan's only recourse is to flee before them. Psalm 68:1, "Let God arise, let his enemies be scattered: let them also that hate him flee before him." We are not weak when we go in the strength of the Lord. All evil must flee away before us when we use the name of Jesus. Our enemies are also God's enemies. Any who would array themselves against us shall be scattered. God is able to make His word accomplish what He set it forth to do. It will not return unto Him void. He is armed with righteousness and salvation, arrayed with vengeance and zeal. His Righteousness will go forth to crush His enemies. Those who are enemies of the cross are our enemies also. He is a mighty general, and the protector of His Company, and we are His Blood-Bought Soldiers!

Again we see the continuity of God's Word and His consistent orderly ways. John 1:1-3, "In the beginning was the Word (Jesus), and the Word was with God, and the Word was God. The same was in the beginning with God. All things were made (created) by him; and without him was not any thing made that was made." That which is made by the Word is subject to the Word. Satan is subject to God's Word for he too (as Lucifer), is a creation of God, however he chose to rebel against the state of his own former perfection. In combat we can defeat this ancient enemy by The Word! Bible scripture is the all-encompassing authority. Jesus provided an example for believers in the power of The Word! Jesus combated Satan's temptations by quoting: "It is written." Our merciful God has given Christians all power over the enemy through the Word. Isaiah 10:15, "Shall the axe boast itself against him that heweth therewith? or shall the saw magnify itself against him that shaketh it? as if the rod should shake itself against them that lift it up, or as if the staff should lift up itself, as if it were no wood." Can one manufactured product be greater than its manufacturer? Certainly not! Lucifer, now Satan, is a created being and being thus, makes him also subject to God and God's authority. Genesis 2:1, "Thus the heavens and the earth were finished, and all the host of them." Lucifer was probably created at this time.

Satan, formerly Lucifer in his original created state, now the Devil that old serpent, was defeated in an attempted coup d'état against God in heaven. Satan tried to overthrow God because he is envious of God, and Satan desires to be the lone object of worship. Only one: The Lord God Almighty is worthy of worship.

At the time of Jesus' birth, Satan devised a plan to have all the babies two years and under killed in an attempt to destroy the newly born Savior. Through King Herod's decree, this atrocity was indeed carried out, but God had forewarned Joseph in a dream and he took baby Jesus and Mary into another country.

Satan was defeated by Jesus Christ's death on the cross. Jesus was victorious over Satan, sin, death, hell, and the grave. When Jesus was hanged on the cross, Satan thought he had bested God. WRONG! Satan was defeated at the cross. Satan was defeated as Jesus arose from the dead. Jesus then defeated Satan by descending into hell and took the keys of death and hell from him. Satan is subject to the Word of God.

Satan will once again encounter defeat in our near future. Scripture proclaims in Revelation 12:11, "And they overcame him (Satan) by the blood of the Lamb, and by the word of their testimony; and they loved not their lives unto the death."

We too have victory through the name and Blood of Jesus. For Jesus said in John 14:11-14, "Believe me that I am in the Father, and the Father in me: or else believe me for the very works' sake. Verily, verily, I say unto you, He that believeth on me, the works that I do shall he (the believer) do also; and greater works than these shall he do; because I go unto my Father. And whatsoever ye shall ask in my name (Jesus), that will I do, that the Father may be glorified in the Son. If ye shall ask any thing in my name, I will do it." After Jesus' ascension into heaven it was foreordained that the power of God's deity, the Holy Spirit, would be sent down to earth and dwell within believers.

We are equipped with God's own Holy Ghost power from upon high. We now have been given power to bind Satan (the strongman) through God's Word using the authority of Jesus' name, and through the provisional force of the Holy Spirit. Matthew 16:19, "And I will give unto thee (us) the keys of the kingdom of heaven: and whatsoever thou shalt bind on earth shall be bound in heaven: and whatsoever thou shalt loose on earth shall be loosed in heaven." We, Christian believers, have been given all authority over the wicked one. As we pray, using this key, we become mighty to the pulling down of strongholds. Example: "Father in the mighty name of Jesus I bring my petitions before your throne. Jesus, as my intercessor is pleading my cause through the blood of the covenant. It is written no weapon formed against me shall prosper. Through the Blood of Jesus, I call my loved ones out from the fields of sin and into a spirit of Godly repentance. In the name of Jesus, I bind the works of darkness, over their lives. I say because of Jesus' blood that I resist the enemy and cast down vain imaginations. I declare, because of Jesus, that my loved ones are delivered from the snare of the fowler. I bind any unclean spirits that would present themselves as hindering spirits and render them bound, powerless, and silenced in Jesus' name. I pray your divine purpose, and your divine will in my life and those that I love. I pray America would have a mighty revival and your Holy name would be lifted up, and many would come to repentance and you would be glorified. I pray for the peace of Jerusalem, as only then will there be true peace here on earth. I give you praise, glory, and honor with thanksgiving. Holy is the Blood of the Lamb. Worthy is the Lamb that was slain, Amen."

Satan contrives to deceive with erroneous dogma or a faulty belief system. It is currently being presented that when a believer prays a prayer with authority, that those are presumptuous prayers. This is Satan's avenue to prevent Christians from obeying God's decree. We must read the Bible for Jesus himself commissioned us believers. Mark 16:15-20, "And he (Jesus) said unto them, Go ye into all the world and preach the gospel to every creature. He that believeth and is baptized shall be saved; but he that believeth not shall be damned. And these signs shall follow them that believe; In my name (Jesus' name) shall they cast out devils (demons); they shall speak with new tongues (prayer language); They shall take up serpents (if accidentally bitten or false teachers); and if they drink any deadly thing (poison or false doctrine), it shall not hurt them; they shall lay hands on the sick, and they shall recover. So then after the Lord had spoken unto them, he was received up into heaven, and sat on the right hand of God. And they (believers) went forth, and preached every where, the Lord working with them (through the indwelling of the Holy Ghost), and confirming the word with signs (operational gifts of the Spirit) following. Amen." These were the last instructions Jesus gave to the believers and they are indisputable. Those who say this is not for today have not read their Bible or they are willful in unbelief. The authority of the believer is incontrovertible.

The order of events becomes clear when one reads the scriptures along with prayer. At the end of Armageddon, the beast and the false prophet will be thrown into the Lake of Fire. Satan will be bound and cast into the bottomless pit for the one thousand years during Christ's Millennial Reign from Jerusalem. Revelation 20:1-3, "And I (John) saw an angel come down from heaven, having the key of the bottomless pit and a great chain in his hand. And he laid hold on the dragon, that old serpent (that had beguiled Eve), which is the Devil, and Satan, and bound him a thousand years, And cast him (Satan) into the bottomless pit, and shut him up, and set a seal upon him, that he should deceive the nations no more, till the thousand years should be fulfilled: and after that he must be loosed a little season." Remember, God Himself is going to honor His own Sabbath Day of Rest, and Satan will be imprisoned in a bottomless pit, and there will be true peace on earth with joy during Jesus' Millennial Reign.

Scripture proves scripture and, through the continuity of God's Word, both the Old Testament and the New Testament prophets foretold Satan's doom. Isaiah 14:15-16, "Yet thou shalt be brought down to hell, to the sides of the pit. They that see thee shall narrowly look upon thee, and consider thee, saying, Is this the man that made the earth to tremble, that did shake kingdoms." Mankind will be witnesses to this and marvel at his demise! By scripture we see that it is through deception and man's willingness to be deceived, that Satan gains the ability to destroy men and the souls of men. Man must purpose in his heart not to be deceived and foolishly follow Satan!

At the completion of The Millennium, Satan will be set loose for a short season, when he will again try to seduce the souls of men. Revelation 17:8, "The beast that thou sawest was, and is not; and shall ascend out of the bottomless pit, and go into perdition: and they that dwell on the earth shall wonder, whose names were not written in the book of life from the foundation of the world, when they behold the beast that was, and is not, and yet is." This explains the short timeframe when Satan is let out of the bottomless pit. The ultimate fulfillment of prophecy that foretells Satan's "final defeat" is recorded. Revelation 20:10, "And the devil that deceived them was cast into the lake of fire and brimstone, where the beast and the false prophet are, and shall be tormented day and night for ever and ever." Hell was created for Satan and his angels. Matthew 25:41, "Then shall he say also unto them on the left hand, Depart from me (Jesus), ye cursed, into everlasting fire (Hell), prepared for the devil and his angels." Satan's fate has been sealed by the spoken word of God and His prophesies are recorded in the Bible and will come to fruition.

All glory is due to our God for this irrefutable and righteous judgment. Satan will suffer eternally the ultimate defeat, the second death which is the Lake of Fire--Hell. The scriptures declare, at that juncture, the beast and the false prophet are already there. They will have been there throughout Jesus' Millennial Reign of wonderful peace here on earth. At the conclusion of the thousand years, Satan will be loosed out of the bottomless pit for a short season. After a short space of time, Satan will then be thrown into the Lake of Fire where the beast and the false prophet will still be there BURNING! The unholy trinity will once again be together, but helplessly tormented and forever consigned to Eternal Hell-Fire! Satan's defeat and his fate are sealed by an edict of the Living God of Israel.

Chapter Eighteen

Fear Not Little Flock

"And ye my flock, the flock of my pasture, are men, and I am your God, saith the Lord GOD."

(Ezekiel 34:31)

Every scripture recorded in the Bible was breathed by God to man and was transcribed through divine inspiration. It is an infallible proof of God's omniscience and omnipresence with mankind. He was in eternity past, He is with us even now at the end of this age, and He is in eternity future. The scriptures were recorded for God's glory and for mankind's good: they are accurate and pluperfect! From the beginning of the Bible to the end, the divine continuity of The Old Testament and The New Testament demonstrates Jesus Christ! The Old Testament pointed to Jesus as the suffering Messiah; and the New Testament documented Jesus throughout His lifetime. He completed the obligatory essentials necessary for fulfilling the Old Testament and then Jesus presented mankind with the New Testament signed in His own blood. Thus giving man an open invitation for salvation, and making a New Covenant between sinful man and a Holy God. Jesus, the Good Shepherd, laid down His life for the sheep.

We now have understanding of the mystery of God in Christ Jesus, and the divine impartation of the Holy Ghost. Deuteronomy 6:4, "Hear, O Israel: The LORD our God is one LORD." God is one in plurality of God The Father, God The Son (The Word-manifested in flesh and blood of God), and God The Holy Ghost.

We are approaching the end of a two thousand year dispensation identified as the Church Age, or Age of Grace, and this is most significant because it will bring to completion Gentile World Domination. God will restore Israel back to Himself and put an end to the present Gentile world powers that are. He wishes all, Jew and Gentile, good and not evil. He has all authority and is keeper of the keys, but we are free moral agents choosing to believe or not believe. Jesus extends to mankind the opportunity to accept His plan of eternal salvation, or to reject it. Since the beginning of time, our Mighty Jehovah God, Savior and Lord has proved Himself trustworthy.

Through Bible Prophecy, God has made known the events that will shortly come to pass. Old Testament prophet Isaiah 22:22, "And the key of the house of David will I (God) lay upon his (Jesus) shoulder; so he shall open, and none can shut; and he shall shut, and none shall open." God corroborates scripture with related scripture. All should read the entire 53rd chapter of Isaiah. It is a prophetic word-picture of Jesus. He fulfilled these prophesies during His first advent. Jesus obtained all authority over all the powers of darkness through the efficacy of The Blood. The New Testament established that Jesus obtained the key of David, and scripture reveals that the key is representative of authority! Jesus is the open door to salvation. The following prophecy is yet future. Revelation 3:7-8, "And to the angel of the church in Philadelphia write; These things saith he that is holy, he that is true, he that hath the key of David, he that openeth, and no man shutteth; and shutteth, and no man openeth; I know thy works: behold, I have set before thee an open door, and no man can shut it: for thou hast a little strength, and hast kept my word, and hast not denied my name."

The door is Jesus Christ and the New Covenant of His Blood, which no man can close. The door that was shut was the door to the Old Testament or Old Covenant that Jesus closed and no man can open it. The door that only Jesus can shut is representative of the completion of the Old Testament. Jesus cried out while hanging on the cross saying, "Father, It is finished." Jesus finished it and the door was shut! No man will again have need of an animal sacrifice, for Jesus is the sacrificial Lamb of God. His sinless blood was shed once for all, and was the perfect atonement for all sin. He fulfilled all the obligations required in the Old Testament to authorize the door to be closed. Same God, New Covenant.

The door that is open and no man can shut is the door of the New Testament. Jesus closed the door of the Old Testament and in chronological order opened the door to the New Testament. Henceforth, Jesus opened the door to salvation, through His Blood

Covenant. He arose from the dead and took back the "authority" from the thief. Satan is the thief, and the robber, who stole the authority over man through deceit while tempting Eve in the garden. John 10:7-11, "Then said Jesus unto them again, Verily, verily, I say unto you, I am the door of the sheep. All that ever came before me are thieves and robbers: but the sheep did not hear them. I am the door (of Salvation): by me if any man enter in, he shall be saved, and shall go in and go out, and find pasture. The thief cometh not, but for to steal, and to kill, and to destroy (mankind): I am come that they might have life, and that they might have it more abundantly. I am the good shepherd: the good shepherd giveth his (Jesus') life for the sheep."

    The door to this present age will be shut just as the door of the Ark was shut at the end of that age, or dispensation. Jesus compared His second coming as to the days of Noah. Matthew 24:36-39, "But of that day and hour (of Jesus' second advent) knoweth no man, no, not the angels of heaven, but my Father only. But as the days of Noe (Noah) were, so shall also the coming of the Son of man be. For as in the days that were before the flood they were eating and drinking, marrying and giving in marriage, until the day that Noe entered into the ark, And knew not until the flood came, and took them all away (drowned); so shall also the coming of the Son of man be." God Himself closed the door of the ark and no man could open it. Genesis 7:16, "And they that went in, went in male and female of all flesh, as God had commanded him (Noah): and the LORD shut him in." The end of that age was completed, and Noah and his family were the only ones left alive on the whole earth. God cleansed the earth from mankind's filthiness with water. When the door of the ark was opened, it is symbolic of the dawning of that new dispensation. There is a chart in chapter sixteen, *Day of Preparation*, which is applicable for reference.

    We are at a pivotal time in Biblical and secular world history. Most alive today will witness the closing of the door of this present time of Gentile World Dominion. The door of the New Millennium will be opened, as Jesus Christ will rule and reign from the Throne of David in Jerusalem. Jesus has the key of David, which is the authority to rule from David's throne. It will be most glorious; scripture states that the Lion shall lay down with the Lamb. This will have a literal fulfillment, but it is also symbolic of Jesus as the Lion of the Tribe of Judah, and the Lamb of God united in peace and unity in God's Kingdom here on earth.

At the time Christ established the New Covenant; He overcame the Devil, and took the keys of the Kingdom back. Matthew 16:19, "And I (Jesus) will give unto thee (believers) the keys of the kingdom of heaven: and whatsoever thou shalt bind on earth shall be bound in heaven: and whatsoever thou shalt loose on earth shall be loosed in heaven."

The authority of Jesus was given to us also. We too have been given all power over the enemy. Recorded in the Bible is a parable of the strongman who is representative of the Devil. Matthew 12:29, "Or else how can one enter into a strong man's house, and spoil his goods, except he first bind the strong man? and then he will spoil his house." If someone is bound, that one is rendered powerless. Jesus has, and also gave to us, the key of operational success. Jesus instituted, and instructed, that we believers take authority over Satan. God chose this avenue that enables believers to do the same works that Jesus did, while here on earth.

We have authority to bind and loose. This is the method Jesus ordained believers to follow. We must follow His example and the instructions of the written word. John 14:12-16, "Verily, verily, I (Jesus) say unto you, He that believeth on me, the works that I do shall he do also; and greater works than these shall he do; because I go unto my Father. And whatsoever ye shall ask in my name, that will I do, that the Father may be glorified in the Son. If ye shall ask anything in my name, I will do it. If ye love me keep my commandments. And I will pray the Father, and he shall give you another Comforter (capitalized, the Holy Ghost revealed as deity), that he may abide with you for ever." This is "the" mandated method that is set before us. The baptism of the Holy Ghost is the divine impartation of God's holiness infused into mortal flesh.

God's order and intentions are that men come to repentance of sins, submit to water baptism, and persevering in prayer wait for the promise of the Father, which is the complete infilling of His Holy Ghost with signs following. The gifts are evidence and signs of the Spirit. 1 Corinthians 12:4-11, "Now there are diversities of gifts, but the same Spirit (capitalized denoting deity). And there are differences of administrations, but the same Lord. And there are diversities of operations, but it is the same God, which worketh all in all. But the manifestation of the Spirit is given to every man to profit withal. For to one is given by the Spirit the word of wisdom; to another the word of knowledge by the same Spirit; To another faith by the same Spirit; to another the gifts of healing by the same Spirit; To another the working of miracles; to another prophecy; to another discerning of spirits (knowing the difference of good or bad spirits); to another divers kinds of tongues (other tongues or languages of men and of angels); to another the interpretation of tongues (understanding when one speaks in their heavenly language): But all these worketh that one and the selfsame Spirit, dividing to every man severally as he (Holy Spirit) will." These scriptures give believers assurance in knowing that this power is only accomplished through the baptism of the Holy Ghost. This is God's order, and there will be signs following those who believe. This is a great reality and should dispel all fear and doubt. This assurance is complete only through faith in knowing Jesus, and being baptized in the Holy Spirit. It is not the Lord's desire that we should be fearful or in need, rather, Jesus fervently wishes us to be blessed with all Spiritual blessings.

We are the sheep of His pasture and He supplies all of our needs. He has instituted a great plan for our salvation and for our sanctification. This plan includes believers being filled with the provisional power to be overcomers in this world. We are living in perilous times, but we must stand in faith and not fear. Matthew 10:16-20, "Behold, I (Jesus) send you forth as sheep in the midst of wolves (evil unbelievers): be ye therefore wise as serpents, and harmless as doves. But beware of men: for they will deliver you up to the councils, and they will scourge you in their synagogues; And ye shall be brought before governors and kings for my sake, for a testimony against them and the Gentiles (in these last days). But when they deliver you up, take no thought how or what ye shall speak: for it shall be given you in that same hour what ye shall speak. For it is not ye that speak, but the Spirit of your Father (Holy Ghost) which speaketh in you." Once one has received the complete infilling of the Holy Spirit we will have signs following. We must not fear what mere man may say or do to us. As believers, we have been commissioned by the Word of God, and given all authority and power over the enemy.

Same chapter verses 26-28, "Fear them not therefore: for there is nothing covered, that shall not be revealed; and hid, that shall not be known. What I tell you in darkness, that speak ye in light: and what ye hear in the ear, that preach ye upon the housetops. And fear not them which kill the body, but are not able to kill the soul (your soul is the eternal you): but rather fear him (God) which is able to destroy both soul and body in hell." We walk in faith that promotes peace knowing our heavenly Father is preserving us in any and all circumstances. He has promised never to leave us or forsake us for He is present with us always, even unto the end.

Continuing in verses 32-34, "Whosoever therefore shall confess me before men, him will I confess also before my Father which is in heaven. But whosoever shall deny me before men, him will I also deny before my Father which is in heaven. Think not that I am come to send peace on earth: I came not to send peace, but a sword." The sword, used in this text, is the Word of God, which is the most powerful weapon. The Word of God stands sure, and therefore is our sure weapon against Satan, and all his low-level devils. We must not fear, but stand firm, lifting high the Blood stained banner and proclaim Jesus as Lord! We combat Satan with the Word, remembering Satan is a created being and subject to the Word of God.

All must have a fear of the Most High God. In this sense, "fear" means reverential fear resulting in obedience and confidence in God. Matthew 10:28, "And fear not them which kill the body, but are not able to kill the soul: but rather fear him (God) which is able to destroy both soul and body in hell."

For me, fear was a prerequisite to my salvation. Reconciliation through faith is necessary for salvation and a successful faith-walk to complete the task Jesus has called us to. Our Lord does not want us to fear our enemies or the uncertain and ever-changing circumstances of life. Everyone must have a reverential fear of the most high and Holy Jehovah God.

Fear and faith are opposites. Logic and faith will always collide. The definition of faith is recorded for our benefit. Hebrews 11:1, "Now faith is the substance of things hoped for, the evidence of things not seen." We cannot proceed victoriously in our Christian service by sight alone, for we will not get very far. We realize greater victories, and receive peace within, through trusting in Jesus despite the circumstances surrounding us. Jesus is present with us even in our most heart-rending midnight hour; we are not alone. Jesus promised never to leave us or forsake us. The Holy Ghost, who is one-third of God's triune Being, is ever-present within, and infuses us with comfort and assurance. God's redeeming power, and keeping power, is promised to those who believe. It is He who has called us and purposed for us this more excellent way. In our darkest of hours, if we are able to see the end result, then we have not attained peace through faith. We have to step out in faith knowing God will provide. Just one step is far enough for faith to see. Trusting God, knowing and understanding Jesus' great love and concern for our well-being triumphs over all life's circumstances. Romans 8:28, "... All things work together for good to them that love God, to them who are the called according to his purpose."

One of the most painful trials anyone endures is the death of a loved one. Most difficult would be experiencing the death of one's child or a young person. Isaiah 57:1, "The righteous perisheth, and no man layeth it to heart, and merciful men are taken away, none considering that the righteous is taken away from the evil to come." We must understand God is the Alpha and Omega, the beginning and the end. He has all knowledge, and possesses all foreknowledge. My mother once used an example; if we lay a yardstick on the floor before us, looking down, we can see the beginning and the end of it. God's ability enables Him to view our lives as we could view the yardstick. The death of mortal man is just the beginning of the eternal man with Jesus Christ the Righteous. The earthly separation brought through death is temporary. We will be reunited with our loved ones, who have preceded us in death. Our birth makes us mortal, but our death makes us immortal.

Psalm 116:15, "Precious in the sight of the LORD is the death of his saints." We view death as an enemy and truly it is. Death is the last enemy, but Jesus will yet conquer this final enemy in the future. 1 Corinthians 15:25-26, "For he (Jesus) must reign, till he hath put all enemies under his feet. The last enemy that shall be destroyed is death." On the Cross, Jesus Christ was victorious over death, hell, and the grave. There are so many beautiful scriptures through which we are to take solace. 1 Corinthians 15:55, "O death, where is thy sting? O grave, where is thy victory?" And verse 57, "... But thanks be to God, which giveth us the victory through our Lord Jesus Christ."

Through faith, and without fear, we can trust Him. These promises, coupled with our prayers, assure us at the appointed time we shall be an unbroken household assembled at God's right hand. Implicit faith is the vital necessity to obtain the promises of God. Hebrews 11:8-10, "By faith Abraham, when he was called to go out into a place which he should after receive for an inheritance, obeyed; and he went out, not knowing whither (where) he went. By faith he sojourned in the land of promise, as in a strange country, dwelling in tabernacles with Isaac and Jacob (his son and grandson), the heirs with him of the same promise: For he looked for a city which hath foundations, whose builder and maker is God." It was by faith Abraham found that city, and through faith we also find our city. Our promised land is heaven enjoying eternal life with Jesus Christ. 1 Corinthians 2:9-10, "But as it is written, Eye hath not seen, nor ear heard, neither have entered into the heart of man, the things which God hath prepared for them that love him. But God hath revealed them unto us by his Spirit: for the Spirit searcheth all things, yeah, the deep things of God." Jesus said in John 14:2-3, "In my Father's house are many mansions: if it were not so, I would have told you. I go to prepare a place for you. And if I go and prepare a place for you, I will come again, and receive you unto myself; that where I am, there ye may be also."

Death is not the end. If we have been saved, and submitted to Jesus, death is the beginning of eternal life with Him! Jesus Christ arose from the tomb and evidenced Himself alive, and to this, were many witnesses and proofs. He was witnessed here on earth after His crucifixion for forty days. In His glorified body, He ate fish and honeycomb. We also, will receive new glorified bodies when this mortal flesh shall put on immortality. These new bodies will never again suffer pain, sickness, hunger, or cold. We are then to be as God intended, enjoying sweet fellowship with our creator.

Many people question if God is God, or if God is good and loving, then why do all these terrible things happen on Earth? The answer is, God never intended for all these miseries to surround us. We, mankind, are to blame for all these calamities we see and suffer. Sin is disobedience to God's word and His commandments. Mankind, and his proclivity to sin, brought earthly calamities. There is a saying; "Life is short, death is sure, sin is the cause, but Christ is the cure!" The result of Adam and Eve's sin: all are born with a sin-nature. Christ lived and never sinned, as a result, when we repent of our sins, and accept Jesus as Savior and Lord, we are assured of everlasting life. Isaiah 25:8, "He will swallow up death in victory; and the Lord GOD will wipe away tears from off all faces; and the rebuke of his people shall he take away from off all the earth: for the LORD hath spoken it." This is a prophecy of Jesus, then future, but was fulfilled through the work Jesus did in life, and on the cross. Scripture proves scripture, and prophecy proves prophecy.

Revelation 7:17, "For the Lamb which is in the midst of the throne shall feed them (Jesus is the bread of life), and shall lead them unto living fountains of waters (symbolic of cleansing): and God shall wipe away all tears from their eyes." This prophecy is also of Jesus and is yet to be fulfilled. It points to His imminent return to earth and His millennial reign from Jerusalem.

We believers are not exempt from hardships, heartaches, mistakes, and failures. However, there is a significant dissimilarity between believers and non-believers. 2 Corinthians 4:8-18, "We are troubled on every side, yet not distressed; we are perplexed, but not in despair; Persecuted, but not forsaken; cast down, but not destroyed; Always bearing about in the body the dying of the Lord Jesus, that the life also of Jesus might be made manifest in our body. For we which live are always delivered unto death for Jesus' sake, that the life also of Jesus might be made manifest in our mortal flesh. So then death worketh in us, but life in you. We having the same spirit of faith, according as it is written, I believed, and therefore have I spoken; we also believe, and therefore speak; Knowing that he which raised up the Lord Jesus shall raise up us also by Jesus, and shall present us with you. For all things are for your sakes, that the abundant grace might through the thanksgiving of many redound to the glory of God. For which cause we faint not; but though our outward man perish, yet the inward man (our Spirit-man) is renewed day by day. For our light affliction, which is but for a moment, worketh for us a far more exceeding and eternal weight of glory; While we look not at the things which are seen, but at the things which are not seen: for the things which are seen are temporal (temporary); but the things which are not seen are eternal."

The believers' acceptance of Christ authorizes the benefit of the Holy Comforter, Who dwells within. John 16:7, "Nevertheless I (Jesus) tell you the truth; It is expedient for you (the believer) that I go away: for if I go not away, the Comforter will not come unto you; but if I depart, I will send Him (The Holy Ghost) unto you." This design signifies oneness with God and a wealth of provisions. The Holy Spirit affords us with comfort, wisdom, and God's power dwelling within. God, in His infinite wisdom, knew mankind had a fallen nature, and without divine intervention, would never withstand temptations and the onslaught of our mortal enemy. Satan wars against man sending forth his minions to do battle against us. In the bleakest of times, and during abject distresses, even in the depths of despair, we are not to be dismayed or give way to fear. The phrase "Fear Not" is written approximately 54 times throughout the Bible! The angel who announced Jesus' birth to shepherds tending their flock proclaimed: "Fear Not." Two angels appeared at Jesus' tomb and said: "Fear Not." On many occasions Jesus, our great Shepherd said: "Fear Not." Jesus does not want us to fear, but to stand stalwart in faith! He is with us in all our trials. He is our burden-bearer and our problem-sharer. In the times of tribulation we press ever closer to Jesus, Who is our source of comfort, strength, and even nourishment to our very souls. Philippians 4:19, "But my God shall supply all your need according to his (God's) riches in glory by Christ Jesus."

An account of the first martyr for the witness of Jesus Christ was Stephen, and the report is recorded in the New Testament book of The Acts of The Apostles. Acts 6:4-5, "But we will give ourselves continually to prayer, and to the ministry of the word. And the saying pleased the whole multitude: and they chose Stephen, a man full of faith and of the Holy Ghost, and Philip, and Prochorus, and Nicanor, and Timon, and Parmenas, and Nicolas a proselyte of Antioch." Same chapter verses 9-10, "Then there arose certain of the synagogue, which is called the synagogue of the Libertines, and Cyrenians, and Alexandrians, and of them of Cilicia and of Asia, disputing with Stephen. And they were not able to resist the wisdom and the spirit (Holy Ghost) by which he spake." They had conspired against Stephen, with witnesses bearing testimony.

Despite the danger of losing his life, Stephen testified of God's truths. He warned the Jews against their persistence in rejecting God's provision. Acts 7:39-60, "To whom our fathers would not obey, but thrust him from them, and in their hearts turned back again into Egypt (representative of the world), Saying unto Aaron, Make us gods to go before us: for as for this Moses, which brought us out of the land of Egypt, we wot not what is become of him. And they made a calf in those days, and offered sacrifice unto the idol, and rejoiced in the works of their own hands. Then God turned, and gave them up to worship the host of heaven; as it is written in the book of the prophets, O ye house of Israel, have ye offered to me slain beasts and sacrifices by the space of forty years in the wilderness? Yea, ye took up the tabernacle of Moloch, and the star of your god Remphan (pray for discernment of the symbol of the Star of David), figures which ye made to worship them: and I will carry you away beyond Babylon. Our fathers had the tabernacle of witness in the wilderness, as he had appointed, speaking unto Moses, that he should make it according to the fashion that he had seen. Which also our fathers that came after brought in with Jesus into the possession of the Gentiles, whom God drave (drove) out before the faces of our fathers, unto the days of David; Who found favour before God, and desired to find a tabernacle for the God of Jacob. But Solomon built him an house. Howbeit the most High dwelleth not in temples made with hands; as saith the prophet, Heaven is my throne, and earth is my footstool: what house will ye build me? saith the Lord: or what is the place of my rest? Hath not my hand made all these things? Ye stiffnecked and uncircumcised in heart and ears (hard hearts and deaf ears to God), ye do always resist the Holy Ghost: as your fathers did, so do ye. Which of the prophets have not your fathers persecuted? And they have slain them which shewed before of the coming of the Just One (Jesus); of whom ye have been now the betrayers and murderers: Who have received the law by the disposition of angels, and have not kept it. When they heard these things, they were cut to the heart, and they gnashed on him (Stephen) with their teeth. But he, being full of the Holy Ghost, looked up steadfastly into heaven, and saw the glory of God, and Jesus standing on the right hand of God, And said, Behold, I (Stephen) see the heavens opened, and the Son of man standing on the right hand of God. Then they cried out with a loud voice, and stopped their ears, and ran upon him with one accord, And cast him out of the city, and stoned him: and the witnesses laid down their clothes at the young man's feet, whose name was Saul (who later became Apostle Paul). And they stoned Stephen, calling (Stephen was calling) upon God and saying, Lord Jesus, receive my spirit. And he kneeled down, and cried with a loud voice, Lord, lay not this sin to their charge. And when he had said this, he fell asleep (died)." Stephen was filled with the Holy Ghost and so fully trusting in the New Covenant that he was willing to die for his beliefs. Reiterating once again, our birth makes us mortal, but our death makes us immortal.

    This true account of the unbelieving Hebrews should make us Gentile believers tremble. The Jews did fail to recognize, or accept, Jesus as their Messiah, but the failures of the Gentiles have far exceeded those of the Jews! We have the revelation knowledge of Jesus Christ. We are advantaged with God's own Holy Ghost and His indwelling Power. In the preceding verse (51), the Jews were accused of resisting the Holy Ghost. We Gentiles are grossly guilty of this even to this very day! We have failed to bring forth these immutable truths, and to perform miracles in the Holy Name of Jesus.

Colossians 1:27-29, "To whom God would make known what is the riches of the glory of this mystery among the Gentiles; which is Christ in you, the hope of glory: Whom we preach, warning every man, and teaching every man in all wisdom; that we may present every man perfect in Christ Jesus: Whereunto I also labour, striving according to his working, which worketh in me mightily." The Gentile Church has become laden with sins and guilty of compromise, failing to continue the works of the early church! We are without excuse! God judged His Hebrew children, and He will judge the Gentiles. Acts 4:29-31, "And now, Lord, behold their threatenings: and grant unto thy servants, that with all boldness they may speak thy word, By stretching forth thine hand to heal (the sick); and that signs and wonders may be done by the name of thy holy child Jesus. And when they had prayed, the place was shaken where they were assembled together; and they were all filled with the Holy Ghost, and they spake the word of God with boldness."

We were commissioned by Jesus to continue His examples of preforming miracles here on earth. We were to be witnesses of this wondrous indwelling power, proving God chose to tabernacle with man. We have revelation knowledge of God's truths, the authorization to use Jesus' name, and overcoming power through the Holy Ghost. Despite every wonderful advantage, men are regretfully wicked. The Church is complacent and caught up with the allures of the world. We are a self-willed and a self-indulgent nation. We must humble ourselves and cry out to our merciful Holy God for forgiveness of our sins, and pray to be filled with His Holy Spirit. We should pray that we be found worthy to escape God's judgments that are coming upon this sin-sick world!

We must not fear man, but have a reverential fear of the Most High God. When we come into right relationship with our Creator, it affords us inner peace. We can have peace in the midst of all the judgments and terrible tribulations coming upon the earth at the end of this age. We are to be strong voices of warning, and living examples of God's grace and salvation here on earth. We must not fear what mere men can do, or the consequences of not obeying man-made laws that are contrary to God's commandments. When our righteous God deems something as sinful, it is, and should be avoided at all cost. Whether we come to the end of our life in full age or, as Stephen, lay down our life as martyrs for our beliefs, we will be rewarded with everlasting life. Just as the door of Noah's Ark was shut by God and no man could open it, the door of this present Gentile age will be shut and no man will be able to open it. Jesus has the key of David and through the "authority of the Word," and "God's grand provisional order," at the appointed time, a new door will open to The Millennial Reign of Peace: The Kingdom Age!

Revelation 14:12-13, "Here is the patience of the saints: here are they that keep the commandments of God, and the faith of Jesus. And I (John the Revelator), heard a voice from heaven saying unto me, Write, Blessed are the dead which die in the Lord from henceforth: Yea, saith the Spirit, that they may rest from their labours; and their works (rewards) do follow them."

Lifelong fears can be replaced by faith and we should "Fear Not," but walk in a new dimension of faith. God desires we should not be in the bondage of fear concerning anything. Philippians 1:28, "And in nothing terrified by your adversaries: which is to them an evident token of perdition, but to you of salvation, and that of God." Our Father doesn't want us to be filled with doubts and fears, which are traits of natural man. Fear is the opposite of faith. Have faith in Jesus; for faith interchanges with reverential trust. We should not dwell on our natural circumstances. Peter walked on the water while looking at Jesus. When he took his eyes off of Jesus, and looked down at the water, his natural reason took over and he began to sink. We all have the natural kind of faith. Regrettably, many people only have faith in the natural sphere rather than true faith, which is in God. The big catch is natural faith will fail you. At some time faith in the natural sphere will fail, but God never fails!

I once had a spiritual dream: in part I saw a small golden plate with a slight edge. As I dreamed, it seemed it was a plate that would fit on a pair of balancing scales. While I looked upon the small golden plate, I observed upon it morsels of different types of food. I understood that pertaining to life there are different experiences shared by all through the commonality of our humanity. We all must partake in our lifetime some experiences that are sweet and pleasant and we all must partake of some that are unpleasant, and at times even bitter. God caused me to understand, as mortals, dwelling in tabernacles of flesh, we all experience good and bad. Many years later I was privileged to attend a Jewish Passover Seder. The symbolism of each food at the Seder was remarkable and I was humbled by the correlations to my dream. The continuity of God's ways, His word, His truths, and the revelation knowledge of these truths, is made known to His people. His truths and precepts are unchanging down through the millenniums.

Jesus taught on faith and the power of faith. Mark 11:22-24, "And Jesus answering saith unto them, Have faith in God. For verily I say unto you, That whosoever shall say unto this mountain, Be thou removed, and be thou cast into the sea; and shall not doubt in his heart, but shall believe that those things which he saith shall come to pass; he shall have whatsoever he saith. Therefore I say unto you, What things soever ye desire, when ye pray, believe that ye receive them, and ye shall have them." Knowing in whom we believe is of paramount importance. God in the plurality of Jesus, Who is The Word, spoke and through the creative force of the Holy Ghost, the world came into existence. Faith is the necessary component in pleasing God. Explicit faith will become evident and will be manifested through our words and actions.

Speak forth faith. The word teaches we can call things into being that are not, or call to naught the things that are. In other words, we can pray and call to naught (or nothing) sickness or disease. We can also call forth, or into effect, things that are not. God enables us by our spoken word, through His indwelling power, to speak forth healing to a sick body and command evil spirits to depart. Acts 5:15-16, "Insomuch that they brought forth the sick into the streets, and laid them on beds and couches, that at the least the shadow of Peter passing by might overshadow some of them. There came also a multitude out of the cities round about unto Jerusalem, bringing sick folks, and them which were vexed with unclean spirits: and they were healed every one."

Man, being created in God's image, also possesses a portion, or a share, of this creative power. God equips believers with the gifts of the Spirit. Christian's lives should also produce fruits and manifest gifts of the Spirit. Considering this similitude of power, we must guard our words. The Bible tells us we will give an account for every idle word. Jesus said in Matthew 12:37, "For by thy words thou shalt be justified, and by thy words thou shalt be condemned." Jesus spoke boldly with the power and authority of the Almighty, and the dead came to life! This demonstrates the power of God's spoken word, and His authority over death and everything pertaining to life. It is a foreshadowing of Jesus' own resurrection. It is an example of Jesus having all authority and power, even over the last enemy that will be destroyed, which is death.

Scriptures explain we must act on our faith. James 2:17, "Even so faith, if it hath not works, is dead, being alone." Something dead has no power. James 1:22, "But be ye doers of the word, and not hearers only, deceiving your own selves." It is crucial to know the word of God, and necessary for the operational gifting of the Holy Ghost.

It is not the Lord's desire for man to be fearful or to be in need. We are the Sheep of His pasture. He has instituted a great plan for our salvation, sanctification, and success. This plan also includes that we be filled with power! Luke 24:49, "And, behold, I send the promise of my Father upon you: but tarry ye in the city of Jerusalem, until ye be endued with the power from on high (the indwelling of the Holy Spirit)."

Following these instructions from Jesus, the Disciples and other believers assembled themselves in the upper room to wait for the promised Holy Ghost and the accompanying power. This account is given in Acts chapter 2 verses 1-4. As the disciples were waiting, praying and expecting, the promise was fulfilled and all these believers were filled with the gift of God's Holy Spirit. Confirming this, 1 Corinthians 6:19, "What? know ye not that your body is the temple of the Holy Ghost which is in you, which ye have of God, and ye are not your own?" This promised gift makes man complete. God's presence and power no longer dwell behind a curtain, but now dwells in these tabernacles of flesh of the redeemed. Same God: New Covenant! Jesus was with The Father in the beginning, "Let us make man in our image." Jesus stepped out of eternity and into time. The deity was presented to us, in the embodiment of Jesus Christ, and at present abides with us through the indwelling Holy Ghost. Colossians 2:9-10, "For in him (Jesus) dwelleth all the fullness of the Godhead bodily. And ye are complete in him, which is the head of all principality and power."

The Heavenly Father is tenderly shepherding His own children. Ezekiel 34:31, "And ye my flock, the flock of my pasture, are men, and I am your God, saith the Lord GOD." Reflecting on this, all should read the Twenty-third Psalm. It portrays our Lord God as the loving Shepherd caring for His flock. Applying this as a personal allegory, it mirrors our daily relationship to Jesus. Under the old law, the sheep died for the shepherd, but under the New Covenant of love, the Shepherd (Jesus) died for his sheep. Sheep without a shepherd are vulnerable to the harsh elements, in need or lack of provisions, in peril of predators, and subject to injury or even wandering lost. Without Jesus as our Shepherd, we too would be in lack, disoriented and losing our way, and vulnerable to the dangers and snares of the predatory enemy of our mortal souls.

Ezekiel 34:11-12, "For thus saith the Lord GOD; Behold, I even I, will both search my sheep, and seek them out. As a shepherd seeketh out his flock ..." The tender mercies of our Shepherd and Savior are graciously renewed every morning. Continuing with a personal application of God's provision for our every need, perhaps today, one is as a lost lamb. Perhaps one, or a loved one, has strayed far from the safety of the fold. Jesus is constantly calling and searching that one who is lost. Possibly one is sick or bruised, Jesus is seeking that one to nurture and bind up their wounds.

Perhaps, one has become tired and weary on this journey of life. Jesus will seek out to find this precious one, and He will carry this one in His own arms. Perhaps, there are others whose needs seem too great to bear. Jesus, as our great Shepherd, states in John 14:27, "Peace I leave with you, my peace I give unto you: not as the world giveth, give I unto you. Let not your heart be troubled, neither let it be afraid." As the Good Shepherd, Jesus will supply all our needs. Maybe one has backslidden or drifted far from the safety of the fold. Jesus is calling that one back to Himself today. Jesus is the restorer of souls.

Revelation 3:18-20, "I counsel thee to buy of me gold tried in the fire, that thou mayest be rich (Spiritually); and white raiment, that thou mayest be clothed (wearing Jesus' righteousness), and that the shame of thy nakedness (sins) do not appear; and anoint thine eyes with eyesalve, that thou mayest see (Spiritually). As many as I (Jesus) love, I rebuke (correct) and chasten (make pure): be zealous therefore, and repent. Behold, I stand at the door (the door of this dispensation), and knock: if any man hear my voice, and open the door (through faith), I will come in to him (through the infilling of the Holy Ghost), and will sup with him, and he with me." These promises are a testament of Jesus' love for the sheep and are great provisional promises, and the One who promises, is Sovereign.

Luke 12:29-32, "And seek not ye what ye shall eat, or what ye shall drink, neither be ye of doubtful mind. For all these things do the nations of the world seek after: and your Father knoweth that ye have need of these things. But rather seek ye the kingdom of God; and all these things shall be added unto you. Fear not, little flock; for it is your Father's good pleasure to give you the kingdom."

We are directed to confess our sins to God, and ask God to forgive us of our sins. In order to become a child of God, or to rededicate your life to Jesus, please pray the "Salvation Prayer" on the next page.

Benediction

Hebrews 13:20-21, "Now the God of peace, that brought again from the dead our Lord Jesus, that great shepherd of the sheep, through the blood of the everlasting covenant, Make you perfect in every good work to do his will, working in you that which is wellpleasing in his sight, through Jesus Christ; to whom be glory for ever and ever. Amen."

Salvation Prayer: A prayer of repentance of sin and acceptance of Jesus as Lord and Savior

"Father, I accept the Blood Covenant you made for me and acknowledge Jesus Christ as the Messiah. I understand that I am a sinner and need salvation. I accept Jesus as your Son and my Savior. I ask you to forgive me of my sins and I invite Jesus to come into my heart and be Lord of my life. I will pray for, and welcome, the baptism of the Holy Ghost, enabling me to live my life to be pleasing to you. I know my name is written, this day, in the Lamb's Book of Life."

Name: _____

Date: _____

www.ingramcontent.com/pod-product-compliance
Lightning Source LLC
LaVergne TN
LVHW022111080426
835511LV00007B/753